D0188707

The Bridge
Across Forever

About the Author

RICHARD BACH is the beloved and bestselling author of *Jonathan Livingston Seagull, Illusions, One, The Bridge Across Forever,* and numerous other books. He lives outside Seattle, Washington, and still flies his own plane whenever he has the chance.

The Bridge
Across

Forever

a true love story

Richard Bach

HARPER

NEW YORK ∙ LONDON ∙ TORONTO ∙ SYDNEY

HARPER

HarperCollins books may be purchased for educational, business, or sales promotional use. For information, please e-mail the Special Markets Department at SPsales@harpercollins.com.

First Harper paperback published 2006.

Library of Congress Cataloging-in-Publication Data is available upon request.

ISBN-10: 0-06-114848-2
ISBN-13: 978-0-06-114848-4

18 19 LSC 15 14 13 12 11 10

For Leslie

who taught me to fly

—how fortunate are you and i, whose home
is timelessness:we who have wandered down
from fragrant mountains of eternal now

to frolic in such mysteries as birth
and death a day(or maybe even less)

e.e. cummings

WE THINK, sometimes, there's not a dragon left. Not one brave knight, not a single princess gliding through secret forests, enchanting deer and butterflies with her smile.

We think sometimes that ours is an age past frontiers, past adventures. Destiny, it's way over the horizon; glowing shadows galloped past long ago, and gone.

What a pleasure to be wrong. Princesses, knights, enchantments and dragons, mystery and adventure . . . not only are they here-and-now, they're all that ever lived on earth!

Our century, they've changed clothes, of course. Dragons wear government-costumes, today, and failure-suits and disaster-outfits. Society's demons screech, whirl down on us should we lift our eyes from the ground, dare we turn right at corners we've been told to turn left. So crafty have appearances become that princesses and knights can be hidden from each other, can be hidden from themselves.

Yet masters of reality still meet us in dreams to tell us that we've never lost the shield we need against dragons, that blue-fire voltage arcs through us now to change our world as we wish. Intuition whispers true: We're not dust, we're magic!

This is a story about a knight who was dying, and the princess who saved his life. It's a story about beauty and beasts and spells and fortresses, about death-powers that seem and life-powers that are. It's a tale of the one adventure that matters most, I think, in any age.

What's written here happened in fact very nearly the way it's turned out in print. I've taken a few liberties with chronology, some people in the book are composites, most of the names are fictitious. The rest I couldn't have invented had I tried; the truth wasn't plausible enough to have been fiction.

As readers see behind writers' masks, you'll see what drove me to put these words on paper. But sometimes, when the light's just so, writers can see behind readers' masks, as well. In that light, perhaps I'll find you and your love walking somewhere along these pages with me and mine.

Richard Bach

one

SHE'LL BE here today.

I looked down from the cockpit, down through wind and propeller-blast, down through half a mile of autumn to my rented hayfield, to the sugar-chip that was my *FLY-$3-FLY* sign tied to the open gate.

Both sides of the road around the sign were jammed with cars. There must have been sixty of them, and a crowd to match, come to see the flying. She could be there this moment, just arrived. I smiled at that. Could be!

I throttled the engine to idle, pulled the nose of the Fleet biplane higher, let the wings stall. Then stomped full rudder, full left rudder and jammed the control-stick back.

The green earth, harvest corn and soybeans, farms and meadows calm as noon, the bottom dropped out and they exploded in the whirling blur of an airshow tailspin, of what would look from the ground like an old flying-machine suddenly burst out of control.

The nose slammed down, the world spun into a color-streak tornado wrapping faster and faster around my goggles.

How long have I been missing you, dear soulmate, I thought, dear wise mystical lovely lady? Today at last, coincidence will bring you to Russell, Iowa, take you by the hand, lead you to that field of alfalfa hay, down there. You'll walk to the edge of the crowd, not quite knowing why, curious to watch a page of history still alive, bright paints spinning in the air.

The two-winger twisted down thuddering, kicking against me on the controls for a thousand feet, the tornado going steeper and tighter and louder every second.

Spin . . . till . . . Now.

I pushed the stick forward, came off the left and stood hard on the right rudder pedal. Blurs going tighter, quicker, one, two times around, then the spin quit and we dived straight down, fast as we could go.

She'll be here today, I thought, because she's alone, too. Because she's learned everything she wants to learn by herself. Because there's one person in the world that she's being led to meet, and that person right now is flying this airplane.

Tight turn, throttle back, switch off, propeller stopped . . . glide down, float soundlessly to land, coast to stop in front of the crowd.

I'll know her when I see her, I thought, bright anticipation, I'll know her at once.

Around the airplane were men and women, families with picnic baskets, kids on bikes, watching. Two dogs, near the kids.

I pulled myself up from the cockpit, looked at the people and liked them. Then I was listening to my own voice, curiously detached, and at the same time I was looking for her in the crowd.

"Russell from the air, folks! See it floating adrift on the fields of Iowa! Last chance before the snows! Come on up where only birds and angels fly. . . ."

A few of the people laughed and applauded for somebody else to be first. Some faces suspicious, full of questions; some faces eager and adventurous; some pretty faces, too, amused, intrigued. But nowhere the face I was looking for.

"You're sure it's safe?" a woman said. "After what I saw, I'm not sure you're a safe driver!" Suntanned, clear brown eyes, she wanted to be sold on this.

"Safe as can be, ma'am, gentle as thistledown. The Fleet here's been flying since December twenty-fourth, nineteen twenty-eight—she's probably good for one more flight before she goes to pieces. . . ."

She blinked at me, startled.

"Just kidding," I said. "She'll be flying when you and I are years gone, I guarantee you that!"

"I'd guess I've waited long enough," she said. "I've always wanted to fly in one of these. . . ."

"You're going to love it."

I swung the propeller to start the engine, showed her the way to the front cockpit, helped her with the safety-belt.

Impossible, I thought. She's not here. Not-here is not possible!

Every day convinced today's-the-day, and every day wrong!

* * *

The first ride was followed by thirty other rides, before the sun went down. I flew and talked till everyone went home to supper and to their nights with each other and left me alone.

Alone.

Is she fiction?

Silence.

A minute before the water boiled, I took the pan from my campfire, tapped in hot-chocolate mix, stirred it with a hay-stem. Frowned, talked to myself.

"I'm a fool, to look for her out here."

I poked last week's cinnamon-roll on a stick, toasted it over shreds of fire.

This adventure, barnstorming through the 1970s with an old biplane, I thought. Once it was spiced with question-marks. Now it's so known and safe I might as well be living in a scrapbook. After the hundredth tailspin I can do them with my eyes closed. After searching the thousandth crowd, I'm beginning to doubt that soulmates appear in hayfields.

There's enough money, passenger-hopping, I'll never starve. But I'm learning nothing new, either, I'm hanging on.

My last real learning happened two summers before. I had seen a white-and-gold Travel Air biplane, another barn-stormer in a field, had landed and met Donald Shimoda, retired Messiah, ex-Saviour-of-the-World. We became friends, and in those last months of his life he had passed along a few secrets of his strange calling.

The journal that I kept of that season had turned into a book sent off to a publisher and printed not long ago. I practiced most of his lessons well, so new tests were rare indeed, but the soulmate problem I couldn't solve at all.

Near the tail of the Fleet, I heard a low crackling; stealthy footsteps crunching in the hay. They stopped when I turned to listen, then crept slowly forward, stalking me.

I peered into the dark. "Who's there?"

A panther? A leopard? Not in Iowa, there haven't been leopards in Iowa since . . .

Another slow step in the night hay. It's got to be . . . . *A timber-wolf!*

I dived for the tool-kit, grabbed for a knife, for a big wrench, but too late. In that instant around the wheel of the airplane popped a black-and-white bandit's mask, bright eyes studying me, furry whiskered nose sniffing inquisitively toward the grocery-box.

Not a timber-wolf.

"Why . . . why, hello there . . ." I said. I laughed at my heart, pounding so, and pretended I was putting the wrench away.

Baby raccoons, rescued and raised as pets in the Midwest, are set free when they're a year old, but pets they are ever after.

There's no wrong, is there, in crackling through the fields, in stopping by after dark to ask if a camper might have, oh, a little something sweet to nibble on, while a night slows by?

"That's OK . . . c'mon, c'mon little fella! Hungry?"

Any little sweet thing would be fine, a square of chocolate or . . . marshmallows? I can tell you have marshmallows. The raccoon stood on its hind feet for a moment, nose twitching, testing the air food-ward, and looked to me. *The rest of the marshmallows, if you won't be eating them yourself, they'd be fine.*

I lifted the bag out, poured a pile of the soft powdery things on my bedroll. "Here y'go . . . come on. . . ."

Settling noisily to dessert, the mini-bear stuffed marsh-mallows into its mouth, chomping them in happy apprecia-tion.

It declined my homemade panbread after half a bite, fin-ished the marshmallows, downed most of my honeyed puffed-wheat, lapped the pan of water I poured. Then it sat for a while, watching the fire, sniffed at last that it was time to be moving on.

"Thanks for stopping by," I said.

The black eyes looked solemnly into mine.

Thank you for the food. You're not a bad human. I'll see you tomorrow night. Your panbread is awful.

With that the fluffy creature trundled away, ring-striped tail disappeared into the shadows, steps crunching fainter and fainter through the hay, leaving me alone with my thoughts and the wish for my lady.

It always comes back to her.

She is not impossible, I thought, she is not too much to hope for!

What would Donald Shimoda tell me, if he were sitting here under the wing tonight, if he knew I hadn't found her yet?

He'd say something obvious, is what he'd say. The strange thing about his secrets was that every one of them was simple.

What if I told him I'd failed, searching for her? He'd study his cinnamon-roll for inspiration, he'd run his fingers through his black hair and he'd say, "Flying with the wind, Richard, from town to town, has it occurred to you that's not a way to find her, that's a way to lose her?"

Simple. And then he'd wait without a word for whatever I had to answer.

I would have said to that, if he were here I would have said, "OK. Flying over horizons is not the way. I give up. Tell me. How do I find her?"

He'd narrow his eyes, annoyed I'd ask him instead of myself.

"Are you happy? Are you doing, this moment, exactly what you most want to do in the world?"

Habit would have answered of course I am, of course I'm running my life just the way I please.

Came the cold of tonight, however, the same question from him, and something had changed. Am I doing this moment what I most want to do?

"No!"

"What a surprise!" Shimoda would have said. "What do you suppose that could mean?"

I blinked, left off imagining and spoke aloud. "Why, it means I'm done barnstorming! This moment I'm looking into my last campfire; the kid from Russell at dusk, he was the last passenger I'll ever fly!"

I tried saying it again: "I'm done barnstorming."

Slow quiet shock. A buzz of questions.

For a moment I tasted my new ignorance, shifted it on my tongue. What am I to do? Whatever will become of me?

After the job security of barnstorming, a surprise new pleasure broke and surged over me like a cool breaker from far deeps. I didn't know what I'd do!

When one door closes, they say, another opens. I can see the door just shut, it's got BARNSTORMING lettered on it and behind are crates and boxes of adventures that changed me from who I was into who I am. And now it's time to move on. Where's the door just opened?

If I were an advanced soul right now, I thought, not Shimoda but an advanced me, what would I say to me?

A moment passed, and I knew what I'd say: "Look at everything around you this moment, Richard, and ask, *'What is wrong with this picture?'* "

I looked around me in the dark. The sky wasn't wrong. What can be wrong with stars exploding diamonds a thousand light-years overhead, and me looking out at the fireworks from a safe place? What's wrong with an airplane so rugged and faithful as the Fleet, ready to take off for anywhere I wish? Nothing wrong.

What's wrong with the picture is this: *She isn't with me!* And I'm going to do something to change that now!

Slowly, Richard, I thought. Be uncharacteristic this one time; please not so fast! Please. Think, first. Carefully.

And sure enough. There was another question in the dark, one I had not asked Donald Shimoda, one he'd not answered.

Why should it be that the most advanced of people, whose teachings, twisted into religions, last for centuries, why should it be that they have always been alone?

Why never do we see radiant wives or husbands or miraculous equals with whom they share their adventures and their love? They're surrounded by their disciples and their curious, these few we so admire, they're pressed by those who come to them for healing and light. But how often do we find their soulmates, glorious and powerful beloveds right close by? Sometimes? Once in a while?

I swallowed, throat suddenly dry.

Never.

The most advanced people, I thought, they're the ones most alone!

The sky turned slow frosty clockworks overhead, uncaring.

Do these perfect ones not have soulmates because they've grown beyond human needs?

No answer from blue Vega, shimmering in her harp of stars.

Attained perfection would not be my problem for a whole lot of lifetimes, but these people are supposed to show us the way. Have they said forget about soulmates because soulmates don't exist?

Crickets chirped slow: could-be, could-be.

Against that wall of stone my evening crashed to its end. If that's what they say, I growled to myself, they're wrong.

I wondered if she'd agree, wherever she was this minute. Are they wrong, my dear unknown?

Wherever she was, she didn't answer.

By the time the frost was melted from the wings next morning I had engine-blanket, tool-kit, grocery-box and cookstove dumped neatly on the front seat, cover brought down and fastened tight. The last of the breakfast cereal I left for the raccoon.

Sleep had found my answer: Those advanced and perfect ones, they can suggest, they can hint whatever they want, but it's me who decides what to do. And I've decided that I am not going to live my life alone.

I pulled on my gloves, swung the propeller, started the engine for the last time, settled down into the cockpit.

What would I do if I saw her now, walking through the hay? On silly impulse, a queer chill in my neck, I turned and looked.

The field was empty.

The Fleet roared up from the earth, turned east, landed at Kankakee Airport, Illinois. I sold the airplane within the day, eleven thousand dollars cash, and stuffed the money into my bedroll.

Touching the propeller for a long minute alone, I told my biplane thanks, told her goodbye, walked swiftly out of the hangar and didn't look back.

Grounded and rich and homeless, I hit the streets on a planet of four billion five hundred million souls, and in that moment I began looking full-time for the one woman who, according to the best people who ever lived, wasn't there at all.

two

*W*HATEVER ENCHANTS, *also guides and protects. Passionately obsessed by anything we love—sailboats, airplanes, ideas—an avalanche of magic flattens the way ahead, levels rules, reasons, dissents, bears us with it over chasms, fears, doubts. Without the power of that love . . .*

"What are you writing?" She looked odd puzzlements at me, as though she had never seen anyone work a pen and notebook, passenging south on the bus to Florida.

Somebody interrupts my privacy with questions, sometimes I answer without explaining, to frighten them silent.

"I'm writing a letter to the me I was twenty years ago: *Things I Wish I Knew When I Was You."*

In spite of my miffment, her face was pleasant to see, lit with curiosity and the bravery to satisfy it. Deep brown eyes, hair a dark brushed waterfall.

"Read it to me," she said, unfrightened.

I did, the last paragraph to where it broke off.

"Is it true?"

"Name one thing you've loved," I said. "Liking doesn't count. What one driving obsessive uncontrollable passion . . ."

"Horses," she said at once. "I used to love horses."

"When you were with your horses, was the world a different color from other times?"

She smiled. "Yeah. I was queen of south Ohio. My mom had to lasso me and drag me out of the saddle before I'd go home with her. Afraid? Not me! I had that big horse under me—Sandy—and he was my *friend* and nobody was going to hurt me as long as he was there! I loved horses. I loved Sandy."

I thought she had stopped talking. Then she added, "I don't feel that way about anything, now."

I didn't answer, and she fell into her own private time, back with Sandy. I returned to my letter.

Without the power of that love, we're boats becalmed on seas of boredom, and those are deadly . . .

"How are you going to mail a letter to twenty years ago?" she said.

"I don't know," I told her, finishing the sentence on the page. "But wouldn't it be terrible, the day comes we learn how to ship something back in time, and we've got nothing to send? So first I thought I'd get the package ready. Next I'll worry about the postage."

How many times had I said to myself, it's too bad I didn't know this at age ten, if only I had learned that at twelve, what a waste to understand, twenty years late!

"Where are you headed?" she said.

"Geographically?"

"Yes."

"Away from winter," I said. "South. The middle of Florida."

"What's in Florida?"

"Not sure. I'm going to meet a friend of mine, and I don't quite know where she is." There, I thought, we have the understatement of the day.

"You'll find her."

At that I laughed and looked at her. "Do you know what you're saying, 'You'll find her'?"

"Yes."

"Explain, please."

"No," she said, and smiled mysteriously. Her eyes shone so dark they were almost black. She had smooth walnut-tan skin, no crease, not a mark to hint who she was; so young she hadn't finished building her face.

" 'No,' it is," I said, smiling back.

The bus boomed along the Interstate, farms rolling past, fall-colored palettes at the edge of the highway. The biplane could have landed in that field, I thought. Telephone-wires high at the edge, but the Fleet could have slipped right down. . . .

Who was this unknown beside me? Was she a cosmic smile at my fears, coincidence sent to melt my doubt? Could be. Anything could be. She could be Shimoda in a mask.

"Do you fly airplanes?" I asked casually.

"Would I be on this bus? Just thinking about it makes me nervous," she said. "Airplanes!" She shuddered, shook her head. "I hate flying." She opened her purse and reached inside. "Mind if I smoke?"

I shrank, cringed from reflex.

"Do I mind? *A cigarette?* Ma'am, please. . . !" I tried to

27

explain, not to hurt her feelings. "You don't mean . . . you're going to blow *smoke* into our little bit of air? Force me who has done you no harm to *breathe smoke?*" If she were Shimoda, she had just found out what I thought of cigarettes.

The words froze her stiff.

"Well, I'm *sorry,*" she said at last. She picked up her purse, moved to a distant seat. Sorry she was, and hurt and angry.

Too bad. Such dark eyes.

I lifted the pen again, to write to the boy long ago. What could I tell him about finding a soulmate? The pen waited above the paper.

I had grown up in a house with a fence around it, and in the fence there was a white smoothwooden gate, two holes bored round and low together in the wood so the dog could see through. One night, the moon high, late for me home from the school dance, I remember that I stopped, hand on the gate, and spoke so quietly to myself and to the woman I would love that not even the dog could have heard.

"I don't know where you are, but you're living right now somewhere on this earth and one day you and I are going to touch this gate where I'm touching it now. Your hand will touch this very wood, *here!* Then we'll walk through and we'll be full of a future and a past and we'll be to each other like no one else has ever been. We can't meet now, I don't know why. But some day our questions will be answers and we'll be caught in something so bright . . . and every step I take is one step closer on a bridge we must cross to meet. Before too long? Please?"

So much of my childhood is forgotten, yet that moment at the gate, word for word, stayed.

What can I tell him about her? Dear Dick: What do you know, twenty years have passed and I'm still alone.

I put the notebook down and looked out the window, not seeing. Surely by now my tireless subconscious has answers for him. For me.

What it had was excuses. It's hard to find the right woman, Richard! You're not so malleable as once you were, you've been through the open-minded stage. Why, things you've chosen to believe, things you'd die for, are to most people funny, or mad.

My lady, I thought, she'll need to have found on her own the same answers that I've found, that this world is not remotely what it seems, that whatever we hold in our thought comes true in our lives, that miracles aren't miraculous. She and I, we'll never get along unless . . . I blinked. *She'll have to be exactly the same as me!*

A lot more physically beautiful than me, of course, for I so love beauty, but she'll have to share my prejudice as well as my passion. I couldn't imagine myself falling into life with a woman who trails smoke and ashes everywhere she goes. If she needs parties and cocktails to be happy, or drugs, or if she were afraid of airplanes or afraid of anything, or if she weren't supremely self-reliant, if she lacked a taste for adventure, if she didn't laugh at the silly things I call humor, it wouldn't work. If she didn't want to share money when we have it and fantasy when we don't, if she didn't like raccoons . . . oh, Richard, this won't be easy. Without all of the above and more, you're better off alone!

In the back of the notebook writing forward, as we rolled in overdrive along Interstate 65 between Louisville and Birmingham, for three hundred miles, I made a list: *The Perfect Woman.* By the ninth page I was getting discouraged. Every line I wrote was important, every line had to be. Yet no one could meet . . . I couldn't meet those standards myself!

A burst of objectivity like cruel confetti around my head: I'm ruined as a mate even before I make it to advanced soulhood, and advancing makes it worse.

The more enlightened we become, the more we can't be lived up to by anybody anywhere. The more we learn, the more we'd better expect to live by ourselves.

I wrote that as fast as I could write. In the blank space at the bottom of the last page I added, barely noticing, *Even me.*

But change my list? Can I say it's wrong? It's OK if she smokes or hates airplanes or if she can't help gulping down a glass of cocaine now and then?

No. That is not OK.

Sunset had been on my side of the bus; now there was dark everywhere. Out in that dark, I knew, were little triangle farms, tiny polygon fields not even the Fleet could land in.

You are never given a wish without also being given the power to make it true.

Ah, *The Messiah's Handbook,* I thought, wherever was it now? Plowed under, most likely, in the weeds where I had thrown it the day Shimoda died. With its pages that opened to whatever a reader most needed to know. I had called it a magic book once, and he had been vexed with me. You can get your answers from anywhere, from last year's newspaper, he had said. Close your eyes, hold any question in mind, touch anything written, and there's your answer.

The nearest printed paper on the bus was my own wrecked copy of the book I had written about him, the page-proof last-chance that publishers give writers to remember that diesel is spelled with the i in front of the e, and was I sure I wanted this to be the only book in the history of English ever to end with a comma.

I put the book on my lap, closed my eyes and asked. How do I find the one most dear, most perfect woman for me? I held the question bright-lit, opened the book, put my finger down and looked.

Page 114. My finger rested on the word "bring": *To bring anything into your life, imagine that it's already there.*

A flash of ice dropped down my back. I hadn't practiced this one for a long time; I had forgotten how well it works.

I looked in the window turned night mirror by the seat-light in the bus, watching for a reflection of what she might be. The glass was empty. I'd never seen a soulmate, I couldn't imagine how to imagine her. Should it be a physical picture I hold in my thought, as though she were a thing? Just this side of tall, is she, long dark hair, eyes seacolor skycolor enchantment knowing, a changing loveliness different every hour?

Or imagine qualities? Iridescent imagination, intuition from a hundred lifetimes remembered, crystal honesty and steel fearless determination? How do I visualize those?

Today, it's easy to visualize them; then, it was not easy. Images flickered and vanished, though I knew I had to hold images clear to make them appear alive around me.

I tried, tried again to see her, but only got shadows, ghosts barely slowing through the school-zone of my thought. I who could visualize the smallest details of anything I dared imagine, could not vaguely picture the one that I wanted to be the most important person in my life.

One more time I tried to see her, imagine her there.

Nothing. Lights from a broken looking-glass, shifting darks. Nothing.

I can't see who she is!

After a time I gave up.

Psychic powers, you can bet on it: when you want 'em, they're out to dinner.

No sooner had I fallen asleep in the bus, tired as death from the ride and the effort to see, a mind-voice shook me, startled me awake:

"YO! RICHARD! If it'll make you feel any better, listen! Your one woman in all the world? Your soulmate?" it said. *"You already know her!"*

three

I GOT off the bus at 8:40 A.M., in the middle of Florida, hungry.

Money was no concern, as it would not be for anyone with so much cash tied into their bedroll. What troubled me was, What happens now? Here's warm Florida. Not only no soulmate waiting at the bus-stop, but no friend, no home, no nothing.

The sign in the café, when I entered, said that it reserved the right to refuse service to anyone.

You reserve the right to do absolutely anything you want to do, I thought. Why put up signs to say so? Makes you look frightened. Why are you frightened? Rowdies come in here, break things up? Organized-criminals? In this little café?

The waiter looked at me and then at my bedroll. My blue-denim jacket had one little torn place on the sleeve where the string was coming loose from my mending, the bedroll had a few tiny spots of grease and clean oil from the Fleet's engine on it, and I realized that he was asking himself if now was the time to refuse service to someone. I smiled hello.

"How you doin', there?" I said.

"Doin' all right." The place was nearly empty. He decided I'd pass. "Coffee?"

Coffee for breakfast? Aak! Bitter stuff . . . they grind it out of bark, or something.

"No thank you," I said. "Maybe a piece of that lemon pie hotted up for a half-minute in the microwave? And a glass of milk."

"Sure thing," he said.

Once I would have ordered bacon or sausage for this meal, but not lately. The more I had come to believe in the indestructibility of life, the less I wanted to be a part of even illusory killings. If one pig in a million might have a chance for a contemplative lifetime instead of being skrockled up for my breakfast, it was worth swearing off meat. Hot lemon pie, any day.

I savored the pie, and looked out the window into town. Was I likely to meet my love in this place? Not likely. No place is likely, against odds in the billions.

How could I already know her?

According to the wisest souls, we know everyone everywhere without having met in person—not much comfort when you're trying to narrow your search. "Hi, there, miss. Remember me? Since consciousness isn't limited by space or time, you'll recall that we're old friends. . . ."

Not a likely introduction, I thought. Most misses know that there are a few strange folks in the world they want to be a little cautious with, and that is definitely a strangefolk introduction.

I brought to mind every woman I had met, going back years. They were married to careers or to men or to different ways of thinking from mine.

Married women sometimes unmarry, I thought, people change. I could call every woman I knew . . .

"Hello," she'd say.

"Hello."

"Who's this?"

"Richard Bach."

"Who?"

"We met at the shopping center? You were reading a book and I said that's a terrific book and you said how do you know and I said I wrote it?"

"Oh! Hello."

"Hi. Are you still married?"

"Yes."

"Well, it's certainly been nice talking to you again. Have a nice day, OK?"

"Ah . . . sure will . . ."

"Bye."

There is better guidance, there has to be, than going through that conversation with every woman . . . When the time is right I'll find her, I thought, and not a second before.

The breakfast came to seventy-five cents. I paid it and strolled into the sun. It was going to be a hot day. Probably lots of mosquitoes tonight. But what do I care? Tonight I sleep indoors!

With that I remembered I had left my bedroll on the seat of the breakfast-booth in the restaurant.

A different life, this staying on the ground. One doesn't just tie things up in the morning and toss them in the front cockpit and fly off into one's day. One carries things around by hand, or finds a roof and stays under it. Without the Fleet, without my Alfalfa Hilton, I was no longer welcome in hayfields.

There was a new customer in the café, sitting in the booth I had left. She looked up, startled when I walked to her table.

"Excuse me," I said, and lifted the bedroll lightly from the other seat. "Left it here just a bit ago. I'd have left my soul if it wasn't tied on with string."

She smiled and went back to reading the menu.

"Careful of the lemon pie," I added. "Unless you like it not too lemony and then you'll love it."

I walked into the sun again, swinging the bedroll at my side before remembering that the United States Air Force had taught me not to swing any hand that was carrying something. Even when we carry a dime, in the military, we do not swing our hands with it.

On impulse, just seeing the telephone in its little glass sentry-box, I decided to make a business call, to someone I hadn't talked with in a long time. The company that had published my book was in New York, but what did I care about long distance? I'd call and reverse the charges. There are privileges in every trade—barnstormers get paid for giving airplane-rides instead of having to pay for them; writers get to call their editors collect.

I called.

"Hi, Eleanor."

"Richard!" she said. "Where have you *been?*"

"Let's see," I said. "Since we talked? Wisconsin, Iowa,

Nebraska. Kansas, Missouri, then back across to Indiana, Ohio, Iowa again and Illinois. I sold the biplane. Now I'm in Florida. Let me guess the weather in the city: six-thousand-foot thin broken stratus, high overcast, visibility three miles in haze and smoke."

"We've been going wild trying to find you! Do you know what's been happening?"

"*Two* miles in haze and smoke?"

"Your book!" she said. "It's selling very well! Extremely well!"

"I know this seems silly," I said, "but I'm stuck on something here. Can you see out the window?"

"Richard, yes. Of course I can see out the window."

"How far?"

"It's hazy. About ten blocks, fifteen blocks. Do you hear what I'm saying? Your book is a best-seller! There are television shows, they want to have you on network television shows; there are newspapers calling for interviews, radio shows; bookstores need you to come and autograph. We are selling hundreds of thousands of copies! All over the world! We've signed contracts in Japan, England, Germany. France. Paperback rights. Today a contract from Spain . . ."

What do you say when you hear that on the telephone? "What nice news! Congratulations!"

"Congratulations yourself," she said. "How have you managed not to hear? I know you've been living in the underbrush, but you're on the *PW* bestseller list, *New York Times*, every list there is. We've been sending your checks to the bank, have you checked your balance?"

"No."

"You should do that. You sound awfully far away, can you hear me all right?"

"Fine. It's not underbrush. Everything west of Manhattan, Eleanor, it's not weeds."

"From the executive dining room I can see to New Jersey, and beyond the river it looks awfully brushy to me."

The executive dining room. What a different land she lived in!

"Sold the biplane?" she said, as though she had just heard. "You're not giving up flying?"

"No, of course not," I said.

"That's good. Can't imagine you without your flying machine."

What a frightening thought: never to fly again!

"Well," she said, getting back to business. "When can you do the TV things?"

"I'm not sure," I said. "Do I want to do them?"

"Think about it, Richard. It would be good for the book, you could tell quite a few people what happened, tell them the story."

Television studios are in cities. Cities, most of them, I prefer to stay out of. "Let me think about it," I said, "and I'll call you back."

"Please call me back. You are a phenomenon, as they say, and everybody wants to see who you are. Do be nice and let me know as soon as you can."

"OK."

"Congratulations, Richard!"

"Thank you," I said.

Aren't you happy?"

"Yes! I don't know what to say."

"Think about the television shows," she said. "I hope you decide to do some, at least. The big ones."

"OK," I said. "I'll call."

I hung up the telephone and looked through the glass. The town was the same as before, and everything had changed.

What do you know, I thought. The journal, those pages sent almost on whim to New York, a best-seller! Hurray!

Cities, though? Interviews? Television? I don't know . . .

I felt like a moth in a chandelier—all at once there were lots of pretty choices, but I wasn't quite sure where to fly.

On impulse I lifted the telephone, coded my way through the maze of numbers required to reach the bank in New York and convinced a bookkeeper that it was me calling and that I wanted to know the balance in my checking account.

"Just a minute," she said, "I have to get it from the computer."

What could it be? Twenty thousand, fifty thousand dollars? A hundred thousand dollars? Twenty thousand. Plus eleven thousand in the bedroll, and I could be very rich!

"Mr. Bach?" she said.

"Yes, ma'am."

"The balance in that account is one million, three hundred and ninety-seven thousand, three hundred and fifty-five dollars and sixty-eight cents."

There was a long silence.

"You're sure of that," I said.

"Yes, sir." Now a short silence. "Will that be all, sir?"

Silence.

"Hm?" I said. "Oh. Yes. Thank you. . . ."

In motion pictures, when we've called somebody and they

hang up, we hear this long buzzy dial-tone on the line. But in real life, when the other person hangs up, the telephone just goes quiet in our hand. Awfully quiet. For as long as we stand there and hold it.

four

*A*FTER A while, I put the telephone back into its holder, picked up my bedroll and started walking.

Has it ever happened, you've seen a striking film, beautifully written and acted and photographed, that you walk out of the theater glad to be a human being and you say to yourself I hope they make a lot of money from that? I hope the actors, I hope the director earns a million dollars for what they've done, what they've given me tonight? And you go back and see the movie again and you're happy to be a tiny part of a system that is rewarding those people with every ticket . . . the actors I see on the screen, they'll get twenty cents of *this very dollar* I'm paying now; they'll be able to buy an ice-cream cone any flavor they want from their share of my ticket alone!

Glorious moments in art, in books and films and dance, they're delicious because we see ourselves in glory's mirror.

Book-buying, ticket-buying are ways to applaud, to say thanks for nice work. We're joyed when a film, when a book we love hits the best-seller list.

But a million dollars for *me?* Suddenly I knew what it was to be on the other end of the gift so many writers had given me, reading their books since the day I sounded out for myself: *"Bam-bi. By Fe-lix Salt-en."*

I felt like a surfer resting on his board, all at once some monster energy wells up, grabs him without asking if he's ready and there's spray flying from the nose of the board, from midships, then from way aft, he's caught on this massive deep power, the wind pulling a smile around his mouth.

There are excitements indeed, having one's book read by many people. One can forget, charging mile-a-minute down the face of a giant wave, that if one isn't terribly skillful, the next surprise is sometimes called a *wipeout.*

five

I CROSSED the street, got directions from the drugstore to a place where I might find what I needed; followed can't-miss-its and Lake Roberts Road under Spanish-moss branches to the Gladys Hutchinson Memorial Library.

Anything we need to know, we can learn it from a book. Reading, careful study, a little practice, and we're throwing knives expertly, overhauling engines, speaking Esperanto like natives.

Touch all the books of Nevil Shute, they're encoded holograms of a decent man: *Trustee from the Toolroom, The Rainbow and the Rose.* The writer printed the person he is on every page of his books, and we can read him into our own lives, if we want, in the privacy of libraries.

The cool hush of the big room, books for walls, I could feel it trembling for the chance to teach me. I couldn't wait,

43

now, to plunge into a copy of *So You've Got A Million Dollars!*

Strangely enough, the title wasn't listed. I looked in the card catalog under *So*, under *Million.* Nothing. In case it was *What To Do When You Suddenly Become Rich*, I checked *What, Rich* and *Sudden.*

I tried a different reference. Your problem isn't that the volume you want is not in this library, said *Books in Print*, it's that it hasn't been printed.

Not possible, I thought. If I've fallen rich, so have a lot of other people, and one of them must have written the book. Not stocks and bonds and banks, those weren't what I needed to know, but what this is supposed to feel like, what opportunities beckoned, what little disasters growled near my ankles, what big ones like vultures might be diving for me this moment. Somebody show me what to do, please.

No answer from the card catalog.

"Excuse me, ma'am . . ." I said.

"Sir?"

I smiled, asking her help. Not since fourth grade had I seen a date-stamper clamped to a wooden pencil, and here's one in her hand this minute, today's date.

"I need a book on how to be a rich person. Not how to earn money. Something on what a person is supposed to do when they get a lot of money. Can you suggest. . . ?"

Clearly she was used to strange requests. Perhaps the request wasn't strange . . . citrus kings, land baronesses, all-at-once millionaires abound in Florida.

High cheekbones, hazel eyes, hair to her shoulders in waves the color of dark chocolate. Businesslike, reserved with those she hasn't known for long.

She looked at me as I asked, then up and to her left, the

place we look when we're remembering old knowledge. Up and to the right (I learned it from a book) is where we look when we are searching for new.

"I can't recall . . ." she said. "How about biographies of rich people? We have a lot of Kennedy books, a Rockefeller book, I know. *The Rich and the Super Rich,* we have."

"Not exactly it, I don't think. Something like *How to Cope with Sudden Wealth?*"

She shook her head solemnly, thoughtfully. Are all thoughtful people beautiful?

She touched an intercom on the desk and spoke softly into it.

"SaraJean? *How to Cope with Sudden Wealth.* Do we have a copy of that?"

"Never heard of it. There's *How I Made Millions in Real Estate,* we've got three copies. . . ."

I wasn't getting through. "I'll sit over here for a while and think about it. Hard to believe. There's got to be this book somewhere."

She looked at my bedroll, which at that moment happened to be in some rather spotty, dirty light, then again at me. "If you don't mind," she said quietly, "could you leave your laundry-bag on the floor? There's new upholstery everywhere . . ."

"Yes, ma'am."

Surely, I thought, in these shelves of books there must be one written about what I'm supposed to do now. The only immediate advice I could think of without a book was that fools and their money are soon parted.

When it comes to slipping a Fleet biplane down to land in a little bit of a hayfield, I was second to few; but at that moment in the Gladys Hutchinson Library I thought that

45

when it comes to herding a fortune I might be second to none at all, I might be an unmatched disaster. Paperwork has always caught and torn in my mind, and I doubted that would suddenly go smooth with money.

Good, I thought. I know myself, and I know for sure—my weaknesses won't change and neither will my strengths. A minor thing like a bank account cannot possibly transform me from the casual, easygoing flyer I've always liked to be.

After ten minutes submerged again in the card catalog, driven at the last to *Luck—Good* and even *Luck—Bad,* I gave up. Not believable! There was no such book as the one I needed!

Lost in doubt, I walked outside into the sun, felt photons and beta-particles and cosmic rays bounce and ricochet at lightspeed, silently zing and whiz through the morning and through me.

I was nearly back to the café part of town when I realized my bedroll was gone. With a sigh, I turned and walked all the way back to the library, ever warmer in the sun, and went to retrieve the thing at the foot of the card catalog.

"Sorry," I said to the librarian.

"I was hoping you hadn't forgotten," she said, and she said it with such relief that she wouldn't have to store this guy's laundry-bag in Lost and Found that I knew that she was telling me true.

"Sorry," I said again.

With all the books we have, so many still waiting to be written! Like fresh deep plums way up in the treetops. Not much fun to climb up some teetery ladder, snake through the branches going way out on limbs to pick 'em, but how delicious they are when the work is over.

What about the television, is that delicious? Or would doing publicity for the book aggravate my crowdophobia? How do I escape when I don't have a biplane waiting to lift me over the trees and away?

I headed toward the airport, the one place in every strange town where an airplane pilot feels at home. I found it by watching the landing pattern, the invisible tracks that small aircraft leave on the way to and from the ground. I was practically under the base-leg-to-final-approach turn, so the airport wasn't much of a walk.

Money is one thing, but crowds, and getting recognized when you want to be quiet and alone, that's something else entirely. Isn't that celebrity, isn't that fame? A little bit might be fun, but what if you can't turn it off? What if you do these television things and everywhere you go, somebody says, "I know you! Don't tell me . . . you're the guy who wrote that book!"

People drove by, people walked by in the near-noon daylight, not looking. I was barely this side of invisible. They didn't know me beyond I was somebody walking toward the airport carrying a neatly tied bedroll, somebody with the freedom to do that without stares.

When someone decides to go famous, they give up such privilege. But a writer doesn't have to do that. Writers can have their books read by a lot of people, they can have their names be known, yet stay unrecognized everywhere. Actors can't. Newscasters can't. Writers can.

If ever I became a Personality, would I be sorry? I knew instantly: *Yes.* Some other lifetime, perhaps, I had tried being famous. *It is not exciting, it is not attractive,* that life warned; *go on television and you will regret it.*

There was the beacon. The green-glass-white-glass spotlight that turns round by night to mark the airport. Perking down final approach flew an Aeronca Champion, a 1946 two-seat paint-and-fabric trainer with a tailwheel at the back instead of a nosewheel in front. I liked the airport without having seen it yet, just from the Champ in the pattern.

What would getting to be slightly famous do to the search for my love? The first answer shot by so fast I never saw the blur: Kill it. You'll never know whether she loves you or your money. Richard. Listen. If you want to find her, do not, ever, become a celebrity, of any kind.

All of that in less time than a breath, and less remembered.

The second answer made so much sense that it was the only one I heard. My bright lovely soulmate, she wasn't driving town to town looking for some guy in a cow-pasture selling biplane rides. My chances of finding her, won't they improve when she knows I exist? Here's a special opportunity, come coincidentally at the moment I need to meet her!

And surely coincidence will lead my forevermate to see the right television show, at the right time, it'll show us how to meet. Then public recognition will fade away. Hide out for a week in Red Oak, Iowa, or Estrella Sailport in the desert south of Phoenix, and I'll get my privacy back and I'll have found her, too! Will that be so bad?

I opened the door to the airport office.

"Hi," she said. "What can we do for you today?" She was writing invoices at the counter, and she had a dazzling smile.

Between the smile and the question, she stopped my hello; I didn't know what to say.

How could I tell her that I was an insider, that the airport and the beacon and the hangar and the Aeronca and even the aeronautical custom of a friendly hi after you land are part of my life, that they had been for a long time and they were slipping now, changing because of what I had done, and I wasn't quite sure I wanted them to change because I knew them and they were my only home on earth?

What could she do? Remind me that home is whatever we know and love, that home is with us wherever we choose to be? Tell me that she knows the one I'm looking for, or that a fellow in a white-and-gold Travel Air landed an hour ago and left a woman's name and address for me? Suggest plans wisely to manage one million four hundred thousand dollars? What could she do for me?

"Don't know quite what you can do," I said. "I'm a little lost, I guess. Are there any old airplanes in the hangar?"

"Jill Handley's Porterfield is out there, that's pretty old. Chet Davidson's Tiger Moth. Morris Jackson has a Waco, but he keeps that locked in a T-hangar. . . ." She laughed. "The Champs are getting pretty old. Are you looking for an Aeronca Champ?"

"It's one of the best airplanes in the history of the world," I said.

Her eyes widened. "No, I was kidding! I don't think Miss Reed would sell the Champs, ever."

I must have sounded like a buyer. Can people sense when a stranger has a million dollars?

She went on with the invoices, and I noticed her wedding ring, woven gold.

"Is it OK to look in the hangar for a minute?"

"Sure," she smiled. "Chet's the mechanic, he should be back there somewhere if he's not across the street for lunch yet."

"Thank you."

I walked down a hall and opened the door into the hangar. It was home, all right. A factory-red-and-cream Cessna 172 in for its annual inspection: engine-cowlings off, spark plugs out, oil in the midst of a change. A Beech Bonanza, silver with a blue stripe down its side, perched delicately on tall yellow jacks for its landing-gear retraction test. Assorted lightplanes, I knew them all. Stories they had to tell, stories I could tell them back. A quiet hangar has the same soft tension as a deep-forest glade . . . a stranger senses eyes watching, action suspended, life holding its breath.

There was a big Grumman Widgeon amphibian there, with two 300-horsepower radial engines, the new one-piece windscreen, mirrors on the wingtip floats so the pilot can check that the wheels are up before landing on the water. When one landed in the bay with its wheels down, the splash of that landing sold a great number of little mirrors to amphibian pilots.

I stood by the Widge and looked into the cockpit, my hands folded respectfully behind me. No one in aviation likes strangers to touch their airplanes without permission—not so much because the airplanes could be damaged as because it is unjustified familiarity, as though a curious stranger might walk by and touch one's wife, to see what she feels like.

Way back by the hangar door was the Tiger Moth, its upper wing standing out above the other airplanes like a friend's handkerchief waved above a crowd. The wing was painted the colors of Shimoda's airplane, it was painted white and gold! The closer I came, threading my way through the labyrinth of wings and tails and shop equipment, the more I was struck with the color of that machine.

The history that's been lived in de Havilland Moths! Men and women who were heroes to me had flown Tiger Moths and Gypsy Moths and Fox Moths from England all around the earth. Amy Lawrence, David Garnett, Francis Chichester, Constantine Shak Lin, Nevil Shute himself—those names and the adventures they'd had, tugged me to the side of the Moth. What a pretty little biplane! All white, gold chevrons ten inches wide, vees pointing forward like arrowheads turning to angled gold stripes all the way out the wings and horizontal stabilizer.

There the ignition switches on the outside of the airplane, sure enough, and if it were a faithful restoration . . . yes, on the floor of the cockpit, a monster British military compass! I could hardly keep my hands behind my back, it was so handsome a machine. Now the rudder pedals should be fitted with . . .

"You like that airplane, do you?"

I nearly cried out, he startled me so. The man had been standing there half a minute, wiping oil from his hands on a shop towel and watching me inspect his Moth.

"Like it?" I said, "It's beautiful!"

"Thank you. She's been finished a year now, rebuilt her from the wheels up."

I looked closely at the fabric . . . there was a haze of texture, showing through the paint.

"Looks like Ceconite," I said. "Nice job." That would be all the introduction we'd need; one doesn't learn in a day how to tell the difference between Grade-A cotton and Ceconite dacron cloth on old airplanes. "And where did you find the compass?"

He smiled, happy I'd noticed. "Would you believe that I found that in a second-hand store in Dothan, Alabama?

Genuine Royal Air Force compass, 1942. Seven dollars and fifty cents. You tell me how it got there, but I'll tell you I got it out!"

We walked around the Moth, me listening while he talked, and as we did I knew I was clinging to my past, to the known and therefore simple life of flight. Had I been too impulsive, selling the Fleet and chopping the ropes of my yesterdays to go searching for an unknown love? There in the hangar, it was as if my world had become a museum, or an old photograph; a raft cut adrift and floating softly away, slowly into history. . . .

I shook my head, frowned, interrupted the mechanic.

"Is the Moth for sale, Chet?"

He didn't take me seriously. "Every airplane's for sale. Like they say, it's a matter of price. I'm more a builder than a flyer, but I'd want an awful lot of money to sell the Moth, I tell you."

I squatted down and looked beneath the airplane. There was not a trace of oil on the cowling.

Rebuilt a year ago by an aircraft mechanic, I thought, hangared ever since. The Moth was a special find, indeed. I had never for a minute intended to stop flying. I could fly clear across the country, in the Moth. I could fly this airplane to the television interviews, and along the way, I might find my soulmate!

I set my bedroll on the floor for a cushion. It crackled when I sat on it. "How much money is a lot of money if it's cash?"

Chet Davidson went to lunch an hour and a half late. I took the Moth logbooks and manuals with me to the office.

"Excuse me, ma'am. You have a telephone, don't you?"

"Sure. Local call?"

"No."

"Pay phone's just outside the door, sir."

"Thank you. You sure have a sweet smile."

"Thank *you,* sir!" A nice custom, wedding-rings.

I called Eleanor in New York and told her I'd do the television.

six

*T*HERE'S LEARNINGFUL serenity, comes from sleeping under airplane-wings in country fields: stars and rain and wind color dreams real. Hotels, I found neither educating nor serene.

There's proper balanced nourishment, mixing panbread-flour and streamwater in the civilized wilderness of farm-land America. Wolfing peanuts in taxicabs careening toward television studios is not so well-balanced.

There's a proud hurray, when passengers step unharmed from an old two-winger back on the ground again, fear of heights turned to victory. TV-talk forced between paid com-mercials and the tick of a second-hand, it lacks the same breath of triumph shared.

But she's worth hotels and peanuts and eye-on-the-time interviews, my elusive soulmate, and meet her I would, if I kept moving, watching, searching through studios in many downtowns.

It did not occur to me to doubt her existing, because I saw almost-hers all about me. I knew from barnstorming that America was pioneered by remarkably attractive women, for their daughters number millions today. A gypsy passing through, I knew them only as lovely customers, sweetly pleasant to watch for the space of a biplane-ride.

My words with them had been practical: The airplane is safer than it looks. If you'll tie your hair with a ribbon before we take off, ma'am, it'll be easier to brush after we land. Yes, it's that windy—ten minutes, after all, in an open cockpit at eighty miles per hour. Thank you. That will be three dollars, please. You're welcome! I liked the ride, too.

Was it the talk-shows, was it the success of the book, was it my new bank account, or was it simply that I was no longer flying without stop? All at once I was meeting attractive women as never I had before. Intent on my search, I met each of them through a prism of hope: she was the one until she proved me wrong.

Charlene, a television model, might have been my soulmate save that she was too pretty. Invisible flaws in her mirror image reminded her that the Business is cruel, only a few years left to earn a retirement, to save for retraining. We could talk about something else, but not for long. Always she came back to the Business. Contracts, travel, money, agents. It was her way of saying she was frightened, and couldn't think her way out of the murderous silvered glass.

Jaynie had no fear. Jaynie loved parties, she loved drinking. Charming as a sunrise, she clouded and sighed when she found I didn't know where the action was.

Jacqueline neither drank nor partied. Quick and bright by

nature, she couldn't take the brightness for true. "High-school dropout," she said, "not a diploma to my name." Without a diploma, a person can't be educated, can she, and without degrees, a person's got to take what comes and hang on, hang on to the security of cocktail-serving no matter how it scrapes her mind. It's good money, she said. I don't have an education. I had to drop out of school, you understand.

Lianne cared not a whit for degrees, or for jobs. She wanted to be married, and the best way to be married was to be seen with me so that her ex-husband would turn jealous and want her again. Up from jealousy would come happiness.

Tamara loved money, and so dazzling was she in her way that she was a fine woman for the price. An artist's-model face, a mind that calculated even while she laughed. Well-read, well-traveled, multi-lingual. Her ex-husband was an investment broker, and now Tamara wanted to start her own broker's shop. A hundred thousand dollars would be enough to get her business off the ground. Just a hundred thousand, Richard, can you help me?

If only, I thought. If only I could find a woman with Charlene's face but with Lianne's body, and Jacqueline's gifts and Jaynie's charm and Tamara's cool poise—there I'd be looking at a soulmate, wouldn't I?

Trouble was that Charlene's face had Charlene's fears, and Lianne's body had Lianne's troubles. Each new meeting was intriguing, but after a day the colors turned dull, intrigue vanished in the forest of ideas that we didn't share. We were pie-slices for each other, incomplete.

Is there no woman, I thought at last, who can't prove in a day that she's not the one I'm looking for? Most of the ones

I was finding had difficult pasts, most were overwhelmed with problems and looking for help, most needed more money than they had on hand. We allowed for our quirks and flaws and, just-met, untested, we called each other friends. It was a colorless kaleidoscope, every bit as changing and as grey as it sounds.

By the time television tired of me, I had bought a short-wing, big-engine biplane to be company for the Moth. I practiced arduously, and later began flying aerobatic performances for hire.

Thousands of people crowd summer airshows, I thought, and if I can't find her on television, perhaps I can find her at an airshow.

I met Katherine after my third performance, in Lake Wales, Florida. She emerged from the crowd around the airplane as though she were an old friend. Smiled a subtle intimate smile, cool and close as could be.

Her eyes were steady level calm even in the glare of bright noon. Long dark hair, dark green eyes. The darker our eyes, it is said, the less we're affected by sunbright.

"Looks like fun," she said, nodding to the biplane, oblivious to the noise and the crowd.

"Beats getting crushed to death by boredom," I said. "With the right airplane, you can escape an awful lot of boredom."

"What's it like to zoom around upside-down? Do you give rides, or just show off?"

"Mostly show off. Not many rides. Sometimes. Once you trust you're not going to fall out, it's fun, zooming around."

"Would you give me a ride," she said, "if I asked in the right way?"

"For you I might, when the show's over." Never saw eyes so green. "What's the right way to ask?"

She smiled innocently. "Please?"

She was not far away the rest of the afternoon, disappeared in the crowd from time to time, then back again, the smile and a secret wave. When the sun was nearly set she was the last one left by the airplane. I helped her into the front cockpit of the little machine.

"Two safety belts, remember," I said. "One by itself will hold you in the airplane no matter what aerobatics we do, but we like to have two, anyway."

I told her how to use the parachute if we had to bail out, smoothed the padded shoulder harness snug over her shoulders, down to lock into the second safety belt. You have beautiful breasts, I nearly said, by way of compliment. Instead: "You want to make sure your harness is pulled as tight as you can get it. Soon as the airplane rolls upside-down, it will feel a whole lot looser than it does now!" She grinned up at me as though I had chosen the compliment.

From the sound of the engine to a sun tilted afire on the rim of the world, from hanging inverted above clouds to floating weightless mid-air to crushing three Gs in loops, she was a natural flyer, she adored the ride.

Landed in twilight, she was out of her cockpit by the time I had the engine stopped and before I knew it she threw her arms around my neck and kissed me.

"I LOVE IT!" she said.

"My goodness . . ." I said. "Why, I don't mind that, myself."

"You're a grand pilot."

I tied the airplane to cables in the grass. "Flattery, Miss, will get you anywhere you want to go."

58

She insisted on taking me to dinner to pay for her ride; we talked for an hour. She was divorced, she told me, and worked as a hostess in a restaurant not far from the lake-house I had bought. Between her job and alimony, she had enough money to get along. Now she was thinking about going back to school to study physics.

"Physics! Tell me what happened to lead you into physics . . ." Such an arresting person—positive, direct, motivated.

She reached for her purse. "You don't mind if I smoke, do you?"

If her question startled, my answer flattened me numb.

"Not at all."

She lit her cigarette and began to talk physics, not noticing the shambles she had made of my mind. RICHARD! WHAT? WHAT DO YOU MEAN NOT AT ALL YOU DON'T MIND? The lady is lighting a CIGA-RETTE! Do you know what that is saying about her values and her future in your life? It says *Road Closed*, it says . . .

Shut up, I said to my principles. She's bright and different, smart as lightning with green eyes, fun to listen to, lovely, warm, exciting, and I'm so tired of thinking alone, sleeping with pretty aliens. Later, I'll talk to her about the smoking. Not tonight.

My principles disappeared so fast it frightened me.

". . . of course rich I won't be, but I'll afford it some-how," she was saying. "I'm going to have my own airplane even if it has to be old and used! Will I be sorry?"

The smoke curled, as any tobacco-smoke will, directly to me. I tugged down mental screens against it, thoughtforms in glass, got myself under control at once.

"You'll get the airplane first," I asked, watching her eyes, "then learn to fly it?"

"Yes. Then I only have to pay for an instructor instead of an instructor and renting an airplane, too. Isn't that cheaper in the long run? Doesn't that sound wise to you?"

We discussed it, and after a while I suggested she might fly with me from time to time in one or another of my airplanes. The new Lake amphibian, I thought, so sleek it looked as if it were built to move through futures and pasts as well as air and water, there's one she'd like.

Two hours later I was stretched out in bed, imagining what she would look like when I saw her next.

I didn't have long to wait. She would look delicious, a tanned curving body covered for a moment by terrycloth.

Then the towel fell away, she slipped under the covers, leaned to kiss me. Not I-know-who-you-are-and-I-love-you did that kiss say, but let's be lovers tonight and see what happens.

What pleasure it was just to enjoy, and not to wish for someone I couldn't find!

seven

"*I*'D JUST as soon you not smoke in the house, Kathy."

She looked up surprised, lighter poised an inch from her cigarette. "You didn't mind last night."

I set our plates in the dishwasher, ran the sponge over the kitchen counter. It was already warm outside, just a few white puffs high in the morning; scattered clouds at six thousand feet, visibility fifteen miles in light haze. No wind.

She was as attractive as she had been the day before; I wanted to know her better. Were cigarettes going to drive away this woman I could touch and with whom I could talk for more than a minute?

"Let me tell you what I think about cigarettes," I said.

I took a long time and told her.

". . . so it's saying to everyone around you," I finished, "it's saying: 'You matter so little to me that I don't care if you can't breathe. Die if you want, I'm lighting up!' Not a courteous habit, smoking. Not something to do around people you like."

Instead of turning into thorns and stalking out the door, she nodded. "It's a terrible habit, I know. I've been thinking about quitting." She closed her purse on cigarettes and lighter.

In time physics fell aside—it was modeling she wanted to try. Then singing. She had a pretty voice, haunting as a mermaid's from a misty sea. But somehow, when she moved past wishing into working toward a career, she lost her dedication and began another dream. Finally it was up to me— why didn't I help her open a little boutique?

Kathy was lighthearted, quick-witted; she loved the amphibian, she picked up flying at once and she was an incurable stranger. She was a foreign body in my system, lovely though she was, and the system moved often to reject her, as gently as it could.

Soulmates we would never be. We were two boats met mid-ocean, each changing course to sail for a while in the same direction over an empty sea. Different boats on our way to different ports, and we knew it.

I had the curious sense that I was marking time, that I was waiting for something to happen before my life could pick up its strange charmed way, its purpose and direction.

Were I a soulmate separated from my love, I thought, I'd expect her to do the best she could without me, till somehow we found each other. In the meantime, my dear undiscovered twin, do you expect the same of me? How close do we allow warm strangers?

A friendship with Kathy is pleasant for the time being, but it must not entangle, interfere, stand in the way of my love, whenever she might come along.

It was sensual, ever-new, my search for the perfect woman. Why this oppressive sense of winter come early? No matter how fast time-the-river thundered over its rocks and depths, my raft was caught in snowy rapids. It's not deadly to be stopped for a while, I hoped over the roar, I don't think it's deadly. But I've chosen this planet and this time to learn some transcendent lesson I don't know what, to meet a woman unlike any other.

In spite of that hope, an inner voice warned that winter could turn me to ice unless I broke free and found her.

eight

*I*T FELT the same as laying out flat on the kitchen table in an airplane two miles up, and then getting kicked out the door. One instant the plane was full-size, inches from my fingers . . . I was falling, but I could grab and get back aboard if I desperately needed to.

The next instant was too late, the closest thing to grab was fifty feet above me, flying away a hundred feet per second. I fell alone, straight down. Now it was straight down, fast.

Oh, my, I thought. Am I sure I want to do this?

When you live for the moment, skydiving is a whale of a lot of fun. It's when you start caring about the next moment that it tarnishes.

I fell down the wild vortex, watching the ground, how big it was, how hard and flat, feeling awfully little, myself. No cockpit, nothing to hang on to.

Not to worry, Richard, I thought. Right here on your chest is the ripcord handle, you can pull it any time you want and out comes the parachute. There's another ripcord on the reserve, if the main chute fails. You can pull it now, if you'd feel better, but then you'd be missing the fun of free-fall.

I glanced at the altimeter on my wrist. Eight thousand feet. Seven thousand five . . .

Way below on the ground was a white-gravel target upon which I aimed to stand in not too many seconds. But look at all that empty air between now and then! Oh, my . . .

Part of us is always the observer, and no matter what, it observes. It watches us. It does not care if we are happy or unhappy, if we are sick or well, if we live or die. Its only job is to sit there on our shoulder and pass judgment on whether we are worthwhile human beings.

Now perched the observer on my reserve harness, wearing his own little jumpsuit and parachute, taking notes on my behavior.

Much more nervous than ought to be at this stage. Eyes too wide; heart-rate too fast. Mixed in with exhilaration is one part too many fright. Grade so far on Jump #29: C-minus.

My observer grades hard.

Altitude five thousand two hundred . . . four thousand eight hundred.

Push my hands ahead of me in the storm of wind and I'd fall feet-down; hands back and I'd dive headfirst toward the ground. This is the way I thought flying without an airplane might be, except for the forlorn wish that I could go up as fast as down. Even a third as fast up would be fine.

Wool-gathering during free-fall. Mind wanders aimlessly. Revised grade: D-plus.

Altitude three thousand seven hundred feet. Still high, but my hand came in for the ripcord, hooked it on the right thumb, pulled hard. The cable slid free; I heard a rattling at my back, which would be the pilot-chute opening.

Pulled early. Too eager to get under canopy. D.

The rattling continued. By now I should have had the falling-into-featherpile shock of the main canopy opening. Instead, I fell unchecked. For no reason, my body started to spin.

Something . . . , I thought, is something wrong?

I looked over my shoulder into the rattling. The pilot-chute thrashed and blurred, caught on a harness-strap. Where the main canopy should have been was a great knot of tangled nylon, reds and blues and yellows roaring in the vortex.

Sixteen seconds—fifteen—to fix it before I'd hit the ground. It looked to me, spinning, as though I were going to hit just shy of the orange grove. Maybe in the trees, but more likely not.

Cut away, I had learned in practice. I'm supposed to cut away from the main canopy now and deploy the reserve from my chest-pack. Is this *fair,* a parachute failure on my twenty-ninth jump? I don't think this is fair!

Mind uncontrolled. No discipline. D-minus.

It was just my luck, then, that time slowed down. A second took a minute to pass.

Yet why is it so hard to get my hands up to the release-latches and cut away from the wreck of the canopy?

My hands weighed tons, and I inched them slow-motion to the latches at my shoulders, an enormous effort.

Is this worth the strain? They didn't tell me it would be so hard to reach the latches! In savage fury at my instructors, I grabbed the last half-inch to the releases and ripped them open.

Slow, slow. Way too slow.

I stopped spinning, rolled over on my back to deploy the reserve, and to my dumb surprise saw the tangled nylon still with me! I was a Roman candle in reverse, tied to a bright cloth flame falling, a rocket fired down from the sky.

"Students, listen," the instructor had said. "This will probably never happen to you, but don't forget: Never deploy your reserve into a fouled main because the reserve will fail, too. It'll barber-pole up the streamer and it won't even slow you down! *ALWAYS CUT AWAY!*"

But I *did* cut away, and there's the main tangled, still jammed in the harness!

My observer snorted in disgust, over his clipboard.

Loses rationality under pressure: F is for Failed.

I felt the ground falling up behind me. The grass would hit the back of my neck at about 125 mph. Certainly a swift way to die. Why aren't I seeing my life flash in front of my eyes, why aren't I leaving my body before I hit, the way it says in books? *PULL THE RESERVE!*

Acts too late. Asks irrelevant questions. Basically poor human being.

I jerked the emergency ripcord, and instantly the reserve burst by my face, up from its pack like a silk snow-shell, cannon-fired into the sky. It streamed alongside the rag of the main; sure enough, I was tied to two Roman candles streaking down.

Then a slamwhite gunshot and the thing was open, full open, and I jerked to a halt in the air four hundred feet above the orange grove, a broken puppet dangling, rescued last-second on its strings.

Time jammed back into high gear, trees whipped by, I hit the ground on my boots and fell in the grass not dead but breathing hard.

Had I already smashed in upside-down killed, I thought, then got myself dragged backwards two seconds in time by a mercy-chute and saved?

Plummeting death was an alternate future I had barely managed not to choose, and as it veered away from me I wanted to wave it goodbye. Wave sadly, almost. In that future, already an alternate past, I had sudden answers to my long curiosity about dying.

Survived the jump. Bungled through with luck and brilliant action from guardian angels. Guardian angels: A. Richard: F.

I gathered up the reserve, hugged it lovingly into a cool foamy pile alongside the failed main. Then I sat on the ground by the trees, lived the last minutes again, wrote into my pocket notebook what had happened and what I had seen and thought, what the mean little observer had said, the sad farewell to death, everything I could remember. My hands didn't shake, writing. Either I felt no shock from the jump, or I was suppressing it with a vengeance.

Home that day, back in my house, there was no one to share the adventure, no one to ask the questions that might show values I'd overlooked. Kathy was out with someone else for the evening on her night off. Brigitte's children had a school play. Jill was tired from work.

The best I could do was long-distance to Rachel, in South Carolina. A pleasure to talk with me, and I was welcome, she said, to stop by whenever I could. I didn't mention the jump, the failed parachute and the other future, my death in the orange grove.

Baked myself a *Kartoffelkuchen* to celebrate, that night, straight from my grandmother's recipe: potatoes and butter-milks and eggs and nutmegs and vanillas, iced it with white frosting and melted bitter chocolate, ate a third of it warm and alone.

I thought about the jump, and concluded at last that I wouldn't have told them anyway, wouldn't have told any-one what had happened. Would I not have been the showoff bragging death escaped? And what could they say? "Good-ness, there's a scary time!" "You must be more careful!"

The observer perched again and wrote. I watched from the corner of my eye.

He's changing. Every day more remote, protected, distant. He builds tests now for the soulmate he hasn't found, bricking wall and maze and mountain fortress, dares her to find him at the hidden center of them all. Here's an A in self-protection from the one in the world he might love and who might someday love him. He's in a race, now . . . will she find him before he kills himself?

Kill myself? Suicide? Even our observers don't know who we are. It wasn't my fault, the streamer. A freak failure, it won't happen again!

I didn't bother to recall that I was the one who had packed that parachute.

A week later, I landed for fuel, late on a day in which everything had been going wrong with my huge fast P-51 Mustang. Radios failing, left brake weak, generator burned out, coolant temperatures unexplainably to redline and unexplainedly recovered. Definitely not the best day, definitely the worst airplane I had ever flown.

Most airplanes you love, but some, you just never get along.

Land and gas, tighten the brake and let's get off again, quick as we can. A long flight, watching engine instruments show things not right behind that enormous propeller. Not one part of the airplane cost less than a hundred dollars, and the parts that were breaking like reeds, they cost thousands.

The wheels of the big fighter-plane floated a foot over the runway at Midland, Texas; then they touched. At once the left tire blew out and the airplane swerved toward the edge of the pavement, in a blink off the pavement into the dirt.

No time. Still moving fast enough to fly, I pressed full throttle and forced her back into the air.

Bad choice. *Not* moving fast enough to fly.

The airplane snarled its nose upward for a second or so, but that was the last it would do. Sagebrush flashed beneath us; the wheels settled and instantly the left main landing gear broke off. The monster propeller hit the ground, and as it bent, the engine wound up, howling, exploding inside.

It was almost familiar, time falling back into slow motion. And look who's here! My observer, with clipboard and pencil! How've you been, guy, haven't seen you in days!

Chats with observer while airplane gets torn to hell in sage-brush. May be worst pilot have ever seen.

Mustang-crashes, I knew full well, are not your everyday left-over-from-dinner airplane-wrecks. The machines are so big and fast and lethal, they go tearing through whatever happens to be in the way and blow up in sudden pretty fireballs of flame-yellow and dynamite-orange and doom-black, detonating bolts and pieces a half-mile round impact center. The pilot never feels a thing.

Slewing toward me eighty miles per hour was impact coming up . . . a diesel-generator shack out in the middle-of-nowhere desert, an orange-and-white checkerboard gen-erator-house that thought it was safe from getting run over by huge fast airplanes crashing. Wrong.

A few more jolts along the way, the other landing gear disappeared, half the right wing was gone, the checkerboard slid huge in the windscreen.

Why is it that I have not left my body? All the books say . . .

I slammed forward in the shoulder harness when we hit and the world went black.

For a few seconds, I couldn't see anything. Painless.

It is very quiet, here in heaven, I thought, straightening, shaking my head.

Completely painless. A calm, gentle hissing . . . What is it in heaven, Richard, that could be *hissing?*

I opened my eyes to find that heaven looks like a demol-ished U.S. Government diesel-generator shack, flattened un-der the wreckage of a very large airplane.

Slow as toad to understand what is going on.

Just a minute! Could it be . . . this isn't heaven? I'm not dead! I'm sitting inside what's left of this cockpit and the airplane hasn't blown up yet! It's going to go VOWNF! in two seconds and I'm trapped in here . . . I'm not going to be exploded to death *I'm going to be burned to death!*

Ten seconds later I was sprinting two hundred yards from the steaming wreckage of what had once been a handsome airplane, if not reliable or cheap or sweet. I tripped and threw myself face-down in the sand the way pilots do in movies just before the whole screen blows apart. Face down, covered my neck, waited for the blast.

Able to move with remarkable speed when finally gets picture.

Half a minute. Nothing happened. Another half.
I lifted my head and peeked.
Then I stood up, casually brushed the sand and sagebrush from the front of my clothes. For no reason, an antique rock-'n-roll tune began brassing my mind. I barely noticed. Trying to be nonchalant?

Son of a gun. Never heard of a '51 that didn't go up like a lit powderkeg, and here the one exception is the disaster scattered over there of which lately I was the pilot. Now there will be a stack of paperwork, reports to file . . . it'll be hours till I can catch an airliner west from here. The tune clattered on.

Doesn't suffer much from shock. B-plus for cool when it's all over.

Flattered, whistling the tune, I walked back to what was left of the Mustang, found my garment-bag and shaving-kit, took them safely aside.

Strong cockpit, got to say that for the thing.

And of course! The airplane hadn't blown up because we were out of gas, landing.

Around that time the observer faded, shaking his head, and the fire-trucks hove into sight. They didn't seem particularly interested in what I had to say about being out of fuel, smothered the wreck in foam, just in case.

I was concerned about the radios, some of which were undamaged in the cockpit, each of which cost more than gold. "Try not to get any foam in the cockpit, please, fellas? The radios . . ."

Too late. As a precaution against fire, they filled the cockpit to its rails.

So what, I thought helplessly. So-what so-what so-what?

I walked the mile to the airport terminal, bought a ticket on the next airline out, filled in the minimum possible incident report, told the wreckers where to sweep the parts of the obstinate machine.

In that moment, writing my address for them, on a desk in the hangar, I remembered the words to the tune that had been bebopping through my head since a moment after the crash.

Sh-boom, sh-boom . . . and a lot of *ya-t-ta ya-t-tas.*

Why should I be humming that song? I wondered. After twenty years, why now?

The song didn't care why, it rattled on: *Life could be a dream/Sh-boom/If I could take you to paradise up-above/Sh-boom* . . .

The song! It was the ghost of the Mustang singing, complete with sound-effects!

Life could be a dream, sweetheart . . .

Of course life is a dream, you tin witch! And you near did take me to paradise up above! *Sh-boom,* you shredded hulk!

Is there nothing goes through our mind that has no meaning? That airplane, it never could take me seriously.

The jetliner taxied past the sagebrush on its way to take-off. From the window by my seat I watched.

The foam-slopped Mustang body was already on a flatbed truck; a crane lifted torn wing-sections.

You want to play games, airplane? You like to have something break every flight, you want to have a clash of wills with me?

You lose! May you find someone who will forget your past and nail you back together someday a hundred years from now. May you remember this hour, and be nice to them! I swear, machine—for you I got no nails.

First the parachute failure, now an airplane-crash. I thought about those, flying west, and after a while decided that I had been divinely guided, protected without a scratch through moments turned a little more adventurous than I had planned.

Anybody else would have seen the opposite. The crash wasn't my protection at work, it was my protection running out.

nine

I WAS drowning in money. People around the world were reading the book, buying copies of other books I had written. Money from every book-sale came from the publisher back to me.

Airplanes I can handle, I thought, but money it makes me nervous. Can money crash?

Palm fronds waved outside his office window, sunlight warmed the reports on his desk. "I can handle this for you, Richard. There's no problem here. I can do it if you want me to." He stood an inch over five feet tall; his hair and beard had turned from red to white over the years, changing a gifted elf to an all-knowing Santa.

He was a friend from my magazine-writing days, editor turned investment counselor. I had liked him from the first story-assignment he had given me, admired his calm sense of business from the first day we had met. I trusted him completely, and nothing he had said all afternoon had flickered that trust.

"Stan, I can't tell you how glad . . ." I said. "It's got to be done right, but I don't know what to do with money; and paperwork and tax-things, I don't know about it, I don't like it. Effective now, Financial Manager, it's your business, full-time, and I'm out of it."

"You don't even want to know about it, Richard?"

I looked again at the graphs of his investing performance. All the lines went straight up.

"Nope," I said. "Well, I want to know if I ask, or if there's any huge decision you're about to make. But so much of what you're doing is so far over my head . . ."

"I wish you wouldn't say that," he said. "It's not magic, it's simple technical analysis of commodity markets. Most people fail in commodities because they don't have the capital to cover a margin call when the market moves against them. You—that is, we—don't have that problem. We start investing cautiously, with a large capital reserve. As we earn money with our strategies, we then become more speculative.

"When we walk into something as obvious as a head-and-shoulders in a commodity, we can move a lot of money and make a fortune. And we don't always go long, a lot of people forget that. There's just as much money to be made short." He smiled, noticed I was lost already.

He touched a graph. "Now you take this chart, which is plywood prices on the Chicago Board of Trade. You see right here's the head-and-shoulders starting, the warning that the bottom is about to fall out, this is last April. At that point we would have sold plywood, sold lots of plywood. Then when the price tumbles way down here, we would have bought lots. Sell high and buy low is the same as buy low and sell high. See that?"

How could we sell . . . "How can we sell before we've bought? Don't we have to buy before we sell?"

"No." He was as calm as a college dean, explaining. "These are commodities *futures*. We promise to sell later at this price, knowing that before the future comes, when we have to do the selling, we will have bought plywood—or sugar, or copper, or corn—at a much lower price."

"Oh."

"Then we reinvest. And diversify. Off-shore investments. An off-shore corporation might be a good idea, as a matter of fact. But CBT will be the place to start, maybe a seat on the West Coast Commodity Exchange. We'll see. Buy a seat on the Exchange, your broker fees go to nothing. Later, diversification; controlling interest in a little company on its way up could be wise. I'll be doing research. But with the amount of money we have to work with, and a conservative strategy for the markets, it'll be pretty hard to go wrong."

I came away convinced. What a relief! In no way can my financial future get tangled, parachute-like.

I'd never be able to handle money the way Stan did. Not patient enough, wise enough, and I don't have charts that shoot moonward.

Yet wise enough am I to know my own weakness, to find a trusted old friend, and give him control of my money.

ten

W<small>E LAY</small> in the sun on the deck, Donna and me, the two of us on my becalmed sailboat, drifting with the current thirty miles north of Key West. "No woman in my life owns me," I told her quietly, patiently, "and I own not one of them. That's terribly important to me. I promise: never will I be possessive of you, never jealous."

"That's a nice change," she said. Her hair was short and black, her brown eyes closed against the sun. She was tanned the color of oiled teak from years of summer since a divorce far northward. "Most men can't understand. I'm living the way I want to. I'll be with them if I want to be with them, I'll be gone if I don't. That doesn't frighten you?" She moved the straps of her bikini, to keep the tan unstreaked.

"Frighten? It delights me! No chains or ropes or knots, no arguments, no boredoms. A present from the heart: *I'm here not because I'm supposed to be here, or because I'm trapped here, but because I'd rather be with you than anywhere in the world."*

The water lapped gently. Instead of shadows, bright lights sparkled up on the sail.

"You will find me the safest friend you have," I said.

"Safest?"

"Because I cherish my own freedom, I cherish yours, too. I am extremely sensitive. If ever I touch you, do anything you'd rather not, you need whisper the gentlest 'No.' I despise intruders and crashers-into-privacy. You ever hint I'm one myself, you'll find me gone before you finish the hint."

She rolled on her side, head on her arm, and opened her eyes. "That does not sound like a proposal of marriage, Richard."

"It isn't."

"Thank you."

"Do you get a lot of those?" I asked.

"A few is too many," she said. "One marriage was enough. In my case, one marriage more than I should have had. Some people are better off married; I'm not."

I told her a little about the marriage I had ended, happy years gone hard and grim. I had learned exactly the lessons she had.

I checked the soft glass table of the Gulf for wind-ruffles. The sea was smooth as warm ice.

"What a shame, Donna, we can't disagree on something."

We drifted for another hour before wind caught the sails and the boat surged ahead. By the time we set foot on land once more we were good acquaintances, hugging farewell, promising to see each other again someday.

As it was with Donna, so with every other woman in my

life. Respect for sovereignty, for privacy, for total independence. Gentle alliances against loneliness, they were, cool rational love-affairs without the love.

Some of my women-friends had never married, but most were divorced. A few were survivors of unhappy affairs, beaten by violent men, terrified, warped by massive stress into endless depressions. Love, for them, was a tragic misunderstanding; love was an empty word left after meaning had been battered away by spouse-as-owner, lover-become-jailer.

Had I gone looking way far back in my thought, I might have found a puzzle: Love between man and woman isn't a word that works anymore. But Richard, is it a meaning?

I wouldn't have had an answer.

Months rippled by, and as I lost interest in love, what it is and isn't, so I lost the motive to look for my hidden soulmate. Gradually her place was taken by a different idea emerging, an idea as rational and flawless as those upon which my business affairs now turned.

If the perfect mate, I thought, is one who meets all of our needs all of the time, and if one of our needs is for variety itself, then *no one person anywhere can be the perfect mate!*

The only true soulmate is to be found in many different people. My perfect woman is partly the flash and intellect of this friend, she's partly the heart-racing beauty of that one, partly the devil-may-care adventure of another. Should none of these women be available for the day, then my soulmate sparkles in other bodies, elsewhere; being perfect does not include being unavailable.

"Richard, the whole idea is bizarre! It will never work!" Had the inner me shouted that, and it did, it would have had rags stuffed in its mouth.

"Show me why this idea is wrong," I would have said,

"show me where it won't work. And do it without using the words *love, marriage, commitment.* Do it bound and gagged while I shout louder than you can about how I intend to run my life!"

What do you know? The perfect-woman-in-many-women design, she won the contest hands-down.

An infinite supply of money. As many airplanes as I wish. The perfect woman for my own. This is happiness!

eleven

*T*HERE ARE no mistakes. The events we bring upon ourselves, no matter how unpleasant, are necessary in order to learn what we need to learn; whatever steps we take, they're necessary to reach the places we've chosen to go.

I lay on the floor, sunk in thick cinnamon carpet, and thought about it. These three years have not been mistakes. I built every year carefully, a million decisions each, into airplanes and magazine interviews and boats and travels and films and business staff and lectures and television shows and manuscripts and bank-accounts and copper-futures. Daylight air displays in the new little jet, nighttime talks and touches with many women, every one lovely, none of them her.

I was convinced she didn't exist, yet she haunted me still. Was she as sure that I didn't exist? Did my ghost disturb her convictions? Was there a woman somewhere this moment lying on plush carpet in a house built over a hangar with five airplanes inside, three more on the lawn and a floatplane tethered at water's edge?

I doubted it. But could there be one alone in the midst of news stories and TV shows, lonely while surrounded by lovers and money, hired friends-become-staff and agents and lawyers and managers and accountants? That was possible.

Her carpet might be a different color, but the rest . . . she could be on the other side of a mirror from here, finding her perfect man in fifty men, and still walking alone.

I laughed at myself. How hard the old myth of one love does die!

An airplane-engine started on the lawn below. That would be Slim, running up the Twin Cessna. A supercharger on the right side was leaking. Retrofit superchargers are retrofit problems, I thought, bolted onto what is otherwise a fine engine.

The Rapide and the motorglider are down there gathering dust. The Rapide is going to need rebuilding before long and that is going to be a monstrous job, a cabin biplane that size. Better sell the thing. I don't fly it enough. Don't fly anything enough. They're strangers to me, like everything else in my life. What is it I am trying to learn? That after a while, and in excess, machines begin to own us?

No, I thought, the lesson is this: To be handed a lot of money is to be handed a glass sword, blade-first. Best handle it very carefully, sir, very slowly while you puzzle what it's for.

The other engine started on the twin. Ground checkout must have been OK, and he's decided to take it up for a check in the air. A windy blast of power while he got the machine moving, then the sweet roar of engines faded as he taxied to the runway.

What else had I learned? That I hadn't survived publicity quite so unchanged as I had thought. I never would have believed, before, that anyone could stay curious about what I think and say and what I look like, where I live, what I do with my time and money; or that it would affect me the way it had, driven me back into caves.

Anyone fallen into camera or print, I thought, they didn't trip. Knowingly or not, they've chosen themselves to be examples for the rest of us to watch, they've volunteered as models. This one has marvels for a life; another is rolling wreckage, loose on deck. This one faces her adversity or her talent with calm wisdom, this one shrieks, this one leaps to his death, this one laughs.

Daily the world ties celebrities to tests and we watch fascinated, unable to turn away. Unable because the tests that our examples face are tests we all must face. They love, they marry, they learn, they quit and begin again, they are ruined; they transport us and they are transported, in plain sight of camera and ink.

The one test they face that others don't is the test of celebrity itself. Even then we watch. Someday it will be us in a spotlight, and examples are always welcome.

Whatever happened, I thought, to the airplane pilot from the fields of the Midwest? Had he turned so swiftly from simple flyer into frilly playboy?

I got up and walked across my empty house to the kitchen, found a bowl of corn chips gradually going stale, walked back to the Eames chair by the picture window and looked out over the lake.

Me, a playboy? Ridiculous. I haven't changed, inside, hardly a bit changed.

Do all frilly playboys say that, Richard?

A Piper Cub from the seaplane school next door practiced glassy-water landings . . . the long slow descent, power-on, and gentle touch on glistening Lake Theresa, then a step-turn and taxi back for takeoff.

The spotlight, it showed me how to hide, where to build walls. Everyone has plates of iron and rows of spikes somewhere inside that say this is as far as you go with me.

For the outgoing, recognition's fun. They don't mind the cameras; cameras come with the territory, and there are some pretty fine people behind those lenses. I can be nice as long as they can be nice, and about two minutes longer.

Such was the height of my wall that day in Florida. Most of the people who knew me from a talk-show here or a magazine cover there or a newspaper story across the way were people who couldn't know how grateful I was for their courtesy, for their respect of privacy.

I was surprised at the mail, glad for the family of readers to whom the strange ideas that I loved made sense. There were many people out there, inquisitive learning men and women every race age nation, every kind of experience. The family was so much larger than I had imagined!

Side-by-side with the delightful letters, once in a while came a few strange ones: write my idea; get me published; give me money or you'll burn in hell.

For the family I felt happy close warmth, sent postcards to reply; against the others was another ton of iron bolted to my wall, daggers welded along the top, rag of a welcome-mat snatched away.

I was a more private person than ever I thought. Had I

not known myself before, or was I changing? More and more, I chose to stay alone at home, that day and that month and those years. Stuck with my big house and nine airplanes and cobweb decisions I'd never make again.

I looked up from the floor to the photographs on the wall. There were pictures of airplanes that mattered to me. Not one human being there, not a single person. What had happened to me? I used to like who I was. Did I like me still?

I walked down the stairs to the hangar, pushed out the airshow biplane and slid into the cockpit. I met Kathy in this airplane, I thought.

Shoulder harness, seat belts, mixture rich, fuel pump ON, ignition ON. Such promise unfulfilled, and she's pushing me now about marriage. As though I've never told her the evils marriage brings, nor shown her I'm only part of the perfect man for her.

"Clear the prop!" I called from habit into the empty place, pressed the starter.

Half a minute after takeoff I was rolling inverted, climbing 2,000 feet per minute, the wind blasting over my helmet and goggles. Love it. A super-slow roll, first, to a sixteen-point. Sky clear? Ready? Now!

The green flat land of Florida; lakes and swamps rose majestically, immensely from my right, turned huge and wide over my head, set to my left.

Level. Then VAM! VAM! VAM! VAM! around went the land in sudden hard jerks, sixteen times. Pull straight up to a hammerhead stall, press left rudder, dive straight down, wind howling in the wires between the stubby wings, and push the stick forward to recover 160 mph upside-down. I threw my head back and looked up at the earth. Stick suddenly full back, hard right rudder, the biplane reared, stalled her right wings and spun twice around, a skygreen earthblue doubletwist; stick forward left rudder and HN! she stopped, wings-level inverted.

A split-S to squash me five Gs into the seat, tunnel my vision to a tiny hole of clear surrounded in grey, dive to a hundred feet over my practice-area and then through the routine again at low-level, airshow-height.

It clears the mind, Spanish moss roaring up toward one's windscreen, a swamp full of cypress and alligators rolling three hundred degrees per second around one's helmet.

The heart stays lonely.

twelve

*T*HERE HAD been not a word between us for minutes.

Leslie Parrish sat quietly on her side of the walnut-and-pine chessboard, I sat on mine. For nine moves in a breath-stopping midgame, the room was silent save for the soft thock of a knight or queen moved into place or out of it, an occasional hm or eek as lines of force swung open on the board, clanged shut.

Chess-players sketch their portraits in the motion of their pieces. Ms. Parrish neither bluffed nor deceived. She played eyes-open straight-on power chess.

I watched her through my laced fingers and smiled, even though she had just captured my bishop and threatened next move to take a knight I could ill afford to lose.

I had first seen that face years before, we had first touched in the most important of ways. By coincidence.

"Going up?" she called, and ran across the lobby to the elevator.

"Yes." I held the door open till she was inside. "Where you headed?"

"Three, please," she said. Three was my floor, too. The door paused a second, softly rumbled shut.

Bluegrey eyes glanced my way in thanks. I held the glance for less than a quarter-second, to tell her that it had been my pleasure to wait, then politely looked away. Darn politeness, I thought. What a lovely face! Had I seen her in movies? Television? I dared not ask.

We rode upward in silence. She was as tall as my shoulder, golden hair swirled and tucked under a spice-color cap. Not dressed like a movie-star: faded work-shirt under a surplus Navy coat, bluejeans, leather boots. Such a beautiful face!

She's here on location for the film, I thought. Is she a technician on the crew?

What pleasure it would be, to know her. But she's so far . . . Isn't it interesting, Richard, how infinitely far away she is? You two are standing thirty inches apart, yet there's no way to bridge the gulf and say hello.

If only we could invent a way, I thought, if only this were a world when unmet people could say you charm me and I'd like to know who you are. With a code: "No thanks," if the charm might not be mutual.

But that world hadn't yet been made. The half-minute ride finished without a word. Softly the door rumbled open.

"Thank you," she said. Barely on the walk side of running, she hurried down the hall to her room, opened the door, entered, closed it behind her and left me alone in the corridor.

I wish you didn't have to leave, I thought, entering my own room, two doors from hers. I wish you didn't have to run away.

By moving my knight, I could shift pressures on the board, blunt her attack. She had an advantage, but she hadn't won, not yet.

Of course! I thought. N-QN5! Threaten NxP, NxR!

I moved the piece, and watched her eyes once more, pleasuring in beauty strangely unflickered by my counterattack.

A year after our meeting in the elevator, I had brought suit against the director of that film, over changes he had made in the script without my approval. Even though he was required by the court to take my name off the credits and reverse some of the worst changes, I could hardly keep from smashing furniture while discussing the matter directly with him. A mediator had to be found with whom each of us could speak.

The mediator turned out to be actress Leslie Parrish, the woman who had shared the ride with me from the lobby to floor three.

Rage melted, talking with her. She was calm and reason—I trusted her at once.

Now Hollywood wanted to turn the latest book into a film. I swore I'd see the story burned before I'd let it be wrecked on screen. If it were to be made, would it best be made by my own company? Leslie was the one person I trusted in Hollywood, and I flew to Los Angeles to talk with her once more.

On the side-table in her office had been a chessboard.

Office chess-sets are most often designers' whims, fancy things with queens like bishops like pawns, pieces scattered in random wrong places. This set was a wooden tournament Staunton, three-and-a-half-inch king on a fourteen-inch board, white-corner square to the players' right, knights facing forward.

"Time for a quick game?" I had said when the meeting was finished. I was not the best chess-player in town; neither was I the worst. I've been playing the game since I was seven, and had a certain arrogant confidence at the board.

She had looked at her watch. "OK," she had said.

That she won the game startled me cold. The way she won, the pattern of her thought on the chessboard, charmed me warm again and then some.

The next meeting, we played for best two games out of three.

The next month we formed a corporation. She set to work to find a way to make the film with the lowest probability of disaster, and we played for best six games out of eleven.

After that there were no meetings required. I'd strap myself into my newest airplane, eight tons of ex-Air Force jet trainer, climb to 35,000 feet and fly from Florida out Jet Fifty to Los Angeles to spend a day at chess with Leslie.

Our games became less tournamental, words allowed, cookies and milk at table.

"Richard, you beast," she frowned over the pieces. Her side of the board was in real trouble.

"Yes," said I smugly. "I am a clever beast."

"But . . . check with the knight," she said, "and check with the bishop, and *guard your queen!* Isn't that a pretty move?"

Blood drained from my face. *Check* I had expected. *Guard-your-queen* was a surprise.

"Pretty indeed," I said, years of emergency-training forcing me casual. "My goodness . . . Hm . . . There's a move to be framed, it's so pretty. But I shall slip like a shadow away. Somehow like a shadow, Ms. Parrish, the Beast shall slip away. . . ."

Sometimes the beast twisted free, others he was herded into a corral and checkmated, only to be reborn half-a-cookie later, trying once more to catch her in his traps.

What strange alchemy between us! I assumed that she had a variety of men for her romances as I had women for mine. Assuming was enough; neither of us pried, each was infinitely respectful of the other's privacy.

Then once in the middle of chess she said, "There's a movie tonight at the Academy that I ought to see. The director might be good for us to think about. Want to come along?"

"Love to," I said absently, tending my defense against her king-side attack.

I had never been inside the theater of the Academy of Motion Picture Arts and Sciences; I was glamour-struck driving past the building. But here was I inside, watching a new film with a crowd of movie-stars. How odd, I thought. My simple life of flying is all at once connected to the inside of Hollywood by a book and a friend who beats me often as not at my favorite game.

After the movie, as she drove us east on Santa Monica Boulevard through the twilight, I was struck by inspiration:

"Leslie, would you care to . . ."

The silence was so tantalizing she said, "Would I care to what?"

"Leslie, would you care for a *hot fudge sundae?*"

She recoiled. "A *what?*"

"Hot . . . fudge . . . sundae. And a round of chess?"

"What a depraved thought!" she said. "The hot fudge, I mean. Haven't you noticed that I live on seeds and raw vegetables and yogurt and only rarely even a chess-cookie?"

"M. Noticed I have. That is why you need a hot fudge sundae. How long has it been? Honest, now. If it was last week you have to say last week."

"Last week? Last *year!* Do I look like I've been eating sundaes? Look at me!"

For the first time, I did. I sat back and blinked to discover what the dimmest male saw at once, that here was an extraordinarily attractive woman, that the thought that had built the exquisite face had also built a body to match.

In the months I had known her, she had been a charming bodyless sprite, a mind that was a dancing challenge, a reference-book of film production, classical music, politics, ballet.

"Well? Would you say I've been living on sundaes?"

"Beautiful! That is, no! That is definitely NOT a hot fudge body! Let me say this for certain . . ." I was blushing. What a stupid thing, I thought, for a grown man . . . Richard, change the subject fast!

"One little sundae," I said swiftly, "it wouldn't be harm,

it would be happiness. If you can make a turn there through traffic, we can get our hands on a pair of hot fudges, small ones, right now. . . ."

She looked at me, flashed a smile to assure me our friendship was safe; she knew that I had noticed her body for the first time, and she didn't mind. But her men-friends, I thought, would mind indeed, and that could bring problems.

Without discussion, without a word to her, I erased the idea of her body from my thought. For romance I had my perfect woman; for a friend and business-partner I needed to keep Leslie Parrish just the way she was.

thirteen

"I T'S NOT the end of the world," Stan said quietly, even before I had settled in the chair on the other side of his desk. "It's what we could call a bit of a reverse. The West Coast Commodity Exchange collapsed yesterday. They filed for bankruptcy. You've lost a little money."

My financial manager was always understated, which is why my jaw tightened at his words. "How little have we lost, Stan?"

"About six hundred thousand dollars," he said, "five hundred ninety-some thousand."

"Gone?"

"Oh, someday you might get a few cents on the dollar from the bankruptcy court," he said. "I'd consider it gone."

I swallowed. "Glad we're diversified. How go things at the Chicago Board of Trade?"

"You've had some setbacks there, too. Temporary, I'm

sure. You're having the longest string of losses I've ever charted. It can't go on like this forever, but for the time being it's not the best. You're down about eight hundred thousand dollars."

He was talking about more money than I had! How could I lose more than I had? On paper, he must mean. It's a paper loss. People cannot lose more money than they have.

If I could learn anything about money, maybe it would be well to pay closer attention to this business. But I would have to study for months, and money-handling is not like flying, it is suffocating dull stuff; even the pictures aren't easy to follow.

"It's not as bad as it sounds," he said. "A loss of a million dollars will cut your taxes to zero; you've lost more than that so you won't be paying a cent of income tax this year. But if I had a choice, I'd choose not to have lost it."

I felt no anger, no despair, as though I had stumbled into a situation comedy, as though by turning fast enough in my chair I'd find television cameras and a studio audience instead of Stan's office wall.

Unknown writer makes millions, loses them overnight. Isn't that some worn cliché? Is this really my life? While Stan explained the disasters, I wondered.

People with million-dollar incomes, they've always been somebody else. I, on the other hand, have always been me. I'm an airplane pilot, a barnstormer selling rides from hayfields. I'm a writer as rarely as possible, when forced by an idea too lovely to let die unwritten . . . what is the likes of me doing with a bank account of more than a hundred dollars which is all anyone could possibly need at one time anyway?

"Might as well tell you, while you're here," Stan went on

quietly. "The investment you made through Tamara, that high-interest, government-backed foreign development loan? Her client disappeared with the money. It was only fifty thousand dollars, but you ought to know."

I couldn't believe it. "He's her friend, Stan! She trusted him! And he's gone?"

"Left no forwarding address, as they say." He studied my face. "Do you trust Tamara?"

Oh, my. Please not *that* cliché! Pretty woman takes rich fool for fifty grand?

"Stan, are you saying that *Tamara* had something to do. . . ?"

"Possible. It looks to me like her handwriting on the back of the check. Different name, same handwriting."

"You're not serious."

He unlocked a file drawer, brought out an envelope, handed me a canceled check. *SeaKay Limited,* it was endorsed, *by Wendy Smythe.* High sweeping capital letters, graceful descenders on the y's. Had I seen those on an envelope, I would have sworn it was a note from Tamara.

"That could be anybody's writing," I said, and handed it back across the desk.

Stan didn't say another word. He was convinced that she had the money. But Tamara was my department; there would be no investigating unless I asked for it. I'd never ask, never say a word about it to her. And I'd never trust her again.

"You do have some money left," he said. "And of course there's new income, every month. After a long streak of bad luck, the market has to turn. Now, you could put the remaining assets in foreign currency. I have a hunch the dollar might fall against the Deutschmark any time now, so that you might earn your losses back, overnight."

"It's beyond me," I said. "Do what you think's best, Stan."

For all the warning-lights flashing and danger-bells clanging, my empire could have been a nuclear powerplant three minutes to melt-down.

At last I stood, picked my flying-jacket from the arm of the couch.

"Someday we'll look back on this as our low point," I told him. "From here on things can only get better, can't they?"

As if he hadn't heard, he said, "One more thing I've been meaning to tell you. It's not easy. Do you know that saying: 'Power corrupts, and absolute power corrupts absolutely'? Well, it does. I think that might be true for me, too."

I didn't know what he meant, and I was afraid to ask. His face was impassive. Stan, corrupted? Not possible. I had looked up to him for years, I couldn't question his honesty. "That might be true for me" could only mean that on an expense account, one time, he might have overcharged a little, by mistake. And corrected it, of course, but felt guilty nevertheless, duty-bound to tell me. And clearly if he were telling me now, he intends no such mistakes again.

"That's OK, Stan. What matters is where we go from here."

"Right," he said.

I put the incident out of my mind. What money remained was being handled by Stan, and by people he knew and trusted, people we paid well for their services. Would people like that let all these complicated money-things drop, a bag of springs off the roof? Of course they wouldn't, especially not now with so much going wrong. Reverses come to all, but my managers are swift of mind, I thought, and will find solutions many and soon.

fourteen

"JET ONE Five Five X-ray," I said, holding the microphone button down, "is out of flight-level three five zero for two seven zero, requesting lower."

I looked down over my oxygen mask seven miles to the afternoon desert of southern California, checking the sky clear below with a long slow-roll.

Technically, I was flying west to give a daylong talk at a Los Angeles university. I was glad, though, to be a few days early.

"Roger Five Five X," came back Los Angeles Center. "Cleared to two five zero, lower shortly."

Going down 400 miles per hour wasn't fast enough. I wanted to get this thing on the ground and see Leslie swifter than any airplane could fly.

"And Five Five X, you're cleared to one six thousand."

I acknowledged that, trimmed the nose of the airplane lower still, and faster. The altimeter needle spun downward.

"Jet Five Five X-ray is through flight-level one eight zero," I said, "and canceling Item Fox."

"Roger, Five X-ray, you are canceled at zero five. Squawk VFR, good day."

The lines from the oxygen mask were still on my face when I knocked on the door of her house at the edge of Beverly Hills. A symphony orchestra boomed on the sound-system inside; the heavy door trembled. I rang the doorbell, the music went quiet. And there she was, eyes of sea and sunshine, sparkling hello. No touch, not even a handshake, and neither of us thought it strange.

"I have a surprise for you," she said, smiling to herself at the thought of it.

"Leslie, I hate surprises. Sorry I never told you this, but I totally and completely hate surprises, despise presents. Anything I want, I buy for myself. If I don't have it, I don't want it. So by definition," I said, tying it up neatly and finally for her, "when you give me a present you are giving me something that I do not want. It's no problem, is it, to return it?"

She walked into the kitchen, her hair splashing lights across her shoulders, down her back. Ambling to intercept came her old cat, convinced it was suppertime. "Not yet," she told it softly. "No dinner yet for the fluffalorium."

"I'm surprised you *haven't* bought one for yourself," she said over her shoulder, with a smile to show that I hadn't hurt her feelings. "You certainly should have one, but if you don't want it, you can throw it away. Here."

The present was not wrapped. It was a large plain bowl from a dime-store, from a cheap dime-store, and there was a painting of a hog on the inside.

"Leslie! Had I seen *this* I would have bought it! This is stunning! What is this nice . . . thing?"

"I knew you'd like it! It's a hoggie-bowl. And . . . a hoggie-spoon!" And there was a spoon in my hand, an eighty-eight-cent steel spoon with the likeness of some anonymous pig stamped upon the handle. "And if you look in the refrigerator . . ."

I swung the thick door open and there stood a two-gallon drum of ice cream and a quart container labeled FUDGE FOR HOT, each with red ribbon and bow. Cold mist gently wafted from frost on the drum, falling silent slow-motion to the floor.

"Leslie!"

"Yes, Hoggie?"

"You . . . I . . . Do you think . . ."

She laughed, as much at herself for the mad caprice of what she had done as for the sounds my mind made while its wheels spun on ice.

It was not the present that stumbled my words but the unpredictability, that she who ate only seeds and a sparing salad would order wild extravagant sweets into her freezer just to watch me trip and numb over them.

I wrestled the tub of stuff from the refrigerator to the kitchen counter, pulled off the top. Full to the edges. Chocolate-chip ice cream. "I hope you got a spoon for you," I said severely, pushing my hog-spoon into the creamy snow. "You have done an unthinkable act, but now it is done and there is nothing for us to do but get rid of the evidence. Come. Eat."

She picked a miniature spoon from a drawer in the kitchen. "Don't you want your hot fudge? Don't you like hot fudge anymore?"

"Crazy about it. But after today, neither you nor I will ever want to see the letters 'hot fudge' so long as we might live."

No one does anything uncharacteristic of who they are, I thought, spooning the mass of fudge into a pan to heat. Could it be that she is characteristically unpredictable? How foolish of me to begin to think that I knew her!

I turned and she was looking at me, spoon in hand, smiling. "Can you really walk on water?" she said. "The way you did in the book with Donald Shimoda?"

"Of course. So can you. I haven't done it yet on my own, in this spacetime. In this my present belief of spacetime. You see, it gets complicated. But I'm working on it."

I stirred the fudge, stuck to the spoon in a half-pound lump. "Have you ever been out of your body?"

She didn't blink at the question or ask me to explain. "Twice. Once in Mexico. Once in Death Valley, on a hilltop at night under the stars. I leaned back to look and I fell up into the stars. . . ." There were sudden tears in her eyes.

I spoke quietly. "Do you remember, when you were in the stars, how easy it was, how natural, simple, right, real-as-coming-home it was, to be free of your body?"

"Yes."

"Walking on the water is the same. It's a power that's ours . . . it's a by-product of a power that's ours. Easy, natural. We have to study hard and remember *not* to use that power, or else the limitations of earth-life get all jangly and undependable, and we're distracted from our lessons. The trouble is that we get so good at telling ourselves we *won't* use our real powers that after a while we think we *can't.* Out there with Shimoda, there were no questions asked. When he wasn't around anymore, I stopped practicing. Little taste of that goes a long way, I guess."

"Like hot fudge."

I looked at her sharply. Was she mocking me?

The chocolate was beginning to bubble in the pan. "No. Hot fudge goes a lot longer than remembering basic spiritual realities. Hot fudge is HERE! Hot fudge does not threaten our comfortable worldview. Hot fudge is NOW! You about ready for some hot fudge?"

"Just a little teeny bit," she said.

By the time we had finished our dessert, we were late, and had to stand in a line two blocks long to buy our movie-tickets.

The wind was from the sea, cooling the night, and not wishing her to feel a chill, I put my arm around her. "Thank you," she said. "I didn't think we'd be outside so long. Are you cold?"

"Not at all," I said, "not cold at all."

We talked about the film we waited to see; mostly she talked and I listened; what to look for, how to notice where money is wasted in a film, and where it's saved. She hated wasting money. In the line we began to talk of other things, too.

"What's it like to be an actress, Leslie? I've never known, always wondered."

"Ah, Mary Moviestar," she said, laughing at herself. "Are you really interested?"

"Yes. It's a mystery to me, what sort of life it is."

"Depends. It's wonderful, sometimes, with a good script, good people who really want to do something worthwhile.

104

That's rare. The rest is just work. Most of it doesn't make much contribution to the human race, I'm afraid." She looked a question at me. "Don't you know what it's like? Haven't you ever been on a set?"

"Only outdoors, on location. Never on a sound-stage."

"Next time I'm shooting, would you like to come and see?"

"I would! Thank you!"

How much there is to know from her, I thought. What has she learned from celebrityhood . . . has it changed her, hurt her, made her build walls, too? There was about her a certain confident, positive grasp of life that was magnetic, deliciously attractive. She's stood on mountaintops I've only sighted from far off; she's seen lights, she knows secrets I've never found.

"But you didn't answer," I said. "Aside from making films—what's the life like, how does it feel, to be Mary Moviestar?"

She looked up at me, guarded for a moment, then trusting.

"It's exciting, at first. You think at first that you're different, that you have something special to offer, and that can even be true. Then you remember you're the same person you've always been; the only change is that suddenly your picture is everywhere and columns are being written about who you are and what you've said and where you're going next and people are stopping to look at you. And you're a celebrity. More accurately, you're a curiosity. And you say to yourself, *I don't deserve all this attention!*"

She thought carefully. "It isn't you that matters to people when they turn you into a celebrity. It's something else. It's *what you stand for, to them.*"

There's a ripple of excitement when a conversation turns valuable to us, the feel of new powers growing fast. Listen carefully, Richard, she's right!

"Other people think they know what you are: glamour, sex, money, power, love. It may be a press agent's dream which has nothing to do with you, maybe it's something you don't even like, but that's what they think you are. People rush at you from all sides, they think they're going to get these things if they touch you. It's scary, so you build walls around yourself, thick glass walls while you're trying to think, trying to catch your breath. You know who you are inside, but people outside see something different. You can choose to become the image, and let go of who you are, or continue as you are and feel phony when you play the image.

"Or you can quit. I thought if being a moviestar is so wonderful, why are there so many drunks and addicts and divorces and suicides in Celebrityville?" She looked at me, unguarded, unprotected. "I decided it wasn't worth it. I've mostly quit."

I wanted to pick her up and hug her for being so honest with me.

"You're the Famous Author," she said. "Does it feel that way to you; does this make sense to you?"

"A lot of sense. There's so much I need to know about this stuff. In the newspapers, have they done this to you? Print things you've never said?"

She laughed. "Things you've not only never said, but never thought, never believed, wouldn't think of doing. A story published about you, with quotes, word for word, made-up. Fiction. You've never seen the reporter . . . not even a phone call, and there you are in print! You pray readers won't believe what they see in some of those papers."

"I'm new at this, but I have a theory."

"What's your theory?" she said.

I told her about celebrities being examples that the rest of us watch while the world puts tests to them. It didn't sound as clear as what she had said.

She tilted her head up to me and smiled. When the sun went down, I noticed, her eyes changed color, to sea-and-moonlight.

"That's a nice theory, examples," she said. "But everybody's an example, aren't they? Isn't everybody a picture of what they think, of all the decisions they've made so far?"

"True. I don't know everybody, though; they don't matter to me unless I've met them in person or read about them or seen them on some screen. There was a thing on television a while ago, a scientist researching what it is that makes a violin sound the way it does. I thought what does the world need with that? Millions of people starving, who needs violin research?

"Then I thought no. The world needs models, people living interesting lives, learning things, changing the music of our time. What do people do with their lives who are not struck down with poverty, crime, war? We need to know people who have made choices that we can make, too, to turn us into human beings. Otherwise, we can have all the food in the world, and so what? Models! We love 'em! Don't you think?"

"I suppose," she said. "But I don't like that word, model."

"Why not?" I said, and knew the answer at once. "Were you a model?"

"In New York," she said, as though it were a shameful secret.

"What's wrong with that? A model is a public example of special beauty!"

"That's what's wrong with it. It's hard to live up to. It frightens Mary Moviestar."

"Why? What's she afraid of?"

"Mary got to be an actress because the studio thought she was so pretty, and she's been afraid ever since that the world is going to find out she isn't that pretty and she never was. Being a model was bad enough. When you call her a public example of being beautiful, it makes it worse for her."

"But Leslie, you *are* beautiful!" I blushed. "I mean, there's certainly no question that you're . . . that you're . . . extremely appealing. . . ."

"Thank you, but it doesn't matter what you say. No matter what you tell her, Mary thinks beauty is an image someone else created for her. And she's a prisoner of the image. Even when she goes to the grocery store, she should be all done up, just so. If not, somebody is sure to recognize her and they'll say to their friends, 'You ought to see her in person! She's not half as pretty as she's supposed to be!' and Mary's disappointed them." She smiled again, a little sad. "Every actress in Hollywood, every beautiful woman I know is *pretending* to be beautiful, she's afraid the world will find out the truth about her sooner or later. Me, too."

I shook my head. "Crazy. You're all crazy."

"The world's crazy, when it comes to beauty."

"I think you're beautiful."

"I think you're crazy."

We laughed, but she wasn't kidding.

"Is it true," I asked her, "that beautiful women lead

tragic lives?" It was what I had concluded from my Perfect Woman, with her many bodies. Perhaps not quite tragic, but difficult. Unenviable. Painful.

She considered that. "If they think their beauty is *them,*" she said, "they're asking for an empty life. When everything depends on looks, you get lost gazing in mirrors and you never find yourself."

"You seem to have found yourself."

"Whatever I've found, it's not by being beautiful."

"Tell me."

She did, and I listened, startled turning astonished. The Leslie she found hadn't been on film, but in the peace movement, in the speakers' bureau she formed and ran. The real Leslie Parrish made speeches, fought political campaigns, struggled against an American government bent on war in Viet Nam.

While I flew Air Force fighter-planes, she was coordinating West Coast peace-marches.

For daring to oppose the institution of war, she was teargassed by the law, attacked by right-wing gangs. She went on afterwards, organizing ever-larger rallies, producing massive fund-raisers.

She had helped elect congresspeople, senators and the new mayor of Los Angeles. She had been a delegate to presidential conventions.

Cofounder of KVST-TV, a Los Angeles television station with special powers built in for the downtrodden minorities of the city, she had taken over as president when the station was in trouble, deep in debt and not a day's patience left among the creditors. Station bills she paid sometimes with money from her film work, and the station survived, it began to prosper. People watched, wrote reviews nationwide about the noble experiment. With success came the power struggle. She was called a racist rich-person; she was fired by the downtrodden. KVST went off the air the day she left, and it never went on again. To this day, she told me, she couldn't see the blank screen on Channel 68 without pain.

Mary Moviestar paid the way for Leslie Parrish. Devout righter-of-wrongs and changer-of-worlds, Leslie had walked alone into late-night political meetings in parts of the city that I didn't have the courage to fly over at noon. She stood in picket lines for the farm workers, marched for them, raised money for them. She had thrown herself, a nonviolent resister, into some of the most violent battles of modern America.

Yet she refused to play nude-scenes in motion pictures. "I wouldn't sit around my living room naked with my friends on a Sunday afternoon. Why should I do it with a bunch of strangers on a movie set? For me, doing something so unnatural for pay would have been prostitution."

When every role in films had its nude-scene, she sank her movie career, switched to television.

I listened to her as though the innocent fawn I touched on a meadow had grown up in the firestorms of hell.

"There was a march, one time, in Torrance, a peace march," she said. "The planning was done, we had our permits. A few days before, we were warned that the right-wing crazies were going to shoot one of our leaders if we dared to march there. It was too late to cancel. . . ."

"It's not too late to cancel!" I said. "Don't do it!"

"Too many people already coming, too short notice. We couldn't reach them all at the last minute. If just a few showed up alone against crazies, that would be murder, wouldn't it? So we called the newspapers and the television networks, we said come on out and watch us get killed in Torrance! Then we marched; we linked arms with the man they said they'd shoot; we surrounded him and marched. They'd have had to kill everybody, to get him."

"You . . . did they shoot?"

"No. Killing us on-camera wasn't part of their plan, I guess." She sighed, remembering. "Those were the bad old days, weren't they?"

I couldn't think what to say. That moment, standing in the movie-line, I had my arm around a rare person in my life: a human being whom I totally admired.

I the retreater was struck dumb with the contrast between us. If others wish to fight and die in wars or in protesting wars, I had decided, that's their freedom. The only world that matters to me is the world of the individual, the world each of us creates to be our own. Sooner I'd try to change history than turn political, than try convincing others to write letters or to vote or to march or to do something they didn't already feel like doing.

She's so different from me, why this awe-full respect for her?

"You are thinking something very important," she said with an important frown at me.

"Yes. Right. You are absolutely right." I knew her so well in that moment, and liked her so well, that I told her what it was. "I was thinking that it is the very difference between us that makes you the best friend I have."

"Oh?"

"We have a little in common—chess, hot fudge, we want to get the film made—but we're so different in every other way that you don't threaten me the way other women do.

111

With them there's the hope of marriage, sometimes, in their minds. One marriage was enough, for me. Never again."

The line inched forward. We'd be inside the theater in less than twenty minutes.

"It's the same with me," she said, and laughed. "I don't mean to threaten you, but that's another thing we have in common. I was divorced a long time ago. I dated hardly at all before I was married, so after my divorce, I went out on dates dates dates! It's impossible to get to know someone that way, don't you think?"

We can get to know them a little, I thought, but better to hear what she thinks.

"I have dated some of the brightest, most glamorous, wealthy men in the world," she said, "but they didn't make me happy. Most of them pull up at your door in a car bigger than your house, they're wearing the right clothes and they take you to the right restaurant where all the other right people have gone, and you get your picture taken and it all looks so glamorous and fun and right! I kept thinking, I'd rather go to a *good* restaurant than the right one, wear clothes I like instead of what designers thought was In, that year. Most of all, I'd rather have a quiet talk or go for a walk in the woods. Different values, I guess.

"We have to deal in a currency that's meaningful to us," she said, "or all the success in the world won't feel good, it won't bring happiness. If someone promised they'd pay you a million scrunchies to walk across the street, and scrunchies had no meaning for you, would you cross the street? If they promised a hundred million scrunchies, so what?

"I felt that way about most of the things highly valued in Hollywood—as if I were dealing in scrunchies. I had all the right things, yet somehow I felt empty, I couldn't seem to care. What's a scrunchy worth? I wondered. All the while, I was afraid if I kept on dating, sooner or later I'd hit the jackpot worth millions of scrunchies."

"What was that?"

"I'd *marry* Mr. Right; wear the right clothes for the rest of my life, play hostess to all the right people at the right parties: his parties. He'd be my trophy and I'd be his. Soon we'd be complaining that the meaning had gone out of our marriage, we weren't as close as we should be—when we'd never had meaning or closeness to begin with.

"Two things I do value a lot, intimacy and the capacity for joy, didn't seem to be on anyone else's list. I felt like the stranger in a strange land, and decided I'd better not marry the natives.

"That's another thing I quit. Dating. And now . . ." she said, ". . . want to know a secret?"

"Tell me."

"Now I'd rather be with my friend Richard than on a date with anybody!"

"Awww . . ." I said. I hugged her for that, a shy one-arm hug.

Leslie was unique in my life: a beautiful sister whom I trusted and admired, with whom I spent night after night over a chessboard, but never a moment in bed.

I told her then about my perfect woman, how well the idea worked for me. I sensed she didn't agree, but she listened with interest. Before she could respond, the line moved into the theater.

Inside the lobby, out of the cold, I took my arm from around her and didn't touch her again.

The movie we saw that night was one we were to watch

eleven times before the end of the year. In that film was a large furry blue-eyed creature from another planet, copilot of a battered spaceship. The creature was called a wookie. We loved him as though we were two wookies ourselves, with our own idol on-screen.

The next time I flew to Los Angeles, Leslie met me at the airport. When I was down from the cockpit she handed me a box, ribbon and bow tied around.

"I know you hate presents," she said, "so I got you one."

"I never give you presents," I gruffed pleasantly. "That's my present to you: I never give you presents. Why. . . ?"

"Open it," she said.

"OK, this one time. I'll open it, but . . ."

"Open it," she said impatiently.

The present was a latex-and-creature-fur wookie-mask, a pullover hat-to-the-neck complete with eye-holes and partly bared teeth—a perfect likeness of our motion-picture hero. "Leslie. . . !" I said. I loved it.

"Now you can tickle all your girlfriends with your soft furry face. Put it on."

"Right here at the airport in public you want me to. . . ?"

"Oh, put it on! For me. Put it on."

She charmed the ice out of me. I put on the mask, to please her, gave her a wookie-roar or two, and she laughed till she cried. Behind the mask I laughed too, and thought how much I cared for her.

"Come on, wookie," she said, brushing tears, impulsively taking my hand. "We'll be late."

True to her word, she drove us from the airport to MGM, where she was finishing a television film. Along the way I noticed people looking frightened at me in the car, and took off the mask.

For one who had never been on a sound-stage, it was the same as being invited to the moon Complexity, that turned about the planet Deadline. Cables and stands and booms and cameras and dollies and tracks and ladders and cat-walks and lights . . . a ceiling so encrusted with enormous heavy lights I swore the beams would crack overhead. Men were everywhere, wrestling equipment into position, adjusting it, or perching in the midst of it waiting for the next ringing bell or flashing light.

She emerged from her dressing room in a gold lamé gown, or the better part of one, and glided to me across the cables and traps in the floor as though they were patterns on a rug. "Can you see OK from here?"

"Sure can." I squirmed in the stares of stagehands watching her; she was oblivious to them. I was nervous, self-conscious, a prairie-horse in a tropic jungle; she was at home. It felt to me as if the temperature was in the low hundreds; she was cool and fresh and bright.

"How do you do it? How can you act, with all this going on, all of us watching? I thought acting was sort of a private thing, somehow. . . ."

"COMING THROUGH! HEADS UP!" The two men were rushing a tree onstage, and had she not touched me on the shoulder to step aside, I would have been branched through the side of a painted street.

She looked at me and at what I thought was chaos around us. "There's going to be an awful lot of waiting around while they're setting up the special effects," she said. "I hope you won't be bored."

"Bored? It's fascinating! And you're just as cool—aren't you the littlest bit nervous, to do it right?"

An electrician on the catwalk above us looked down at her and called across the ceiling, "Sure can see those mountains clear today, George! *Beautiful!* Oh, hi, Miss Parrish, how you doin', down there?"

She looked up and pressed the top of the gold lamé to her chest. "Go on, you guys," she laughed. "Is that all you have to do?"

The electrician winked at me, shook his head. "Workman's compensation!"

She continued without so much as a frown. "The producer's nervous. They're a day and a half behind. We might stay late tonight to make it up on overtime. If you get tired and I'm in the middle of something, run on back to the hotel and I'll call you later, if it's not too late."

"Doubt I'll get tired. Don't let me talk to you if I shouldn't be, if you want to study your lines. . . ."

She smiled. "No problem," she said, and glanced toward the set. "I ought to get in there now. Have fun."

Next to the camera, a fellow shouted, *"First team! Places, please!"*

Why wasn't she at least a little tense about remembering her lines? I'm lucky to remember words I've written myself, without reading them over and over again. Why wasn't she nervous, with so much to remember?

The shooting began, one scene and then another, then one more. Not once did she look at her script. I felt as if I were a friendly spirit, watching the role she played in the drama onstage. She didn't miss a line. Watching her at work was watching a friend who was at the same time a stranger. I felt a curious warm apprehension—my own sister, centered in lights and cameras!

Does it change the way I feel about her, I thought, to see her there?

Yes. There is something magical going on. She has skills and powers I haven't learned, and never will. I wouldn't have liked her less if she weren't an actress, but I did like her more because she was. There has always been electricity for me, pleasure in meeting people who can do things that I can't. That Leslie was one of them pleasured me indeed.

Next day in her office, I asked a favor. "Can I borrow your telephone? I want to call the Writers' Guild. . . ."

"Five five oh, one thousand," she said absently, pushing the phone toward me as she read a financing proposal from New York.

"What's that?"

She looked up. "The telephone number of the Writers' Guild."

"You know the number?"

"M-hm."

"How come you know it?"

"I know lots of numbers." She went back to the proposal.

"What does that mean, 'I know lots of numbers'?"

"I just know lots of numbers," she said sweetly.

"What if I wanted to call . . . Paramount Studios?" I said suspiciously.

"Four six three, oh one hundred."

I squinted at her, sideways. "A good restaurant?"

"Magic Pan's good. It has a no-smoking section. Two seven four, five two two two."

I reached for a telephone book, turned to a listing. "Screen Actors Guild," I said.

"Eight seven six, three oh three oh." She was right.

I began to understand. "You haven't . . . Leslie, the script yesterday, you don't have a photographic memory, do you? You haven't memorized . . . *the entire telephone book?*"

"No. It's not a photographic memory," she said. "I don't see, I just remember. My hands remember numbers. Ask me for a number and watch my hands."

I opened the huge book, turned pages.

"City of Los Angeles, Office of the Mayor?"

"Two three three, one four five five."

The fingers of her right hand moved as though she were dialing a push-button telephone in reverse, taking numbers off instead of putting them in.

"Dennis Weaver, the actor."

"One of the sweetest human beings in Hollywood. His home number?"

"Yes."

"I promised I'd never give it out. How about *The Good Life*, his wife's health-food store?"

"OK."

"Nine eight six, eight seven five oh."

I looked up the number; of course she was right again. "Leslie, you're scaring me!"

"Don't be scared, wookie. It's just a funny thing that happens with me. I memorized music when I was little, and every license plate in town. When I came to Hollywood, I memorized scripts, dance routines, phone numbers, schedules, conversations, anything. The number of your pretty yellow jet airplane is N One Five Five X. Your hotel number

118

is two seven eight, three three four four; you are staying in room two one eight. When we left the studio last night you said, 'Remind me to tell you about my sister in show business.' I said, 'Can I remind you now?' and you said, 'I think you might as well because I really want to tell you about her.' I said, 'Do I know . . .' " She broke off remembering and laughed at my astonishment. "You're looking at me as if I'm a freak, Richard."

"You are. But I like you anyway."

"I like you too," she said.

Late that afternoon, I was working on a television screenplay, rewriting the last few pages, knocking them out on Leslie's typewriter while she slipped into the garden to care for her flowers. Even there, so different we were. Flowers are pretty little things, all right, but to put so much time into them, to have them depending on you to water them and feed them and wash them and whatever else flowers need . . . dependence is not for me. I'd never be a gardener, she'd never be otherwise.

There among the plants in her office were shelves of books reflecting mists of the rainbow that she was, there above her desk the quotes and ideas that mattered to her:

Our country right or wrong. WHEN RIGHT, TO BE KEPT RIGHT; WHEN WRONG, TO BE PUT RIGHT.
   —Carl Schurz.
No smoking, here or anywhere.
Hedonism is no fun.
I tremble for my country when I reflect that God is just.
   —Thomas Jefferson.
Suppose they gave a war, and no one came?

The last was a quote from herself. She had it printed as a bumper-sticker, and then it had been picked up by the peace movement and spread fast as television around the world.

I studied those from time to time between paragraphs of my script, knowing her better with every spade-crunch, scissor-snip, rake-scratch from her garden, the muffled hiss of water through pipes and hose, gently slaking the thirst of her flower family. She knew and loved each separate blossom.

Different different different, I thought, finishing the last paragraph, but my, I admire that woman! Have I ever, for all our differences, had a friend like her?

I stood and stretched, walked through the kitchen and the side door into her garden. Her back was to me as she watered the flower-beds, the long hair pulled into a work-time ponytail. I walked quietly and stood a few feet behind her. She was singing softly to her cat.

"You are a pussycat, oh yes you are/my fluffalorium, my little star/and if you leave me, don't go far. . . ."

Her cat clearly enjoyed the song, but it was too intimate a moment for me to be standing there unseen, so I spoke as if I had just arrived.

"How are your flowers doing?"

She whirled about, hose in hand, eyes blue-saucer fright that she wasn't alone in her private garden. The nozzle of the hose was pointed chest-high, but it was set to drench a cone several feet in diameter, from my mouth to my belt. Neither of us said a word, neither moved while the hose poured water into me as though I were a tall fire escaped.

She was stricken with fright, first from my sudden words, then from what the water was doing to my coat and shirt. I stood without moving, because I thought it unseemly to scream and run, because I hoped that before long she might decide to turn the hose in some other direction than point-blank on my city-clothes.

As well she held a sandblaster, the scene is so clearly etched today . . . the sunlight, the garden around us, her eyes enormous astonishment at this polar bear broken into her flower-patch, a hose her only defense. If you water a polar bear long enough, she must have been thinking, it will turn and dash away.

I didn't feel like a polar bear, except for the ice-water spraying over me, soaking in. I saw her horror, finally, at what she was doing to what was not a polar bear but a business-partner friend and guest in her home. Though she was still frozen aghast, she gained control of her hose-hand and slowly turned the water away.

"Leslie!" I said into a dripping silence, "it was only me. . . ."

Then she was crying with laughter, her eyes helpless merry blurred shock, imploring forgiveness. She fell laughing, sobbing, against my coat, which squished water from the pockets.

fifteen

"ATHY CALLED today from Florida," said Leslie, moving her chesspeople to their places for another game. "Is she jealous?"

"Not possible," I said. "Jealousy is not part of my agreement with any woman."

I frowned to myself. After all these years, I still have to mutter "Queen-on-Her-Own-Color" to set my pieces right.

"She wanted to know if you have some special girlfriend out here, you've been coming to Los Angeles so much lately."

"Oh, come on," I said. "You're not serious."

"Honest."

"What did you tell her?"

"I told her not to worry. I told her that when you're here, you don't go out with *anybody*, you spend all your time with me. I think she felt better, but maybe you ought to go over your no-jealousy agreement with her one more time to be sure."

She left the table for a minute to puzzle over her tape collection. "I have Brahms's First by Ozawa, by Ormandy and by Mehta. Any preferences?"

"Whatever will be most distracting to your chess."

She considered for a moment, chose a tape and slid it into the intricate electronics of her sound-system.

"Inspiring," she corrected. "For distraction, I have other tapes."

We played for half an hour, a tough game from the first move. She had just reread her *Modern Ideas in the Chess Opening,* which would have powdered me had I not finished *Chess Traps, Pitfalls and Swindles* two days earlier. We played nearly to a draw; then a brilliant move on my part, and the game teetered in the balance.

As far as I could see, any move but one would be disaster. Her only escape was an obscure pawn advance, to control the hidden square around which I had built a towering delicate strategy. Without that square, my effort would collapse in rubble.

The part of me that takes chess seriously hoped she would see the move, demolish my position and force me to fight for my hand-carved wooden life (I play best when my back is to the wall). Yet I couldn't imagine how I would recover if she blocked this scheme.

The part of me that knew it was just a game hoped she wouldn't see it, because it was such a pretty, such an elegant strategy I had coming up. A Queen sacrifice, and five moves to checkmate.

I closed my eyes for a minute, while she considered the

board, opened them, struck head-on by a remarkable thought.

There in front of me was a table and a window full of color; beyond, the twilight flickerings of Los Angeles, the last of June fading into the sea. Silhouetted against twinkles and color was Leslie misted in thought, as still as a warned deer over a chessboard melted honey and cream in the shadows of an evening still to come. A warm soft vision, I thought. Where did it come from, who's responsible for it?

A quick little trap of words, a net of ink and pocket notebook over the idea before it vanished.

From time to time, I wrote, *it's fun to close our eyes, and in that dark say to ourselves, "I am the sorcerer, and when I open my eyes I shall see a world that I have created, and for which I and only I am completely responsible." Slowly then, eyelids open like curtains lifting stage-center. And sure enough, there's our world, just the way we've built it.*

I wrote that at high speed in dim light. Then closed my eyes, tested once more: *I am the sorcerer* . . . slowly opened my eyes again.

Elbows on chess-table, face cupped in hands, I saw Leslie Parrish, eyes large and dark looking directly into my own.

"What did the wookie write?" she said.

I read it to her. "The little ceremony," I said, "is a way of reminding ourselves who's running the show."

She tried it, *"I am the sorceress . . ."* She smiled when she opened her eyes. "Did that just come to you now?"

I nodded.

"I created you?" she said. "I'm responsible for bringing you onstage? Movies? Sundaes? Chessgames and talks?"

I nodded again. "Don't you think so? You're the cause of me-as-you-know-me. Nobody else in the world knows the

Richard that's in your life. No one knows the Leslie that's in mine."

"That's a nice note. Would you tell me some other notes, or am I prying?"

I turned on a light. "I'm glad you understand that these are very private notes. . . ." I said it lightly, but it was true. Did she know it was another ribbon of trust between us, first that she who respected my privacy would ask to hear the notes and next that I'd read them to her? I had a notion that she knew it well.

"We have some book titles," I said, *"Ruffled Feathers: A Birdwatcher's Exposé of a National Scandal.* Here's one could be a five-volume set—*What Makes Ducks Tick?"*

I turned the page back, skipped a grocery list, turned another page.

"Look in a mirror, and one thing's sure: what we see is not who we are. That was after your talk about mirrors, remember?

"When we look back on our days, they've passed in a flash. Time doesn't last, and nobody's got long to live! SOMETHING bridges time—What? What? What?

"You can tell that all of these aren't quite finished yet. . . .

"The best way to pay for a lovely moment is to enjoy it.

"The only thing that shatters dreams is compromise.

"Why not practice living as though we were extremely intelligent? How would we live if we were spiritually advanced?"

I reached the first page of the month's notes. *"How do we save the whales? WE BUY 'EM! If whales were bought, and then made American citizens, or French or Australian or Jap-*

anese, there's no country in the world dare lay a hand on 'em!'"

I raised my eyes to hers, over the notebook. "That's about it so far this month."

"We buy 'em?" she said.

"I don't have the details of that worked out. Each whale would carry the flag of the country it belongs to, a giant passport, sort of. Waterproof, of course. The money from the sale of citizenships goes to a big Whale Fund, something like that. It could work."

"What do you do with them?"

"Let 'em go where they want. Raise little whales . . ."

She laughed. "I mean what do you do with your *notes.*"

"Oh. End of every month, I read them through, see what they're trying to tell me. Maybe a few will wind up in a story or a book, maybe they won't. To be a note is to lead a very uncertain life."

"These notes tonight, do they tell you anything?"

"I don't know yet. A couple of them are saying I'm not too sure this planet is home. Do you ever have the feeling you're a tourist on earth? You'll be walking down the street and suddenly it's like a moving postcard around you? *Here's how the people live here, in big house-shaped boxes to keep off 'rain' and 'snow,' holes cut in the sides so they can see out. They move around in smaller boxes, painted different colors, with wheels on the corners. They need this box-culture because each person thinks of herself and himself as locked in a box called a 'body,' arms and legs, fingers to move pencils and tools, languages because they've forgotten how to communicate, eyes because they've forgotten how to see. Odd little planet. Wish you were here. Home soon.* Has that ever happened to you?"

"Once in a while. Not quite that way," she said.

"Can I get you anything from your kitchen?" I said, "a cookie or something?"

"No, thank you."

I got up and found the cookie-jar, put a leaning tower of chocolate-chips on a plate for each of us. "Milk?"

"No, thank you."

I brought the cookies and milks to the table.

"The notes remind. They help me remember that I'm a tourist on earth, remind me the funny customs they have here, how fond I am of the place. When I do that, I can almost recall what it's like where I came from. There's a magnet that's pulling on us, pulling us against the fence of this world's limits. I have this strange feeling that we come from the other side of the fence."

Leslie had questions about that, and she had answers I hadn't thought of. She knew a world-as-it-ought-to-be, that I bet her was a warless world-as-it-is on some parallel dimension. The idea bemused us, melted the clock away.

I picked a chocolate-chip cookie, imagined it warm, attacked it gently. Leslie sat back with a curious little smile, as though she cared about my notes, about the thoughts that I found so interesting.

"Have we talked about writing before?" I said.

"No." She reached for a cookie at last, her resistance broken by the patient ruthless proximity of her favorite morsel. "I'd love to hear. I'll bet you started early."

How odd, I thought. I want her to know who I am!

"Yep. Everywhere at home, when I was a kid, books. When I learned to crawl, there were books at nose-level. When I could stand, there were books that went on out of sight, higher than I could reach. Books in German, Latin, Hebrew, Greek, English, Spanish.

"My dad was a minister, grew up in Wisconsin speaking German, learned English when he was six, studied Bible languages, speaks them still. My mother worked in Puerto Rico for years.

"Dad would read stories in German and translate them for me as he read; Mom would chat with me in Spanish even when I couldn't understand, so I grew up sort of basted in words. Delicious!

"I loved opening books to see how they'd begin. Writers create books the way we write lifetimes. A writer can: lead any character, to any event, for any purpose, to make any point. What does this writer do, or this one, I wanted to know, with a blank Page One? What do they do to my mind and my spirit, when I read their words? Do they love me or despise me or don't they care? Some writers are chloroform, I found out, but some are cloves and ginger.

"Then I went to high school, learned to hate English Grammar, so bored with it I'd yawn seventy times in a fifty-minute class, walk out at the end slapping my face to wake up. Came my senior year at Woodrow Wilson High School, Long Beach, California, I picked Creative Writing to duck the torment of English Literature. Room four-ten, it was. Sixth-period Creative Writing."

She moved her chair out from behind the chess table, listening.

"The teacher of the class was John Gartner, the football coach. But John Gartner, Leslie, he was also a writer! In person, a real writer! He wrote stories and articles for outdoor magazines, books for teenagers: *Rock Taylor—Football Coach, Rock Taylor—Baseball Coach.* A bear, he was, stood about six-foot-five, hands this big; tough and fair and funny and angry sometimes, and we knew he loved his work and he loved us, too." All at once there was a tear in my eye, and I wiped it away, swiftly, thinking how strange. Haven't thought of Big John Gartner . . . he's been dead ten years and now there's this odd feeling in my throat. I hurried on, trusting she wouldn't notice.

" 'OK, you guys,' he said the first day. 'I know you're in here so you don't have to take English Literature.' There was this guilty murmur you could hear among us, and the class kind of looked the other way. 'Let me tell you,' he said, 'the only way that anyone in this class gets an A on their report card is to show me the check from a piece of writing that you have written and sold this semester.' A chorus of groans and whines and howls . . . 'Oh, Mister GART-NER that's not fair, we're poor little high-school kids, how could you possibly expect—that's not FAIR, Mister Gart-ner!' which he silenced with a word that sounded like, 'GROWL.'

" 'There's nothing wrong with a grade of B. B is Above Average. You can be Above Average without selling what you write, can't you? But A is Superior. Don't you agree that if you sell something that you have written it would be superior and you would be worth an A?' "

I picked the second-to-last cookie from my plate. "Am I telling you more than you want to know?" I asked her. "Honest, now."

"I'll say when to stop," she said. "Unless I ask you to stop, go on, OK?"

"Well. I was highly grade-oriented, in those days."

She smiled, remembering report-cards.

"I wrote a lot and sent articles and stories to newspapers

and magazines and just before the end of the semester sent a story to the Sunday supplement of the *Long Beach Press-Telegram*. It was a story about a club of amateur astronomers. *They Know the Man in the Moon.*

"Imagine the shock! I come home from school, bring in the trash can from the street, feed the dog, and Mom hands me a letter from the *Press-Telegram!* Instant ice in all veins! I tremble it open, gulp through the words, start again and read from the beginning. *They bought my story!* Check enclosed for twenty-five dollars!

"Can not sleep, can not wait for school to open in the morning. Finally it opens, finally sixth period, I whomp it dramatically on his desk, WHOMP! 'There's your check, Mister Gartner!'

"His face . . . his face lit up and he shook my hand so I couldn't move it for an hour. Announced to the class Dick Bach sold an article, to make me feel about a quarter-inch high. Got my A in Creative Writing, no further effort required. And I figured that was the end of the story."

I thought about that day . . . twenty years ago or yesterday? What happens to time, in our minds?

"But it wasn't," she said.

"It wasn't what?"

"It wasn't the end of the story."

"Nope. John Gartner showed us what it was to be a writer. He was working on a novel about teachers. *Cry of September*. Wonder if he finished it before he died. . . ." Again, a queer tightening in my throat; I thought it best to press on and finish this story and change the subject.

"He'd bring in a chapter every week from his book, read it aloud and ask us how we'd write it better. It was his first novel for grown-ups. It had a lovestory in it, and his face would get bright red, reading parts of it, he'd laugh and shake his head in the middle of a sentence he thought was a little too true and tender for a football-coach to be sharing with his writing class. He had a terrible time writing women. Whenever he got too far from sports and the outdoors, we could hear it in his writing; telling about women was creaking along thin ice. So we'd criticize gleefully; we'd say, 'Mister Gartner, the lady doesn't seem quite as real to us as Rock Taylor does. Is there some way you can *show* her to us instead of *tell* her to us?'

"And he'd bellow with laughter and pat his handkerchief over his forehead and he'd agree, he'd agree. Because always Big John drove it into us, he'd pound his fist on the table: 'Don't TELL me, SHOW me! *INCIDENT!* and *EXAMPLE!*' "

"You loved him a lot, didn't you?"

I smashed away another tear. "Ah . . . he was a good teacher, little wookie."

"If you loved him, what's wrong with saying that you loved him?"

"I never thought of it that way. I did love him. I do love him."

And then before I knew what I was doing, I was kneeling in front of her, arms around her legs, head down in her lap, sobbing for a teacher whose death I had heard fifth-hand without a blink, years before.

She stroked the back of my head. "It's all right," she said softly, "it's all right. He must be so proud of you, and your writing. He must love you, too."

What a strange feeling, I thought. This is what it's like to cry! It had been so long since I had done more than clench my jaw and bring down steel against sorrow. The last time I had cried? I couldn't remember. The day my mother died, a month before I became an aviation cadet, off to earn my wings in Air Force pilot training. From the day I joined the military, intensive practice in emotional control: Mr. Bach, henceforth you will salute all moths and flies. Why will you salute all moths and flies? You will salute all moths and flies because they have their wings and you do not. There is a moth on yonder window. Mister Bach, Laiuff: FACE! Fowurd: HAR! And: HALT! Face moth: FACE! Hand: SALUTE! Wipe that smile off your mouth, Mister. Now step on that smile, kill that smile, KILL IT! Now pick it up and carry it outside and bury it. You think this program's a joke? *Who's in control of your emotions, Mister Bach!"*

That was the center of my training, that's what mattered: who's in control?

Who's in control? I am! I the rational, I the logical, screening and weighing and judging and picking the way to act, the way to be. Never did I-the-rational consider I-the-emotional, that despised minority, never allowed him to take the wheel.

Until tonight, sharing a sliver of my past with a best-friend sister.

"Forgive me, Leslie," I said, straightening, wiping my face. "I can't explain what happened. Never done that before. I'm very sorry."

"Never done what before? Never cared about someone's dying or never cried?"

"Never cried. Not for a long time."

"Poor Richard . . . maybe you should cry more often."

"No, thank you. I don't think I'd approve of me if I did too much of that."

"Do you think it's bad, for men to cry?"

I moved back to my chair. "Other men can cry, if they want. I don't think it's right for me."

"Oh," she said. I felt that she was thinking about that, judging me. What kind of person would judge against another for wishing to control his emotions? A loving woman might, one who knew a lot more about emotions and how to express them than I did. After a minute, no verdict returned, she said, "So what happened then?"

"Then I dropped out of my first and only waste-of-a-year in college. Wasn't wasted. Took a course in archery, and there met Bob Keech, my flight instructor. The college was a waste, the flying lessons changed my life. But I stopped writing, after high school, till I was out of the Air Force, married, and discovered that I couldn't hold a job. Any job. I'd go wild with boredom and quit. Better starve than live with the *stam!* of the time clock, twice a day.

"Then at last, I finally understood what John Gartner had taught us: *This is what it feels like to sell a story!* Years after he died, I got his message. If the high-school-kid can sell one story, why can't the grown-up sell others?"

I watched myself, curious. Never had I talked this way, to anyone.

"So I started collecting rejection slips. Sell a story or two, earn a mass of rejections till the writing-boat sank and I was starving. Find a job letter-carrying or jewelry-making or drafting or tech-writing, hold it till I could stand it no longer. Back to writing, sell a story or two, rejections till the boat sank again; get a different job. . . . Over and over. Each time the writing-boat sank slower, until finally I was barely able to survive, and I never much looked back. That's how I got to be a writer."

She had a stack of cookies left on her plate, I had crumbs.

I licked my fingertip and touched the crumbs, eating them in neat order, one after the other. Without comment, listening, she moved her cookies to my plate, saving only one for herself.

"I had always wanted an adventurous life," I said. "It took a long time to realize that I was the only one who was going to make an adventurous life happen to me. So I did the things I wanted to do, and wrote about them, books and magazine stories."

She studied me carefully, as though I were a man she had known a thousand years before.

I felt suddenly guilty. "On and on I go," I said. "What have you done to me? I tell you I'm a listener and not a talker and now you won't believe it."

"We're both listeners," she said, "we're both talkers."

"Better finish our chess-game," I said. "Your move."

I had forgotten my elegant trap, took me as long to remember what it was as it took her to consider her position and move.

She did not make the pawn advance that was essential for her survival. I was sad and delighted. At least she would see my marvelous satin trap spring shut. That's what learning is, after all, I thought, not whether we lose the game, but how we lose and how we've changed because of it and what we take away from it that we never had before, to apply to other games. Losing, in a curious way, is winning.

Even so, part of me stayed sad for her. My queen moved and lifted her knight from the board, even though the knight was guarded. Now her pawn would take my queen, for the sacrifice. Go ahead and take the queen, you little devil, enjoy it while you can. . . .

Her pawn did not take my queen. Instead, after a moment, her bishop flew from one corner of the board to the other, her night-blue eyes watched mine for response.

"Checkmate," she whispered.

I turned to ash, unbelieving. Then studied what she had done, reached for my notebook and wrote half a page.

"What did you write?"

"A nice new thought," I said. *"That's what learning is, after all: not whether we lose the game, but how we lose and how we've changed because of it and what we take away from it that we never had before, to apply to other games. Losing, in a curious way, is winning."*

She sat lightly on the sofa, shoes off, her feet drawn cozily beneath her. I sat on the chair opposite and placed my shoes carefully on the coffee-table, not to leave marks on the glass.

Teaching Horse-Latin to Leslie was like watching a new water-skier stand up on her first tow. Once through the principles of the language, she spoke it. Days, it had cost me as a kid, learning this, neglecting algebra to do it.

"Wivel, Liveslivie," I said, *"civan yivou ivundiverstivand whivat ivI'm sivayiving?"*

"Ivi civerti . . . Ivi civerti . . . vanlivy civan!" she said. *"Hivow divo yivou sivay 'Fuzzalorium' ivin Hivorse Livativin?"*

"Whivy, ivit's 'Fivuzz-iva-livor-ivi-ivum,' ivof civorse!"

How swiftly she learned, what a pleasure of mind she was! The only way to keep up with her was to have studied something she had never seen, to invent new rules of communication, or to lean way out on sheer intuition. I leaned, that night.

"I can tell, just looking, that you have played the piano

for a long time, Ms. Parrish. Just looking at the music there, the Beethoven sonatas on the yellowed paper with the old pencilmarks in amongst the notes. Let me guess . . . since you were in high school?"

She shook her head no. "Before that. When I was a little girl I made a paper keyboard to practice at, since we didn't have money for a piano. Before that, before I could walk, my mother says I crawled to the first piano I ever saw and tried to play it. From then on, music was all I wanted. But I didn't get it for a long time. My parents were divorced; my mother got sick; my brother and I bounced from foster-home to foster-home for a while."

I clenched my jaw. There's a grim childhood, I thought. What's it done to her?

"When I was eleven, my mother got out of the hospital and we moved to what you'd call the ruins of a pre-Revolutionary War house, crumbling great big thick stone walls, rats, holes in the floors, boarded-up fireplace. We rented it for twelve dollars a month, and Mom tried to fix it up. One day she heard about an old upright piano for sale, and she bought it for me! It cost her a fortune, forty dollars. But it changed my world; I was never the same again."

I inched out on another limb. "Do you remember the lifetime when you played the piano before?"

"No," she said. "I'm not too sure I believe in other lifetimes. But there is one funny thing. Music that's no later than Beethoven, than the early 1800s, it's as if I'm relearning, it's easy, I seem to know it at first sight. Beethoven, Schubert, Mozart—like meeting old friends. But not Chopin, not Liszt . . . that's new music to me."

"Johann Sebastian? He was an early composer, early 1700s. . . ."

"No. I have to study him, too."

"If somebody played the piano in the early 1800s," I asked, "they'd have to know Bach, wouldn't they?"

She shook her head. "No. His music was lost, it was forgotten till the mid-1800s, when his manuscripts were rediscovered and published again. In 1810, 1820, nobody knew anything about Bach."

The hair quivered at the back of my neck. "Would you like to find out if you lived then? I read it in a book, a way to remember lifetimes. Want to try it?"

"Maybe sometime . . ."

Why is she reluctant? How can such an intelligent person not be sure that there is more to our being than a flash-bulb in eternity?

Not long after that, at something past eleven in the evening, I checked my watch. It was four o'clock in the morning.

"Leslie! Do you know what time it is?"

She bit her lip, looked for a long moment to the ceiling. "Nine?"

sixteen

*W*AKING AT seven to fly to Florida is not going to be pleasant, I thought, after she dropped me back at my hotel and drove away in the dark. To stay up past ten P.M. was unusual for me, remnants of the barnstormer who rolled up under the wing an hour past sundown. To go to sleep at five, wake at seven and fly three thousand miles will be a challenge.

But there had been so much to hear from her, so much to say!

It won't kill me to go without a little sleep, I thought. With how many people in this world can I listen and talk till four, till long after the last cookie has disappeared, and not feel the least tired? With Leslie, and with whom else? I asked.

I fell asleep without an answer.

seventeen

"LESLIE, FORGIVE me for calling so early. Are you awake?" It was the same day, just past eight A.M. on my watch.

"I am now," she said. "How are you this morning, wookie?"

"Do you have time today? We didn't talk long enough last night, and I thought if your schedule allows, we might have lunch. And dinner, maybe?"

There was a silence. I knew at once I was imposing on her, and winced. I shouldn't have called.

"You said you were flying back to Florida today."

"Changed my mind. I'll go tomorrow."

"Oh, Richard, I'm sorry. I'm going to have lunch with Ida, then I have a meeting this afternoon. And a dinner-meeting, too. I'm sorry, I'd love to be with you, but I thought you'd be gone."

That'll teach me, I thought, for making assumptions. What made me think she's got nothing to do but sit and talk with me? I felt instantly alone.

"No problem," I said. "It's better I take off, anyway. But may I tell you how much I enjoyed our evening last night? I could listen to you, talk with you till the last cookie in the world is crumbs. Do you know that? If you don't know that, let me tell you!"

"Me too. But all those cookies that Hoggie feeds me, I've got to starve for a week till you'll be able to recognize me again, I'm so fat. Why can't you like seeds and celery?"

"Next time I'll bring celery seeds."

"Don't forget."

"You go back to sleep. I'm sorry I woke you. Thanks for last night."

"Thank you," she said. " 'Bye."

I hung up the telephone, began laying clothes into my garment-bag. Is it already too late to leave Los Angeles and fly so far east before dark?

I did not relish night-flying in the T-33. An engine flame-out, any forced landing in a heavy fast airplane is difficult enough in the daytime; black night outside would turn it thoroughly unpleasant.

If I'm wheels-up by noon, I thought, I'll be in Austin, Texas, by five, their time, off at six, Florida by nine-thirty, ten o'clock their time. Any light left at ten o'clock? None.

Oh, so what? The T has been a reliable airplane so far . . . one small mystery hydraulic-leak, the only problem I haven't fixed. But I could lose all the hydraulic fluid and it wouldn't be a disaster. Speed-brakes wouldn't work, ailerons would get hard to move, wheel brakes weak. But it'd be controllable.

There was the faintest foreboding, as I finished packing and thought my way through the flight. I couldn't see myself landing in Florida. What could go wrong? Weather? I promised never to fly through thunderstorms again, so I probably wouldn't do that. Electrical system failure?

That could be a problem. Lose electrical power in the T and I lose fuel boost pumps from the main-wing and leading-edge tanks, that leaves tiptanks and fuselage fuel only to fly on. Most of the instruments go out. All radio and all navigation equipment fails. No speed-brakes, no wing-flaps. Electrical failure means a high-speed landing, needs a long runway. All the lights are gone, of course.

The generator, the electrical system has never failed, hasn't whispered that it plans to fail. This airplane is not the Mustang. What am I worried about?

I sat on the edge of the bed, closed my eyes, relaxed and visualized the aircraft, imagined it floating in front of me. Scanned it smoothly from nose to tail, watching for something wrong. Just a few minor spots showed up . . . the tread on one tire was nearly smooth, a dzus fastener on the plenum chamber door was worn, the tiny hydraulic leak way in the middle of the engine compartment that we hadn't found. Definitely no warning, telepathically, that the electrical system or any system was going to blow up. And yet, when I tried to visualize myself arriving in Florida tonight, I couldn't do it.

Of course. I wouldn't go to Florida. I'd land before dark, somewhere else.

Even so. I could not see myself walking away from the T-33 this afternoon anywhere. Such an easy thing, it ought to be, to watch that in my mind. There I am, engine shut down; can you see that, Richard? You're shutting the engine down at some airport where you've landed. . . .

I couldn't see it.

How about final approach? Surely you can see the turn, the runway swinging majestically up from earth, landing gear is down, three little wheel-down pictures to show it's locked?

Nothing.

Well, heck, I thought. Not my electrical powers failed today but my psychic ones.

I reached for the phone and called the weather station. It would be fine all the way to New Mexico, the lady said, then I'd overtake a cold front, thunderstorms with tops to 39,000 feet. I'd clear the thunderstorm-tops at 41,000 if the T could stagger up that high. Why couldn't I visualize myself landing safely?

One more call, to the hangar.

"Ted? Hi, it's Richard. I'll be down in about an hour— would you roll out the T, make sure she's got full fuel? Oxygen's OK, oil's OK. She might take half a pint of hydraulic fluid."

On the bed I laid out maps, took notes of the navigation frequencies, headings, altitudes I'd need in flight. I computed times en route, fuel burned. We could climb to 41,000 if we had to, but just barely.

I picked up maps and baggage, checked out of the hotel and took a taxi to the airport. It will be nice to see my Florida ladies again. I suppose it will be nice.

Baggage stowed in the airplane, gun-bay doors double-locked and safetied, I climbed the ladder to the cockpit, took my helmet from its bag and hung it on the canopy bow. Hard to believe. In twenty minutes this airplane and I will be climbing up through four miles high, closing on the Arizona border.

"RICHARD!" Ted yelled from the office door. "TELEPHONE! YOU WANT TO TAKE IT?"

"NO! TELL 'EM I'M GONE!" And then from curiosity, "WHO IS IT?"

He asked the phone and shouted back. "LESLIE PARRISH!"

"TELL HER JUST A MINUTE!" I left the helmet and oxygen mask hanging and ran to answer.

By the time she picked me up at the airport, the airplane's ground-safety pins were pushed back in place; intake and tailpipe covers on; canopy closed, locked and covered and the big machine rolled back into the hangar for another night.

That's why I couldn't visualize myself landing, I thought, I couldn't visualize that future because it wasn't going to happen!

Baggage in the trunk, I slid into the seat next to her. "Hi, little tiny wookie just like all the other wookies only an awful lot smaller," I said, "I'm glad to see you! How come your schedule got cleared up?"

Leslie drove a sand-colored fluff-velvet luxury car. After we had seen the film with the wookie in it, the car got renamed *Bantha,* after a fluffy-mammoth sand-creature in the same picture. It pulled smoothly away from the curb, carrying us into a river of different-color Banthas migrating everywhere at once.

"For as little time as we have together, I thought I could shift things around a bit. I do have to pick up some things at the Academy, and then I'm free. Where would you like to take me for lunch?"

"Anywhere. Magic Pan, if it's not crowded. It has a no-smoke place, didn't you say?"

"It'll be an hour waiting, at lunchtime."

"How much time do we have?"

"How much do you want?" she said. "Dinner? Movie? Chess? Talk?"

"Oh, you sweetie! Did you cancel your whole day for me? You don't know how much that means."

"It means that I'd rather be with a visiting wookie than with anyone else. But no more hot-fudge and no more cookies and no more nothing bad! You can eat bad things if you want, but I am back on a diet to pay for my sins!"

As we drove, I told her about the curious experience of the morning, about my extrasensory aircraft and flight checks, about strange times in the past when they had been remarkably accurate.

She listened courteously, carefully, as she did whenever I talked about experiments with the paranormal. I sensed behind the courtesy, though, that she listened to find explainings for events and interests she dared not consider before. Listened as though I were some friendly Leif Ericson, returned with snapshots of a land she'd heard about but not explored.

Car parked near the offices of the Motion Picture Academy, she said, "I won't be a minute. You want to wait or come in?"

"I'll wait. Take your time."

I watched her from a distance, in a noontime crowd of sidewalkers in the sun. Modestly dressed, she was, a white summer blouse over a white skirt, but my, how heads did turn! Every male in a moving hundred-foot circle about her slowed to watch. The honey-wheat hair flew loose and bright as she hurried to catch the last seconds of the walk signal. She waved thank-you to a driver who waited for her, and he waved back, well rewarded.

What a captivating woman, I thought. Too bad we aren't more alike.

She disappeared into the building, and I stretched out across the seat, yawned. To use this time, I thought, why not get a full night's sleep? That will require an autohypnotic rest of about five minutes.

I closed my eyes, took one deep breath. *My body is completely relaxed: now.* Another breath. *My mind is completely relaxed: now.* Another. *I am in a deep sleep: now. I shall waken the instant Leslie returns; as refreshed as from eight hours of deep, normal sleep.*

Autohypnosis for rest is especially powerful when one hasn't slept but two hours the night before. My mind plunged into darkness; sound in the streets faded away. Caught in deep black tar, time stopped. Then in the midst of that charcoal dark,

!!LIGHT!!

As if a star fell on me, ten times ten brighter than the sun, and the blast from the light of it knocked me deaf.

No shadow no color no heat no glare no body no sky no earth no space no time no things no people no words just

LIGHT!

I floated numb in glory. It isn't light, I knew, this immense unstopping brilliance bursting through what once had been me, it isn't light. The light, it merely represents, it stands for something else brighter than light, it stands for *Love!* so intense that the idea of intense is a funny feather of thought next to how huge a love engulfed me.

145

I AM!
   YOU ARE!
     AND LOVE: IS ALL: THAT MATTERS!

Joy exploded through me and I tore apart, atom from atom, in the love of it, a matchstick fallen into sun. Joy too intense to bear, not another instant! I choked. Please, no!

The moment I asked, Love retreated, faded into the night of noontime Beverly Hills, northern hemisphere third planet smallish star minor galaxy minor universe tiny twist of one belief in imagined spacetime. I was a microscopic life-form, infinitely large, stumbled backstage of its playhouse, caught a nanosecond glance of its own reality and nearly vaporized in shock.

I woke in the Bantha, heart pounding, my face soaked in tears.

"AI!!" I said aloud. *"AI-ai-ai!"*

Love! So intense! If it were green, it would be a green so transcendently green that even the Principle of Green couldn't have imagined . . . like standing on a huge ball of, like standing on the sun but not the sun, there were no ends, no horizons to it, so bright and NO GLARE, I looked eyes open into the brightest . . . and yet I had no eyes I COULDN'T STAND THE JOY of that *Love.* . . . It was as if I dropped my last candle in a black cavern and after a while a friend, to help me see, she lit a hydrogen bomb.

Next to the light, this world . . . ; next to that light, the idea of living and dying, it is simply . . . irrelevant.

I sat blinking in the car, gasping air. Lordy! It took ten minutes' practice, learning to breathe again. What . . . Why . . . Ai!

146

There a blonde-and-smile flash above the sidewalk, heads turning in the crowd to watch, and in a moment Leslie opened the door, piled envelopes on the seat, slid behind the wheel. "Sorry to be so long, wook. It was mobbed. Did you melt to death out here?"

"Leslie, I've got to tell you. The most . . . something just happened . . ."

She turned in alarm. "Richard, are you all right?"

"Fine!" I said. "Fine fine fine fine."

I stabbed at saying, told her in fragments and fell silent. "I was sitting here, after you left, closed my eyes . . . Light, but it wasn't light. Brighter than light, but no glare, no hurt from it. LOVE, not the fake broken syllable, but Love that IS! like no love I've ever imagined. *AND LOVE! IS ALL: THAT MATTERS!* Words, but they weren't words, or even ideas. Has this ever . . . do you know?"

"Yes," she said. And after a long moment remembering, she went on. "Up in the stars, when I left my body. A oneness with life, with a universe so beautiful, a love so powerful the joy made me cry!"

"But why did it happen? I just, I was going to catch a quick hypno-nap, done it a hundred times! This time, POW! Can you imagine joy so much you can't stand it, you beg to turn it off?"

"Yes," she said. "I know. . . ."

We sat together, wordless for a while. Then she started the Bantha and we lost ourselves in traffic, already celebrating our time together.

eighteen

EXCEPT FOR chess between us, there's no action. We don't climb mountains together or run rivers or fight revolutions or risk our lives. We don't even fly airplanes. The most adventurous thing we share is a plunge into the traffic down La Cienega Boulevard after lunch. Why does she charm me so?

"Have you noticed," I asked as she turned west on Melrose for home, "that our friendship is completely . . . actionless?"

"Actionless?" She looked at me as startled as if I had touched her. "Oh, you. Sometimes it's hard to know when you're kidding. Actionless!"

"No. Really. Shouldn't we be skiing cross-country, surfing to Hawaii, something energetic? Heavy exercise for us is lifting a chess-queen and saying 'Check' at the same time. Just an observation. I've never had a friend quite like you, before. Aren't we awfully cerebral; don't we talk too much?"

"Richard," she said, "chess and talk, *please!* Not throwing parties, throwing money around, which is the preferred exercise in this town."

She turned the car onto a side-street, into her driveway, stopped the engine.

"Pardon me for a minute, Leslie. I'm going to run home and burn every dollar I have. It'll take a minute. . . ."

She smiled. "You don't have to burn it. It's fine if you have money. The thing that matters to a woman is whether you use it to try to buy her. Be careful you never try that."

"Too late," I said. "I've already done it. More than once."

She turned to me, leaning back against the door of the car. She made no move to open it.

"You? Why do I find that such a surprise? Somehow I can't see you doing . . . Tell me. Have you bought any good women?"

"Money does strange things. It scares me to watch, to see it happening firsthand to *me,* not a movie but nonfiction firsthand, real life. It's as if I'm the odd man in a love-triangle, trying to force myself between a woman and my money. A lot of cash is still a new thing to me. Along comes some very nice lady who doesn't have much to live on, who's just about broke, her rent's overdue, do I say, 'I won't spend a dime to help you'?"

I needed an answer to that one. Part of my perfect woman at the moment included three comely friends, struggling to survive.

"You do what you think is right," she said. "But don't fool yourself that anybody's going to love you because you pay their rent or buy their groceries. One way to be sure they will not love you is to let them depend on you for money. I know what I'm talking about!"

I nodded. How does she know? Does she have men out to get her money?

"It's not love," I said. "None of them love me. We enjoy each other. We're happy mutual parasites."

"Grf."

"Pardon?"

"*Grf:* expression of distaste. 'Happy mutual parasites' makes me see bugs."

"Sorry. I haven't solved the problem yet."

"Next time don't tell them you've got money," she said.

"Doesn't work. I'm a terrible deceiver. I reach for my notebook and these hundred-dollar bills tumble out on the table and she says, 'What the hey, you said you were on welfare!' What can I do?"

"Maybe you're stuck. But be careful. There's no town like this one to show you the many ways people crash who can't handle money." She pushed her door open at last. "Would you care for a salad, something healthy? Or will it be hot fudge for Hoggie?"

"Hoggie's off hot fudge. Could we split a salad, between us?"

Inside, she put a Beethoven sonata on low, made a huge vegetable-and-cheese salad, we fell to talking again. Missed sunset, missed a research-movie, played chess, and our time together was gone.

"It must be early takeoff tomorrow that's on my mind," I said. "Does it seem to you that my play is up to form, losing three out of four like that? I don't know what's happened to my game. . . ."

"Your game is as good as ever," she said with a wink.

"But mine is improving. July eleventh you will remember as the day you won your last chess-game from Leslie Parrish!"

"Laugh while you can, mischievess. The next time you encounter this mind, it will have memorized *Wicked Traps in Chess* and every one of them will be waiting for you on the board." I sighed without knowing it. "I'd best be on my way. Will my Bantha-driver give me a ride to the hotel?"

"She will," she said, but she didn't move from the table.

To thank her for the day, I reached for her hand and held it, lightly, warmly. For a long time we looked at each other and no one talked, no one noticed time had stopped. The quiet itself said what we had never considered in words.

Then somehow we were holding each other, kissing softly, softly.

It didn't occur to me then, that by falling in love with Leslie Parrish I was destroying the only sister I'd ever have.

nineteen

I WOKE in the morning to sunlight filtered and goldened through her hair cascading across our pillows. I woke to her smile.

"Good morning, wookie," she said, so close and warm I barely caught the words. "Did you sleep well?"

"M!" I said. "My! Yes. Yes, thank you, slept very well! Had this dream all in glories, last night, that you were going to take me to the hotel? Couldn't help but give you a little kiss, and then . . . what a beautiful dream!"

For once, for blessed once the woman next to me in bed was not a stranger. For once in my life, this person belonged exactly where she was, and so did I.

I touched her face. "It'll be just a minute, won't it, and you'll turn into air? Or the clock will go off or the telephone will ring and it will be you asking if I slept well. Don't call yet. I want to dream some more, please."

" 'Ring . . .' " she said in a tiny voice. She threw her covers back, held a light nothing-telephone to her ear. The sunlight on her smile, on her bare shoulders and breasts brought me very much awake. " 'Ring . . .' Hello, Richard? How did you sleep last night? Hm?"

She changed herself that instant to innocent seductress, pure and wholesome—a star-bright mind in a sex-goddess body. I blinked at the intimacy of what she did with a move, a sentence, with a flicker in her eyes.

Life with an actress! I hadn't imagined—how many different Leslies can be stirring in this one, how many might there be to touch, to know, appearing in sudden spotlights on the stage of this one person?

"You are . . . so . . . lovely!" I stumbled after words. "Why didn't you tell me you are this . . . beautiful?"

The telephone vaporized from her hand, the innocent turned to me with a quizzical smile. "You never seemed interested."

"This is going to surprise you, but you'd better get used to it because I am a wordsmith and I can't help but just blurt out poetry now and then, it's my nature and I can be no other way: *I think you're terrific!*"

She nodded slowly, solemnly. "That is very good, wordsmith. Thank you. I think you are terrific, too." Split-second, a sultry different idea took her mind. "Now for practice, let's say the same thing without words."

Shall I die of happiness now, I thought, or shall I linger for a while?

Lingering seemed the better way. I floated on the edge of death-by-joy, nearly wordless, not quite.

I could not have invented a woman so perfect for me, I thought, yet here's the real one alive, hidden in the acquaintance of Ms. Leslie Parrish since years ago, masked within my business partner, my best friend. Just that fragment of wonderment surfaced, to be swept away by the sight of her in the sun.

Light and touch, soft shadows and whispers, that morning-turned-noon-turned-evening, with our way found to meet again after a lifetime apart. Cereal for dinner. And finally we could talk once more in words.

How many words, how long does it take to say Who Are You? How long to say why? Longer than we had before three in the morning, before sunrise again. The scenery of time vanished. It was light outside her house or it was not-light, it rained or it was dry, clocks pointed ten and we didn't know which ten of which day of which week it might happen to be. We woke in our mornings to stars over silent city dark; the midnights we held each other and dreamed were Los Angeles rush-hours and lunch-times.

A soulmate can not be possible, I had learned in the years since I turned the Fleet to money and built my walled empire. Not possible for people who run ten directions ten speeds at once, not possible for life-hogs. Could I have learned wrong?

I walked back into her bedroom, one of our mornings around midnight, balancing a tray of apple-slices and cheeses and crackers.

"Oh!" she said, sitting up, blinking her eyes awake, smoothing her hair so it fell only a little tousled over bare shoulders. "You sweetie! Thoughtful as can be!"

"I could have been thoughtfuller still, but your kitchen doesn't have the buttermilk or the potatoes for kartoffelkuchen."

"*Kartoffelkuchen!*" she said, astonished. "When I was a

little girl, my mother made kartoffelkuchen! I thought I was the only person left in the world who remembers! Can you make it?"

"Recipe is safely locked within this extraordinary mind, handed down from Grandma Bach. You're the only human being who's said that word back to me in fifteen years! We ought to list all the things we have in . . ." I fluffed some pillows, settled myself so that I could see her clearly. My, I thought, how I love the beauty of her!

She saw me looking at her body, and deliberately she sat very straight in bed for a moment, to watch me catch my breath. Then she brought the sheets to her chin.

"Would you answer my ad?" she said, suddenly shy.

"Yes. What ad is that?"

"It's a classified ad." She placed a transparent slice of cheese on half a cracker. "Do you know what it says?"

"Tell me." My own cracker creaked under its cheeseweight, but I judged it structurally sound.

"Wanted: a one hundred percent man. Must be brilliant, creative, funny, capable of intense intimacy and joy. Want to share music, nature, peaceful quiet joyful life. No smoking no drinking no drugs. Must love learning and want to grow forever. Handsome, tall, slim, fine hands, sensitive, gentle, loving. Affectionate and sexy as can be."

"What an ad! Yes! I answer!"

"I'm not done yet," she said. *"Must be emotionally stable, honest and trustworthy and a positive constructive person. Highly spiritual, but no organized religion. Must love cats."*

"Why, that's me to the letter! I even love your cat, though I suspect the feeling isn't mutual."

"Give him time," she said. "He's going to be a little jealous for a while."

155

"Ah. You gave it away."

"Gave what?" she said, letting the sheet fall, leaning forward, adjusting the pillows.

The effect of that simple act, the effect of her leaning forward, was for me a push into ice and fire. As long as she was still, she was as sensual as I could stand. When she moved, the softs and curves and lights of her *changing,* every word in my mind jarred into happy wreckage.

"Hm. . . ?" I said, watching.

"You animal. I said, 'What did I just give away?' "

"If you stay very still, please, we can have a nice talk. But I must tell you that unless you are dressed, a small amount of that pillow-moving tends to run me off my rails."

I was sorry at once. She pulled the sheet to cover her breasts, held it there with her arms, and looked at me primly over her cracker.

"Oh. Well, yes," I said. "What you gave away by saying that your cat would be jealous for a while was that you think I meet the requirements of your advertisement."

"I meant to give it away," she said. "I'm glad to see you took it."

"Aren't you afraid that if I know that, I will take advantage of you?"

She let the sheet loose an inch, arched an eyebrow. "Would you like to take advantage of me?"

With enormous mental effort, I reached to her and moved the white linen upward.

"I noticed it was falling, there, ma'am, and in the interest of having a minute to talk with you I thought perhaps I'd best be sure that it doesn't come down too much farther."

"How good of you."

"Do you believe," I asked her, "in guardian angels?"

"To protect and watch over us and help guide us? Sometimes, yes."

"Then tell me: why should a guardian angel care about our love-life? Why should they guide our romances?"

"Easy," she said. "To a guardian angel, loving is more important than anything else. To them, our love-life is more important than any other kind of life we have! What else should angels care about?"

Of course, I thought, she's right!

"Do you think it might be possible," I said, "for guardian angels to take human form for each other, to be lovers every few lifetimes?"

She took a bite from her cracker, thinking about it. "Yes." And in a moment, "Would a guardian angel answer my ad?"

"Yes. For certain. Every male guardian angel in the country would answer that ad, if they knew it was you, advertising."

"I just want one," she said, and after a moment, "Do you have an ad?"

I nodded, and surprised myself. "Been writing it for years: *Wanted: a one hundred percent female guardian angel in human body, please. Independent, adventurous, extreme wisdom required. Prefer ability to initiate and respond creatively in many forms of communication. Must speak Horse-Latin.*"

"Is that it?"

"No," I said. "*Only angel with glorious eyes, stunning figure and long golden hair need apply. Require brilliant curiosity, hungry capacity for learning. Prefer professional in several creative and business fields, experience in top management positions. Fearless, willing to take all risks. Happiness guaranteed in long run.*"

157

She listened carefully. "The stunning-figure-long-golden-hair part. Isn't that too earthy for an angel?"

"Why not a guardian angel with stunning figure and long hair? Does that mean she's any less angelic, any less perfect for her mortal, any less capable at her job?"

Well, why *can't* guardian angels be that way? I thought, wishing for my notebook. Why not a planet of angels, lighting each other's lives with adventure and mystery? Why not a few, at least, who could find each other now and then?

"So we create whatever body our mortal finds most delicious?" she said. "When teacher is pretty, we pay attention?"

"Right!" I said. "Just one second . . ."

I found the notebook on the floor by the bed, wrote what she said, put a dash and an L-for-Leslie after it. "Do you ever notice, after you've known someone for a while, how their appearance changes?"

"He can be the handsomest man in the world," she said, "but he turns plain as popcorn when he has nothing to say. And the plainest man says what matters to him and why he cares and in two minutes he's so beautiful you want to hug him!"

I was curious. "Have you gone out with many plain men?"

"Not many."

"If they get beautiful to you, why not?"

"Because they see Mary Moviestar all spifflicated and pretty, on her marks for the camera, and they figure she only looks at Harry Handsome. They rarely ask to go out with me, Richard."

The poor fools, I thought. *They rarely ask.* Because we believe the surface, we forget that surfaces aren't who we are. When we find an angel dazzling of mind, her face grows lovelier still. Then "Oh, by the way," she tells us, "I have this body . . ."

I wrote it into the notebook.

"Someday," she said, moving the tray of breakfast to the nightstand, "I am going to ask you to read me more notes." In the act of moving, the sheet fell away again. She raised her arms, stretching luxuriously.

"I won't ask now," she said, moving closer. "No more quizzes today."

As I could no longer think, that was just as well.

twenty

*I*T WASN'T music, it was saw-edge snag-metal discord. She had barely turned from her stereo controls, from fine-tuning the volume as loud as it could go, than I was a kettle of complaints.

"That's not music!"

"PARDON ME?" she said, lost in sound.

"I SAID THAT'S NOT MUSIC!"

"BARTÓK!"

"WHAT?" I said.

"BÉLA BARTÓK!"

"COULD YOU TURN IT DOWN, LESLIE?"

"CONCERTO FOR ORCHESTRA!"

"COULD YOU TURN THE VOLUME DOWN JUST A LITTLE BIT OR A LOT? COULD YOU TURN THE VOLUME DOWN A LOT?"

She didn't catch the words, but she got the idea and turned it down.

"Thank you," I said. "Wookie, is that . . . do you honestly consider—that—to be music?"

Had I watched carefully, beyond the delicious figure in the flowered bathrobe, hair tied and covered in a towel-turban to dry, I would have seen disappointment in her eyes.

"You don't like it?" she said.

"You love music, you have studied music all your life. How can you call that inharmony we're hearing, that rat sort of discord, how can you call that music?"

"Poor Richard," she said. "Lucky Richard! You have so much to learn about music! So many beautiful symphonies, sonatas, concertos that you get to hear for the first time!" She stopped the tape, rewound it and took it from the machine.

"Maybe it's a little soon for Bartók. But I promise you. The day will come when you will listen to what you have just heard and you will call it glorious."

She looked over her collection of tapes, chose one and put it into the machine where the Bartók had been. "How would you like to hear some Bach . . . would you like to hear your great-grandaddy's music?"

"You are probably going to throw me out of your house inverted for saying this," I told her, "but I can only listen to him for half an hour, then I get lost and a little bored."

"Bored? Listening to Bach? Then you don't know how to listen; you've never learned to listen to him!" She pressed a rocker-switch and the tape began; Grandaddy on some monster organ, it was clear. "First you have to sit right. Here. Come sit here, between the speakers. This is where we sit when we want to hear all the music."

It felt like musical kindergarten, but I loved being with her, sitting very close to her.

"The complexity of it alone should make it irresistible for you. Now, most people listen to music horizontally, following along with the melody. But you can listen *structurally*, too; have you ever done that?"

"Structurally?" I said. "No."

"Early music was all linear," she said over a landslide of organ-notes, "simple melodies strung out one at a time, primitive themes. But your grandaddy took complex themes, with tricky little rhythms, and spun them out together at odd intervals so they created intricate structures and made vertical sense as well—*harmony!* Some Bach harmonies are as dissonant as Bartók, and Bach was getting away with them a hundred years before anyone even thought of dissonance."

She stopped the tape, slid onto the piano-bench, and without a blink of her eye there was the last chord from the speakers in her hand on the keyboard.

"There." It sounded clearer on the piano than it had on the speakers. "See? Here's one motif . . ." She played. "And here's another . . . and another. Now watch how he builds this. We start with the A theme in the right hand. Now A enters again four bars later in the left hand; do you hear it? They go on together until . . . here comes B. And A is subordinate to it just now. Here's A entering again in the right. And now . . . *C!*"

She set out themes, one by one, then put them together. Slowly at first, then faster. I barely followed. What was Simple Addition for her was Advanced Calculus to me; by closing my eyes and squashing my forehead together with my hands I could nearly understand.

She started again, explaining every step. As she played, a light began to glow through an inner symphony-hall that had been dark all my life.

She was right! There were themes among themes, dancing together, as if Johann Sebastian had locked secrets into his music for the private pleasure of those who learned to see beneath surfaces.

"Aren't you a joy!" I said, excited to understand what she was saying. "I hear it! It's really there!"

She was as glad as I, and forgot to get dressed or brush her hair. She moved sheet-music from the back of the music-shelf on the piano to the front. *Johann Sebastian Bach,* it said, and then a thunderstorm of notes and sweeps and dots and sharps and flats and ties and trills and sudden commands in Italian. Right at the beginning, before the pianist could get her wheels up and fly into that storm, she was hit with a *con brio,* which I figured meant she had to play either with brightness, with coldness, or with cheese.

Awesome. My friend, with whom I only recently emerged from warm sheets and voluptuous shadows, with whom I spoke English with ease, Spanish with laughter, German and French with much puzzlement and creative experiment, my friend had all at once burst out singing a new and vastly complicated language that I was on my first day's learning to hear.

The music broke from the piano like clear cold water from a prophet-touched rock, pouring and splashing around us while her fingers leaped and spread, curled and stiffened and melted and flickered in magic pass and streaked lightning above the keyboard.

Never before had she played for me, claiming that she was out of practice, too self-conscious even to uncover the keys of the instrument while I was in the room. Something had happened between us, though . . . because we were lovers, now, was she free to play, or was she the teacher so desperate to help her deaf one that nothing could keep her from music?

Her eyes traced every raindrop of that hurricane-on-paper; she had forgotten that she had a body, except that the hands remained, the blurred fingers, a spirit that found its song in the heart of a man died two hundred years ago, raised triumphant from his tomb by her wish for living music.

"Leslie! My God! Who are you?"

She turned her head only a little toward me and half-smiled, her eyes and her mind and her hands still on the music storming upward.

Then she looked at me; the music stopped instantly but for strings trembling harplike inside the piano.

"And so on and so on," she said. The music shimmered in her eyes, in her smile. "Do you see what he's doing there? Do you see what he's done?"

"A little bit, I see," I said. "I thought I knew you! You whelm the daylights out of me! That music is . . . it's . . . you're . . ."

"I'm way out of practice," she said; "the hands aren't working the way they . . ."

"Leslie, no. Stop. Listen. What I have just heard is pure . . . listen! . . . pure radiance, that you took from cloud-linings and sunrises and distilled into light that I can hear! Do you know how good, how lovely that is, that you make the piano do?"

"Don't I wish! You know that was my chosen career, the piano?"

"It's one thing to know that in words, but you never played, before! You give me one more whole different . . . heaven!"

She frowned. "THEN DO NOT BE BORED WITH YOUR GRANDADDY'S MUSIC!"

"Never again," I said meekly.

"Of course never again," she said. "Your mind is too much like his, not to understand. Every language has its key, and so does your grandaddy's language. Bored! Indeed!"

She accepted my promise to improve, having flattened me in awe, and went to brush her hair.

twenty-one

SHE TURNED from the typewriter, smiled at me where I had settled with my cup of chocolate and a draft screenplay.

"You don't have to gulp it down all at once, Richard, you can sip it slowly. That way you can make it last longer."

I laughed at me, with her. To Leslie, I thought, I must look like a pile of jackstraws on her office couch.

Her desk organized, her files trim, not a paper-clip out of place. She looked just as neat, herself: snug beige pants, transparent blouse tucked in, a brassiere as sheer as the blouse, outlined in filmy white flowers. Her hair was brushed gold. Here, I thought, is the way neatness ought to look!

"Our drinks are not paperweights," I said. "Hot chocolate, most people drink it. Yours, you befriend. I can drink enough hot chocolate to hate the taste of it for the rest of my days in the time it takes you to get acquainted with one cup!"

"Wouldn't you rather drink something friendly," she said, "than something you've hardly met?"

Intimate with her chocolate, with her music, with her garden, her car, her house, her work. I was linked to the things I knew by a network of silken threads; she was bound to hers by braided silver cables. To Leslie, nothing close was unvalued.

Acting-dresses and gowns hung in her closets, sorted by color and by shade of color, clear-plastic dust-covers over each. Shoes to match on the floor below, hats to match on the shelf above.

Books in their cases by subject; phonograph records and tapes by composer, conductor and soloist.

A hapless clumsy spider tripped and fallen in the sink? Everything stops. Down slides a papertowel spidey-ladder to the rescue, and when the creature steps aboard, it's lifted outside and set gently in the garden, tucked away with soothing words and soft warnings that sinks are not safe places for spiders to play.

I was so much the opposite. Neatness, for instance, had a lower priority. Spiders do need to be saved from sinks, of course, but they don't have to be pampered. Taken outside and dropped on the porch, they ought to count their lucky stars.

Things, they disappear in the blink of an eye; a wind ruffles them and they're gone. Her silver cables . . . attach ourselves so strongly to things and to people, when they're gone, doesn't part of us go, too?

"Better far to attach ourselves to forever-thoughts than to here-now gone-now things," I told her as she drove us toward the Music Center. "Don't you agree?"

She nodded, driving five miles above the speed limit, catching green lights.

"Music is a forever thing," she said.

Like a rescued cat, I was fed on top-cream classical music, for which she insisted I had ear and aptitude.

She touched the radio and at once violins flowed, the midst of some perky air. Another quiz coming up, I thought. I liked our quizzes.

"Baroque, classical, modern?" she asked, sweeping into an open lane toward city center.

I listened to the music with intuition as well as with new training. Too deep-structured to be baroque, not combed and formal enough to be classical, not crinkly enough to be modern. Romantic, lyric, light . . .

"Neoclassical," I guessed. "Feels like a major composer, but he's having fun with this one. Written, I'd say—1923?"

I was convinced Leslie knew epoch, date, composer, work, movement, orchestra, conductor, concertmaster. Once she had heard a piece of music, she knew it; she sang along with every one of the thousand performances she had collected. Stravinsky, as unpredictable to me as a rodeo bronc, she hummed, hardly aware she did.

"Good guess!" she said. "Close! Composer?"

"Definitely not German." It wasn't heavy enough; it didn't have enough wheels on the road to be German. Playful, so it wasn't Russian. Nor did it taste French nor feel Italian nor look British. It wasn't colored like Austria, not enough gold in it. Homey, I could hum it myself, but not American homey. It was dancing.

"Polish? Sounds to me like it was written in the fields east of Warsaw."

"Nice try! Not Polish. Little bit farther east. It's Russian." She was pleased with me.

The Bantha didn't slow; green lights were Leslie's servants.

"Russian? Where's the yearning? Where's the pathos? Russian! My goodness!"

"Not so quick with generalities, wookie," she said. "You haven't heard any happy Russian music, till now. You're right. This one, he's playful."

"Who is it?"

"Prokofiev."

"What do you know!" I said. "Rus . . ."

"GODDAMN IDIOT!" Brakes shrieked, the Bantha swerved wildly, missed the black-lightning streak of sudden truck by a yard. *Did you see that son of a bitch?* Straight through the light! He nearly killed . . . what the HELL does he think . . ."

She had reflexed like a racing driver to miss the thing and now it was gone, a quarter-mile down Crenshaw Boulevard. What stunned me was not the truck but her language.

She looked at me, frowning still, saw my face, looked again, puzzled, struggled to suppress a smile, failed.

"Richard! I've shocked you! Did I shock you with *Goddamn Hell?*" She smothered her mirth with immense effort. "Oh, my poor baby! I cursed in front of it! I'm sorry!"

I half-raged, half-laughed at myself.

"All right, Leslie Parrish, this is it! You enjoy this mo-

169

ment because this is the last time you will ever see me shocked over *goddamn hell!*"

Even as I said the last words, they sounded strange in my mouth, awkward syllables. Like a nondrinker saying *martini;* a nonuser saying *cigarette* or *joint* or any of the jargon that comes easy to addicts. No matter the word, if we never use it, it sounds awkward. Even *fuselage* sounds funny, coming from one who doesn't like airplanes. But a word is a word is a sound in the air and there is no reason why I shouldn't be able to say any word I want without feeling like a goat.

I didn't talk for a few seconds, while she twinkled at me.

How does one practice swearing? To the melody of Prokofiev, still on the radio, I practiced, quietly. "Oh . . . damn, damn hell, damn-damn-hellllll/damn-damn-hell-oh damn-damn-hell, DAMN-DAMN HELLLLLL/Oh, damdam-hel-hel-dam-dam-hell-oh-dam-dam-hel-hel dammmn; Oh dammmmmmn. . . . *HELL!*"

When she heard what I was singing, and the earnest determination with which I sang, she dissolved against the wheel in merriment.

"Laugh if you want, damn it hell, wookie," I said. "I'm going to learn this damn stuff right! Hell! What's the name of the damn music?"

"Oh, Richard," she gasped, wiping tears. "It's *Romeo and Juliet* . . ."

I went on with my song regardless, and sure enough, after a few stanzas the words lost their meaning altogether. Another few verses and I'd be damning and helling with the worst of them! And other words beyond, to conquer! Why hadn't I thought of curse-practice thirty years ago?

She got me to curb my profanity by the time we entered the symphony hall.

It wasn't till we were back in the car after an evening of front-row Tchaikovsky and Samuel Barber, Zubin Mehta conducting Itzhak Perlman and the Los Angeles Philharmonic, that I could express my feelings.

"That was hot damn hellacious fine music! Don't you think it was, god . . . I mean, damn?"

She looked to heaven, imploring. "What have I done?" she said. "What am I creating?"

"Whatever the hell you're creating," I said, "you're doing a damn fine job of it!"

Business partners still, we insisted some work get done in those weeks together, so we chose a film to research and left early to stand in line for the afternoon show. The traffic sighed and hummed in the street while we waited, yet the traffic wasn't there, as though an enchanted mist began at arm's-length around us, everything beyond turned ghostly as we talked on our private planet.

I hadn't noticed the woman watching us, not far away in the mist, but all at once she made a decision that frightened me. She walked directly to Leslie, touched her shoulder, demolished our world.

"You're Leslie Parrish!"

At once, my friend's bright smile changed. Still a smile, but suddenly frozen; inside she had retreated, cautious.

"Excuse me, but I saw you in *The Big Valley* and *Star Trek* and . . . I love your work and I think you're beautiful. . . ." She was sincere and shy, so that the walls thinned.

"Oh—thank you!"

The woman opened her purse. "Could you . . . if it isn't too much trouble, would you mind signing an autograph for my daughter Corrie? She'd kill me if she knew I was this close to you and didn't . . ." She wasn't having much luck finding paper to write on. "There's got to be something here. . . ."

I offered my notebook, and Leslie nodded, accepting it. "Here we are," she said to the lady. "Thank you, sir," to me.

She wrote a greeting to Corrie and signed her name, tore off the sheet of paper and handed it to the woman.

"You were Daisy Mae in *Li'l Abner*, too," the woman said, as though Leslie might have forgotten, "and *The Manchurian Candidate*. I loved it."

"You remember, after all this time? That's so nice of you. . . ."

"Thank you, very much. Corrie will be so happy!"

"Give her a hug for me."

It was quiet for a moment after the woman went back to her place in line.

"Don't you say a word," Leslie growled at me.

"That was touching!" I said. "I'm not kidding. Really."

She softened. "She's sweet and sincere. The ones who say, 'Aren't you somebody?' I just say no and try to get by. 'No, you're somebody, I know you're somebody, what have you done?' They want you to list your credits. . . ." She shook her head, perplexed. "What do you do? There's no sensitive way to deal with insensitive people. Is there?"

"Interesting. I don't have that problem."

"You don't, wookie? You mean that you've never had one rude person crash into your privacy?"

"Not in person. To writers, insensitive people send written demands, and they send manuscripts. About one percent is that way, maybe not that much. The rest of the mail is fun."

I resented the speed of the ticket-line. In less than an hour we had to cut off our discoveries to walk into the theater on business and sit down and watch a movie. There's so much to gain from her, I thought, holding her hand in the dark, my shoulder touching hers, more to say than ever there was! And now lived the wild gentility of sex between us, changing us, completing us.

Here is a woman unequaled in my history, I thought, looking at her in the dark. I cannot imagine what it would take to shatter, to threaten the warmth of being close to her. Here is the one woman, of all the women I know, with whom there can never be any question, any doubt of the bond between us, for so long as we both shall live.

Isn't it strange, the way certainty always comes before shatterings?

twenty-two

THERE WAS the lake once more, Florida sparkling under my windows. Seaplanes like sun-color watermoths practicing, gliding on water and air. Nothing changed about the place, I thought, laying down the garment-bag on the couch.

A movement at the edge of my eye and I jumped, to see him in the doorway, another me that I had forgotten: armored, defended and at the moment, disgusted. Like coming home from a walk in the meadow, daisies in my hair, pockets empty of apple-snacks and sugar-cubes for the deer, to find a mailed warrior standing coldly await in the house.

"You are seven weeks late!" he said. "You did not tell me where you were. You will be hurt by what I must say, and I could have saved you pain. Richard, you have seen quite enough of Leslie Parrish. Have you forgotten everything you've learned? Don't you see danger? The woman threatens your entire way of life!" The chain-steel cape moved, the armor creaked.

"She's a beautiful woman," I said, then knew he'd miss the meaning, remind me that I knew many beautiful women.

Silence. Another creak. "Where's your shield? Lost it, I suppose. Luck, that you made it back alive!"

"We got to talking . . ."

"Fool. Do you think we wear armor for fun?" Eyes glowered, within the helmet. A mailed finger traced dents and blows on the metal. "Every mark was made by some woman's design. You were nearly destroyed by marriage, you escaped by miracle, and were it not for armor you would have been cut ten times since by friendships turned obligation turned oppression. One miracle you deserve. Dozens you had better not count on."

"I've worn my armor," I growled at him. "But you want me to . . . *all the time?* Every moment? There's a time for flowers, too. And Leslie is special."

"Leslie *was* special. Every woman is special for a day, Richard. But special turns to commonplace, boredom sets in, respect vanishes, freedom's lost. Lose your freedom, what more is there to lose?"

The figure was massive, but quicker than a cat in battle, immensely strong.

"You built *me* to be your closest friend, Richard. You did not build me pretty, or laughing, or warm and pliant. You built me to protect you from affairs turned ugly; you built me to guarantee your survival as a free soul. I can save you only if you do as I say. Can you show me a single happy marriage? One? Of all the men you know, is there one whose marriage would not go happier through instant divorce, and friendship instead?"

I had to admit. "Not one."

"The secret of my strength," he said, "is that I do not lie. Until you can out-reason me, change my fact to fiction, I shall be with you, and I shall guide and protect you. Leslie is beautiful to you today. Other women were beautiful to you yesterday. Every one of them would have destroyed you in marriage. There is one perfect woman for you, but she dwells in many different bodies. . . ."

"I know. I know."

"You know. When you find one woman in the world who can give you more than many women can, I'll disappear."

I didn't like him, but he was right. He had saved me from attacks that would have killed who I was this moment. I didn't like his arrogance, but arrogance came from certainty. It was chilly to stand in the same room with him, but to ask him to thaw was to become casualty to each discovery that this woman or that one is not my soulmate, after all.

As long as I could remember, freedom equaled happiness. A little protection, that's small price to pay for happiness.

Naturally, I thought, Leslie has her own steel person to guard her . . . many more men had planned her capture and marriage than women planned mine. If she lived without armor, she'd be married today, without a prayer of the glad lovership we had found. Her joy was founded on freedom, too.

How we frowned at the married ones who sometimes looked to us for extramarital affairs! Act as you believe, no matter what—if you believe in marriage, live it honestly. If you do not, un-marry yourself fast.

Was I marrying Leslie, spending so much of my freedom on her?

"I'm sorry," I told my armored friend. "I won't forget again."

He gave me a long dark look before he left.

I answered mail for an hour, worked on a magazine article that had no deadline. Then, restless, I wandered downstairs to the hangar.

Over the great hollow place hung the faintest veil of something wrong . . . so light a vapor that there was nothing to see.

The little BD-5 jet needed flying, to blow the cobwebs from its control surfaces.

There are cobwebs on me, too, I thought. It is never wise to lose one's skill in any airplane, to stay away too long. The baby jet was demanding, the only aircraft I had flown more dangerous on takeoff than landing.

Twelve feet from nose to tail, it wheeled out of the hangar like a hot-dog pushcart without the umbrella, and as lifeless. Not quite lifeless, I thought. It was sullen. I'd be sullen, too, left alone for weeks, spiders in my landing gear.

Canopy cover removed, fuel checked, preflight inspection done. There was dust on the wings.

I should hire someone to dust the airplanes, I thought, and snorted in disgust. What a lazy fop I have become—hire somebody to dust my airplanes!

I used to be intimate with one airplane, now there's a tin harem; I'm the sheikh come to visit now and then. The Twin Cessna, the Widgeon, the Meyers, the Moth, the Rapide, the Lake amphibian, the Pitts Special . . . once a month, if then, do I start their engines. Only the T-33 had recent time in its logbook, flying back from California.

Careful, Richard, I thought. To be distant from the airplane one flies is not to invite longevity.

I slid into the baby-jet's cockpit, stared at an instrument panel turned unfamiliar with time.

Used to be, I spent every day with the Fleet, crawled upside-down in the cockpit reaching hay off the floor, streaked my sleeves with oil cleaning the engine and setting the valves just so, tightening cylinder hold-down bolts. Today, I'm as intimate with my many airplanes as I am with my many women.

What would Leslie think about that, she who values everything? Weren't we intimate, she and I? I wish she were here.

"Tailpipe clear!" I called the warning from habit, and pressed the start switch.

The igniters fired TSIK! TSIK! TSIK!, and at last a rumble of jet fuel lighting off in burner cans. Tailpipe temperature swept up its gauge, engine rpm turned round on its tiny dial.

So much is habit. Once we learn an airplane, our hands and eyes know how to make it run long after our minds have forgotten. Had someone stood at the cockpit and asked how to start the engine, I couldn't have said . . . only after my hands finished the starting sequence could I have explained what they had done.

The rough perfume of burning jetfuel sifted into the cockpit . . . memories of a thousand other flights sifted along with it. Continuity. This day is part of a lifetime spent mostly flying.

You know another meaning for *flying*, Richard? *Escaping*.

Running away. What am I escaping, and what am I finding, these days?

I taxied to the runway, saw a few cars stop at the airport fence to watch. There wasn't much for them to see. The jet was so small that without the airshow smoke system on, it would be out of sight before it reached the far end of the runway.

Takeoff is critical, remember. Lightly on the control stick, Richard, feather lightly. Accelerate to 85 knots, then lift the nosewheel one inch and let the airplane fly itself off. Force it off and you are dead.

Pointed down the white runway centerline, canopy closed and locked, I pressed full throttle and the little machine crept forward. With its tiny engine, the jet gathered speed about as fast as an Indian oxcart. Halfway down the runway it was moving, but still asleep . . . 60 knots was far too slow to fly. A long time later we were going 85 knots, wide open, and most of the runway was behind us.

I eased the nosewheel off the concrete, and a few seconds later we were airborne, barely, low and sluggish, off the end of the runway, straining to clear the trees.

Wheels up.

Mossy branches flashed ten feet below. Airspeed up to 100 knots, 120 knots, 150 knots and at last the machine woke up and I began to relax in the cockpit. At 180 the little thing would do anything I wanted it to do. All it needed was airspeed and free sky and it was a delight.

How important was flying to me! It stood for all I loved. Flight seems magic, but it's a learned, practiced skill with a learnable lovable partner. Principles to know, laws to follow, disciplines that lead, curiously enough, to freedom. So much like music, is flying! Leslie would love it.

Away off airways to the north a line of cumulus built toward thunderstorms. Ten minutes and we were skating on their smooth-dome tops, off the edge into thin air, two miles down to the wilderness.

When I was a kid I'd hide in the weeds and watch clouds, see another me perched way up high on just such an edge as this, waving a flag to the boy in the grass, shouting HI DICKIE! and never being heard for the height. Tears in his eyes, he wanted so much to live one minute on a cloud.

The jet turned at the notion, climbed, then shot toward the cloudtop, an Austrian down a ski-jump. We plunged our wings briefly into the hard mist, pulled up and rolled. Sure enough, dwindling behind us, a curling white flag of cloud to mark the jump. *Hi Dickie!* I thought, louder than a shout. Hi Dickie crosstime to the kid on the ground thirty years before. Hold your passion for the sky, kiddo, and I promise: what you love will find a way to sweep you up from the earth, high into its joyful scary answers for every question you can ask.

A level rocket, we were, cloudscape changing highspeed around us.

Did he hear?

Do I remember hearing then the promise I just this minute gave the kid watching from the grass of a different year? Maybe. Not the words, but the dead-sure knowing that I would someday fly.

We slowed, rolled inverted, plunged straight down for a long way. What a thought! What if we could talk between us, from one time to another, Richard-now encouraging Dickie-then, touching not in words but in way-deep

180

rememberings of adventures yet to be. Like psychic radio, transmitting wishes, hearing intuitions.

How much to learn if we could spend one hour, spend twenty minutes with the us-we-will-become! How much could we say to us-we-were!

Smoothly smoothly, with the gentlest touch of one finger on the control stick, the little airplane eased out of its dive. At redline airspeed one does nothing sudden with an aircraft, lest it become a puff of separate parts stopped midflight, fluttering here and there into swamps.

Lower clouds shot past like bursts of peaceful flak; a lonely road flicked below and was gone.

Such an experiment that would be! To say hello to all the other Richards flown out ahead of me in time, to find a way to listen to what they'd say! And the alternate me's in alternate futures, the ones who made different decisions along the way, who turned left at corners I turned right, what would they have to tell me? Is their life better or not? How would they change it, knowing what they know now? And none of this, I thought, is to mention the Richards in other lifetimes, in the far futures and the far pasts of the Now. If we all live Now, *why can't we communicate?*

By the time the airport was in sight, the little jet had forgiven me my neglects and we were friends again. It was harder to forgive myself, but so it usually is.

We slowed and entered the landing pattern, that same pattern that I had seen the day I got off the bus and walked to the airport. Can I see him now, walking there with his bedroll and news he was a millionaire? What do I have to say to him? Oh, my, what do I have to say!

As easy to land as it was tricky to take off, the BD-5 hushed down final approach, touched its miniature wheels

181

to the ground, rolled long and straight to the last taxiway. Then primly she turned and in a minute we were back at the hangar, engine-fire off, turbine spinning slower and slower and stopped at last.

I patted her canopy-bow and thanked her for the flight, the custom of any pilot who's flown longer than he or she thinks they've deserved.

The other airplanes watched enviously. They wanted to fly, too; needed to fly. Here the poor Widgeon, oil leaking from the nose-case of her right engine. The seal had dried from being still for so long.

Could I listen to airplane's futures, as well as my own? Had I practiced and known her future then, I would not have felt sad. She would become a television-star airplane, opening each episode of a wildly popular TV series, flying to a beautiful island, landing on the water, taxiing to dock sparkling and pretty, no oil leaks anywhere. And she couldn't have that future without the present she lived right now, dusty in my hangar after flying her few hundred hours with me.

So was there some future ahead for me that could not possibly happen without my first having lived this free lonely present.

I climbed the stairs back to the house, absorbed in the possibility of contact with the other aspects of me, Richards-before and Richards-yet-to-be, the I's of other lifetimes, other planets, other hypnotic space-times.

Would any of them have looked for a soulmate? Would any of them have found her?

Intuition—the future/past always-me—whispered back, that moment on the stairs:

Yes.

twenty-three

I OPENED the cupboard, took out a soup-can and some noodles, planned me a fine Italian lunch in a minute. May not have been quite Italian. But hot and nourishing of the kind of inquiring I had to do.

Look around you this moment, Richard. What you see, is it the kind of life you most wish to have?

It's awfully lonely, I thought, putting the soup in a pan on the stove, forgetting to turn on the fire. I miss Leslie.

There was a rattling of armor, and I sighed.

Don't worry, I thought, don't bother; I know what you are going to say, I cannot fault your logic. Togetherness is drab destruction. I do not miss Leslie, I suppose. I miss what she represents for me at this time.

The warrior left.

There came another idea in its place, a thought altogether

kind: *The opposite of loneliness, Richard, it's not together-ness. It is intimacy.*

The word floated loose, a silver bubble cut free from the floor of a dark sea.

That!

Is what I miss!

My many-bodied perfect woman is as warm as ice in the freezer. She's communication without caring; she's sex with-out love; she's friendship without commitment.

Just as she can't hurt or be hurt, so is she incapable of loving or being loved. She is incapable of *intimacy*. And intimacy . . . might that be as important to me as freedom itself? Is that why I stayed seven weeks with Leslie, when three days were too much to spend with any other woman?

I left the soup cold on the stove, found a chair and sat, knees pulled under my chin, looking out the window over the lake. The cumulus were full cumulonimbus now, block-ing sunlight. Florida in summertime, you can set your clock by the thunderstorms.

Twenty minutes later I stared into a wall of rain, barely noticing.

I had somehow talked today with Dickie, so far in my past; somehow I had gotten a message through to him. How can I get in touch with a future Richard? What does he know about intimacy? Has he learned love?

Surely the other aspects of who we are, they must be closer friends than anyone . . . who can be closer to us than ourselves in other bodies, ourselves in spirit-forms? If we're each of us spun about an inner golden thread, which strand is it in me that runs to all the others?

I went heavier and heavier, sinking down into the chair and at the same time rising above it. What a curious feeling,

I thought. Do not fight it, do not move, do not think. Let it take you where it will. It would help so much, to meet . . .

I stepped from a bridge of quiet silver light into a huge arena, empty seats curving away in semicircles, vacant aisles like spokes raying out from centerstage. Not on the stage but near it, a single figure sat, chin on knees. I must have made some sound, for he looked up, smiled, unfolded, waved hi.

"Not only punctual," he said, "you're early!"

I couldn't see the face clearly, but the man was about my height, dressed in what looked like a snowmobile suit, a black one-piece nylon coverall, bright yellow and orange across the chest and down the sleeves. Zippered pockets, zippered leather boots. Familiar.

"Sure enough," I told him back, casual as could be. "Doesn't look like the show will be starting for a bit." What was this place?

He laughed. "The show is started. Just now got its wheels up. Do you mind if we get out of here?"

"Fine with me," I said.

On the grass of the park outside the arena was a spidery little aircraft that might have weighed two hundred pounds with its pockets full. It had a high wing covered in orange and yellow nylon, tall bright rudders at each wingtip, same-painted canard elevator perched on aluminum tubes ahead of the seats, a small pusher engine mounted behind. I knew a lot of airplanes, but never had I seen anything like this.

It wasn't a snowmobile suit he was wearing, it was a flight suit, to match his airplane.

185

"Left seat, if you want." How courteous, how trusting of him, to offer me the pilot's place!

"I'll take the right," I said, and threaded my way into the passenger-spot. A snug fit, because everything about the airplane was small.

"Whatever. You can fly it from either side. Standard controls, but you see you've got no rudder pedals. It's all in the stick. Sensitive elevator, that canard. Pretend it's as sensitive as a helicopter cyclic stick, and you'll have it down."

He called the propeller clear, reached to an overhead handle, pulled once and the engine was running, quiet as an electric fan. He turned to me. "Ready?"

"Go," I said.

He pushed forward on a throttle smaller than the baby jet's, and with no more sound than a softly rising breeze, the machine lunged ahead. In fifty feet it was airborne, tilted back, climbing like a big-engine uphill racer. Ground fell away, a wide green floor cut loose from us, falling clear a thousand feet per minute. He touched the control stick forward, eased the throttle back till the fan whisked quietly behind us in the wind. He took his hands off the controls, motioned that I could fly the airplane. "You've got it."

"Thank you."

It was like flying a parachute, except we weren't dropping out of the sky. We were moving perhaps thirty miles per hour, judging by the wind, in a little delight of a machine more eight-dollar lawn-chair than airplane. Without walls or floor, it was so open-cockpit that biplanes were locked tombs, compared. I turned the *airplane, and climbed. It was as sensitive as he had warned.*

"Can we shut the engine down? Can we soar this thing like a sailplane?"

"Sure." He touched a switch on the throttle and the engine stopped. We glided noiseless through what must have been rising air . . . there was no altitude loss that I could measure.

"What a perfect little airplane! This is lovely! How do I get one of these for my own?"

He looked at me strangely. "Haven't you guessed, Richard?"

"No."

"Do you know who I am?"

"Sort of." I felt a brush of fright.

"Just for the fun of it," he said, "walk through the wall between what you know and what you dare to say. Do that, and tell me whose airplane this is and who you're flying with."

I tilted the control stick to the right, and the airplane banked smoothly, turned toward a cumulus at the top of its thermal. It was second nature, engine off, to look for lift even though the featherweight machine wasn't losing height.

"If I had to guess, I would say that this airplane is mine from the future, and you're the fellow that I'm going to be." I dared not look at him.

"Not bad," he said. "I'd guess the same."

"You'd guess? Don't you know?"

"It gets complicated if you think about it much. I'm one of your futures, you're one of my pasts. I think you're the Richard Bach in the midst of the money-

storm, aren't you? The new celebrity author? Nine airplanes, isn't it, and a flawless idea you've designed for a perfect woman? You're straight-arrow faithful to her, and still she leaves you cold?"

We touched the lift of a thermal with the right wing, and I banked steeply into it.

"Don't wrap it too tight," he said. "It's got such a small turning radius anyway, just a little bank will keep you in the lift."

"OK." This joy of an airplane would be mine! And he would be me. What things he must know!

"Look," I said, "I've got some questions. How far in my future are you? Twenty years?"

"More like five. Seems like fifty. I could save you forty-nine if you'd listen. There's the difference between us. I've got the answers you need, but there's not a prayer you'll listen before you get yourself flattened by the Great Steamroller of Experience."

My heart sank. "You think I'm scared of what you'll say, you're _sure_ I won't hear you?"

"Will you?"

"Who can I trust more than you?" I said. "Of course I'll listen!"

"Listen you might; act you won't. We get to meet now because we're both curious, but I doubt you'll let me help."

"I will!"

"You won't," he said. "It's like this airplane. In your time, it doesn't have a name, it hasn't been invented yet. When it is invented, it'll be called an ultralight, and it's going to revolutionize sport aviation. But you're not going to buy this machine finished, Richard, or hire anybody to

188

build it for you. You're going to build it yourself: piece by piece, Step One, Step Two, Step Three. Same with your answers, exactly the same. You can't buy them finished, you won't take them if I give them to you free, if I tell you word for word what they are."

I knew he was wrong. "You've forgotten," I said, "how fast I learn! Give me an answer and watch what I do with it!"

He tapped the control stick, a signal that he wanted to fly our kite for a while. We had gained a thousand feet in the thermal, nearly to cloudbase. Fields meadows forests hills rivers away down below us, lime and rolling velvet. No roads. Soft fuffling whisper, the gentlest of winds about us while we glided upward.

With the calm smile of a gambler calling a bluff: "You want to find your soulmate?"

"Yes! Since always, you know that!"

"Your armor," he said. "It shields you from any woman who would destroy you, sure enough. But unless you let it go, it will shield you as well from the only one who can love you, nourish you, save you from your own protection. There is one perfect woman for you. She is singular, not plural. The answer you're looking for is to give up your Freedom and your Independence and to marry Leslie Parrish."

It was well he had taken the controls before telling me.

"You're saying . . . WHAT?" I choked on the thought. "You . . . You're saying . . . MARRY? I cannot possibly . . . Do you know what I think about marriage? Don't you know I say in lectures that after War and

*Organized Religion, Marriage brings more unhapp . . .
you think I don't believe that? Give up my FREEDOM!!
My INDEPENDENCE? You are telling me that my
answer is to GET MARRIED? Are you . . . I mean
. . . WHAT?"*

*He laughed. I saw nothing funny. I looked away to
the horizon.*

*"You're really scared, aren't you?" he said. "But
there's your answer. If you'd listen to what you know
instead of what you fear . . ."*

"I don't believe you."

*"Maybe you're right," he said. "I'm your most
probable future, not your only one." He turned in his
seat, reached back to the engine, pulled a mixture-
enrichment lever. "But it's pretty likely, I think, that my
wife Leslie is one day going to be yours. She's asleep,
right now, in my time, as your friend Leslie is asleep in
your time, a continent away from you. Each of your
many women, what you've learned from them, gives you
the gift of this one woman, do you understand that? Do
you want more answers?"*

*"If that's a taste," I said, "I'm not sure that I do.
Give up my freedom? Mister, you have no idea who I
am. Answers like that I can do without. Please!"*

*"Don't worry. You'll forget this flight; you won't
remember till much later."*

"Not me," I said. "Memory like a steel claw."

*"Old friend," he said quietly. "I know you so well.
Don't you ever get tired of being contrary?"*

*"Deathly tired. But if that's what it takes to live my
life the way I want to live it, contrary shall I be."*

He laughed, and let our flying machine slide off the

thermal-top. We coasted slowly cross-country, more
balloon than aircraft. I didn't care for his answers, they
threatened and frightened and angered me. But the
details of the ultralight, the aluminum tube and fittings,
the reflex curve of the wing, the attachment of stainless-
steel cables, even the curious pterodactyl insignia painted
on the canard I printed in memory, to build from
nothing if I had to.

He found some sinking air and rode it down in circles
as we had ridden the rising air upward. The meeting was
not going to last much longer.

"OK," I said. "Hit me with some more answers."

"I don't think so," he said. "I wanted to warn you,
but now I don't think so."

"Please. I'm sorry I was contrary. Remember who I
am."

He waited a long moment, decided at last to talk.

"With Leslie, you'll be happier than you've ever been,"
he said. "Which is fortunate, Richard, because
everything else is going straight to hell. Together, the two
of you will be hounded by the government for money
your managers have lost. You will not be able to write,
lest the Internal Revenue Service seize the very words you
put on paper. You will be wiped out, bankrupt. You will
lose your airplanes, every one; your house, your money,
everything. You'll be stuck on the ground year after year.
Best thing that ever happened to you. That will ever
happen to you."

My mouth went dry, listening. "That's an answer?"

"No. Out of that will come an answer."

He broke off over a meadow on the crest of a hill,

looked down. Waiting at the edge of the grass was a woman. Watching us, waving at the sight of the airplane.

"Want to land it?" he said, offering the controls to me.

"Field's a little small for a first-time landing. You do it."

He stopped the engine dead, turned in a wide circle, gliding. As we crossed the last trees before the meadow, he plunged the nose down, dived to the grasstops, smoothly tilted the nose up again. Instead of climbing, the ultralight floated for a second, touched its wheels and rolled to a stop by a Leslie even more breathtaking than the one I had left in California.

"Hello, you two," she said. "I thought I'd find you here, with your airplane." She leaned to kiss the other Richard, ruffle his hair. "Are you telling him his fortune?"

"His loss of one, his gain of another," he said. "So lovely, sweet! He'll think you're a dream!"

Her hair was longer than I knew it, her face gentler. She was dressed in lemon-gossamer silk, a high-neck flowing blouse that would have been prim had the silk not been so sheer. A wide sunlight sash for a belt at her waist. Slacks of white sailcloth, seamless to the grass, covering all but the toes of her sandals. My heart nearly stopped, my walls nearly shattered right there. If I'm to spend my years on earth with one woman, I thought, let this be the one.

"Thank you," she said. "Got dressed for the occasion. Not often we get to meet our ancestors . . . not often in the middle of a lifetime." She put her arm around him as he stepped from the airplane, then turned to me and smiled. "How are you, Richard?"

"Deeply envious," I said.

"Envy not," she said. "The airplane will be yours."

"I don't envy your husband his airplane," I said. "I envy him his wife."

She blushed. "You're the one who hates marriage, aren't you? Marriage is 'boredom, stagnation, inevitable loss of respect'!"

"Maybe not inevitable."

"That's encouraging," she said. "Think you'll change your mind about marriage, someday?"

"If I'm to believe your husband, I will. I don't see how, except when I look at you."

"No fair looking, after today," said the future Richard. "You'll forget this meeting, too. You've got to learn your own way, for better or for worse."

She looked up at him. "For richer or for poorer."

He smiled the trace of a smile at her. "Till death brings us closer still together." They mocked me gently with their words, and I loved them both.

Then, to me, he said, "Our time's up. There's the answer for you to forget. Fly the airplane, if you want. We have to run along back to the land of the waking, in a year so far from yours, so close to yours. I'm in the midst of writing the new book and if I'm lucky I'll reach out first thing I wake and get this dream on paper."

He reached his hand slow-motion toward her face, as though to touch her, and disappeared.

The woman sighed, sad the time was gone. "He's awake, and I will be, too, in a minute."

She floated a step toward me and, to my astonishment, kissed me softly.

"It won't be easy for you, poor Richard," she said.

"Won't be easy for her, either, the Leslie I was. Hard times ahead! Fear not. If you want magic, let go of your armor. Magic is so much stronger than steel!"

Eyes like the twilight sky. She knew, so much!

In the midst of her smile she vanished. I was left alone in the meadow with the ultralight. I didn't fly it again. I stood in the grass remembering everything that had happened, burning it into my mind—her face, her words—until the scene melted.

When I woke, the window was black, speckled with raindrops and a curved line of house-lights on the far side of the lake. I unfolded my legs and sat in the dark, trying to remember. By the chair was a notepad and pen.

Flying dream. Prehistoric flying beast, colored feathers, and it brought me to land face to face with the most beautiful woman I've ever seen. One word, she said: "Magic." The most beautiful face . . .

Magic. There was more, I knew, but I couldn't remember. The feeling that stayed in me was love love love. She was no dream. That was a real woman I had touched! Dressed in sunlight. A living woman, and I can't find her!

Where are you?

I burst in frustration, threw the notepad against the window. It bounced, fluttered, pages flying, crashed to a stop against my instrument-landing charts for southern California.

"Now, damn it! Where are you NOW?"

twenty-four

I WAS in Madrid when it happened, faltering gamely through a publicity tour for the Spanish edition of the book, giving interviews in that language which made the television hosts, the news reporters smile. Why not? Wasn't I charmed when a Spanish visitor to America, or a German or French or Japanese or Russian, spurned translators, did her or his own interviews in English? So the syntax is a little odd, the words chosen not quite the way a native would choose them, but how nice to watch these people bravely balanced on tightropes, trying to talk to us!

"The events and ideas of which you write, Señor Bach, believe you them, work they for you?" The camera had the faintest hum, waiting, while I translated the question for my mind.

"Not there is a writer in all the world," I said slowly at my top speed, "that she or he can to write a book of ideas in which she or he not to believe. We can to write truly only it that we believe truly. Not I am so good in the . . . how itself it says *proving* in Spanish? . . . living of the ideas as I desire, but I am more and more good every day!"

Languages are fluffy big pillows stuffed between nations—what others say is muffled and nearly lost in them, and when we speak their grammar we get feathers in our mouth. It's worth it. What pleasure to phrase an idea, even in child's words, slowly, and sail it across the gulf in another language, to a different-speaking human being!

The hotel phone rang late at night, and before I could think of the Spanish, I said hello.

A faint little voice on long long distance. "Hello wookie, it's me."

"What a wonderful surprise! Aren't you a sweetie to call!"

"I'm afraid we have some terrible problems here, and I had to call."

"What problems?" I could not imagine problems that would be so important for Leslie to telephone Madrid at midnight.

"Your accountant is trying to reach you," she said. "Do you know about the IRS? Has anyone told you? Did your business manager say anything?"

The long line crackled and hissed.

"No. Nothing. What I.R.F.? What's going on?"

"The Internal Revenue Service. They want you to pay them a million dollars by Monday or they're going to seize everything you have!"

It was a threat so huge that it couldn't possibly be true.

"Seize everything?" I said. "By Monday? Why Monday?"

"They sent a certified notice three months ago. Your business manager didn't tell you. He says you don't like bad news. . . ."

She said it so sadly I knew she wasn't kidding. What did I have a business manager for, a financial manager . . . why did I hire these professionals? Surely I didn't need to hire experts for anything so simple as getting my property seized by the IRS. I could have done that by myself.

"Can I help you, Richard?" she said.

"I don't know." What a strange feeling it will be, to see locks hanging on the airplanes, on the house.

"I'll do anything you want," she said. "I've got to be able to do something. I think I should see a lawyer."

"Good idea. Call my lawyer in Los Angeles, see if he's got anybody in his office who knows taxes. And don't worry. It's got to be a mistake. Can you imagine, a million dollars in TAXES? What's happened is I've *lost* a million dollars and there will be *no* taxes. A wire got crossed. I'll talk to the IRS when I get back and see what's going on, and we'll straighten the whole thing out."

"OK," she said, doubtfully. "I'll call your lawyer and go from there. Hurry home, please, soon as you can." She sounded tense and scared.

"I have to stay two more days. Don't you worry. We'll get this settled and I'll see you soon!"

"Don't you worry, either," she said. "I'm sure I can do something. . . ."

How strange, I thought, back under my covers in Madrid. She's taking it so seriously! As if it matters to her, as if she cares!

I thought of the managers I had hired. If this were true,

every one of them had failed. I'll bet that woman has more business sense in her hair-ribbon than the rest of us tied together in a knot.

What do you know—I hadn't bought trustworthiness with trust. Or with big salaries or with titles or with responsibilities or with expense accounts. And when hired hands fail, I suddenly realized, it's not them but me who gets vaporized!

Ay, Richard, *qué tonto! Estoy un burro, estoy un burro estúpido!*

Interesting, I thought. Less than two weeks in Spain, and already I'm thinking in the language!

twenty-five

*I*T WAS in a file marked *Richard* on her desk,
and assuming it for me, I opened the file and read.

> *Dawn's peaceful, luminous blue*
> *Intensified with the day*
> *As did happiness,*
> *Blue . . . bluer . . . bluest,*
> *White puffs of delight,*
> *Joy overflowing,*
>
> *Until sunset*
> *Wrapped us in tender pink*
> *And we fused in a*
> *Passionate magenta goodbye,*
> *Earth-soul and Cosmic-soul*
> *Bursting with beauty.*

When night came,
A baby moon
Laughed sideways in the dark.
I laughed back
And thought:

Partway across the world
Your sky
Is filled with this same
Golden laughter,
And hoped that you,
Twinkling Blue Eyes,
Saw and heard,

So that somehow we three
Were joined in our gladness,
Each in our own space,
Together apart,
Distance meaningless.

And I slept
In a world
Full of smiles.

I read it once, and again, and then once more, slowly.

"Little wookie," I called. "Who wrote the poem with the baby moon laughing sideways in the dark? In the file on your desk. Did you write that?"

She answered from her living room, where she had surrounded herself with mountains of investment-transaction forms, prairies of ledger-sheets, rivers of canceled checks; a settler in hostile country, circled by paper wagons.

She had managed to forestall the IRS seizure. Now she

was working topspeed to organize facts so negotiations could begin, two weeks from Thursday.

"Excuse me?" she said. "I did. Oh, DON'T READ IT, PLEASE!"

"Too late," I said, quiet enough for her not to hear.

We wonder sometimes if ever we can know our closest friend, what she thinks and feels in her heart. And then we find she's written her heart to a secret paper, clear as a mountain spring.

I read it again. It was dated the day I had left for Spain, and now the day after I returned I was learning how she had felt, telling no one but this paper. What a poet she was! Intimate on paper, gentle, unafraid. Writing moves me when it is intimate; flying does, film, talk, touches that seem accidental but aren't.

No one had I met but her, with whom I dared be as childish as sometimes I felt, as silly, as knowing, as sexual, as close and touching. If love wasn't a word twisted and mutilated by possession and hypocrisy, if it was a word that meant what I wanted it to mean, I might be on the edge of believing that I was in love with her.

I read her words again. "That's a beautiful poem, Leslie." Sounds so weak and condescending. Does she know I mean it?

Her voice was a silver chain, swung hard. "Damn it, Richard! I asked you not to read it! That is *private!* When I want you to read it I will let you know! Now will you come out of the office, *please* come out of there and help me?"

The poem shattered in my mind, a clay disk shot point-blank. Lightning fury. Who are you to shout at me, lady! NO ONE shouts at me and sees me again, ever! You don't

want me, you don't got me! Bye . . . Bye . . . BYE . . .
BYE!

That two-second spike of rage, then hot anger at myself. I who most value privacy had read her private poem! I had broken into her private writing—how would I feel if she'd broken into mine? Unthinkable, to do that. She had every right to throw me out of her house forever, and I hated so to have it end because she was the closest person ever to touch . . .

I clamped my jaw tight, said not a word, walked to the living room.

"I'm very sorry," I said, "I deeply apologize. That was unforgivable and I will never do it again. I promise you that." Fury cooled, molten lead dumped into ice. The poem stayed broken dust.

"Don't you care about this?" She was angry, desperate. "The lawyers can't do anything to help you until they have something to work with, and this . . . mess! . . . is supposed to be your records!"

She shuffled papers, sorted one stack here, one there. "Do you have copies of your tax returns? Do you know where your tax returns are?"

I hadn't a clue. If I abhorred anything next after War, Organized Religion and Marriage, it might have been Financial Paperwork. To see a tax return was to meet Medusa head-on: instant stone blank.

"They must be here somewhere," I said lamely. "I'll give a look for them."

She checked a clipboard list on her lap, lifted her pencil. "What was your income last year?"

"I don't know."

"Approximately. Plus or minus ten thousand dollars."

"I don't know."

"Richard! Come on! Plus or minus fifty thousand, a hundred thousand dollars?"

"Honest, Leslie, I really truly don't know!"

She put the pencil down, looked at me as though I were some biology sample brought in from arctic mud. "Within a million dollars," she said, very slowly and clearly. "If you earned less than a million dollars last year, say, 'Less than a million dollars.' If you earned more than a million dollars, say, 'More than a million dollars.'" Patiently, as though talking to a stupid child.

"Maybe more than a million," I said, "but maybe less and maybe two."

Her patience snapped. *"Richard! Please! This isn't a game! Can't you see I'm trying to help?"*

"CAN'T YOU SEE I *DON'T KNOW?* I DON'T HAVE THE FAINTEST IDEA HOW MUCH MONEY I EARNED, I DON'T CARE HOW MUCH MONEY I EARNED! I HAVE . . . I HAD PEOPLE I TRUSTED TO KNOW ALL THAT STUFF, I HATE KEEPING TRACK OF IT, *I DON'T KNOW HOW!"* It sounded like a scene from a script. "I don't know."

She touched the eraser to the corner of her mouth, looked at me, and after a long silence, she said, "You really don't know, do you?"

"No." I felt sullen, misunderstood and alone.

"I believe you," she said gently. "How can you not know within *a million dollars?"*

She saw my face and waved her hand to take back what she had said. "OK, OK! You don't know."

I pawed through boxes for a while, hating it. Papers, look

at all these papers. Numbers in unknown handwritings, from different typewriters, yet they were supposed to have something to do with me. Investments, commodities, brokers, taxes, bank accounts . . . "Here's taxes!" I said. "A whole folder of taxes!"

"Good boy!" she said, as though I were a cocker spaniel dug up a lost bracelet.

"Bark," I said. She didn't reply, scanning the titles of the returns, checking the entries there.

It was quiet while she read, and I yawned without opening my mouth, a trick I had learned in high school English. Hating paperwork so, was this to be required learning for me now, more deadly than grammar? Why? I hadn't ignored the paperwork, I had hired people to do it! After hiring them and paying them, why is it me stirring this mess, looking for tax-forms; why is it Leslie catching the load dropped by six high-paid employees? It's not fair!

When somebody writes a best-seller or sings a glorious song or acts a lovely film, they should be issued a heavy grey manual, along with their checks and fanmail and bushels of money:

INTRODUCTION AND WARNING

Congratulations for doing whatever you did to earn all this cash. Although it seems to be yours and you think it ought to be yours for giving whatever gift you gave to society, only about one-tenth of it might actually wind up under your control IF YOU ARE SKILLED IN PAPERWORK.

The rest goes to agents and taxes and accountants and lawyers and staff and governments and guilds and employees that you are going to have to hire to keep track of all this and to pay the employment taxes for the employees. It doesn't matter that you don't know where to hire the people to do this, that you don't know whom to trust or that you don't know all the bodies that you have to pay; you have to pay them, anyway.

Please begin on Page One and read straight through to page 923, memorizing every line. Then you can go out and have a deductible dinner if you take a business-person with you, talk business, keep the receipt and write who joined you for the meal. If you don't do that you have actually spent twice the amount you thought you did when you paid it.

Hereafter, live your life in strict accord with the rules herein, and we your government might allow you to exist a little longer. Otherwise, abandon hope all ye who enter here.

Not even a pamphlet. Every person who writes a song to enchant us is presumed a competent accountant, record-keeper, guardian of credits and debits payable to invisible agencies of city and state and nation. If one or two of those persons are not suited to these tasks or not blessed with an orderly mind that understands careful record-keeping, their star in the firmament is netted and stuffed into a jail cell. There they must turn their full talent to learning the ways of cells, to mastering this boresome stuff no matter how it tastes like cardboard; they must spend years in stifled darkness before their star may shine again if there is a spark of it left.

Such energy wasted! What other films, what other books, what other songs go unsung while those hours and months and years pour down plush rat-hole offices of attorneys and accountants and advisers and counselors and consultants paid in desperation for help?

Calm, Richard. You are peeking at your future. If you choose to stay in this country, careful attention to money and its records will be a choke-chain at your neck. Lunge against it, fight it and you will strangle. Just take it nice and easy, walk along slow, agree with every bureau and agent you meet, smile sweetly . . . do that and you will be allowed to breathe without being hanged dead on that chain.

But my *freedom!* I lunged. Aaak! Wheeze. Yike, that is a ferocious collar!

My freedom is a choice now between escape to some other country and careful, slow working out this heap of broken crockery that was my empire. Richard-then made some blind decisions and stupid mistakes that Richard-now will have to pay for.

I watched Leslie studying the tax returns, jotting page after page of notes for the lawyers.

Richard-now, I thought, is not doing a damn thing. Leslie-now is doing it, and she isn't the tiniest bit responsible for what happened. Leslie didn't get to fly the fast airplanes; she didn't even get a chance to save the empire from disaster. Leslie gets to sweep up the pieces if she can. What a reward, for making a friend of Richard Bach!

And then he gets mad at her because she raised her voice to him when he read her private poetry!

Richard, I thought, have you considered the possibility that you may in fact be a god damned worthless son-of-a-bitch? For the first time in my life, I considered that, seriously.

twenty-six

*T*HE ONLY difference might have been that she was quieter than usual, but I didn't notice that.

"I can't believe you don't have your own airplane, Leslie. A meeting in San Diego, it's only half an hour away!" I checked the oil in the engine of the Meyers 200 that I had flown west this time to see her, checked that the fuel caps were on tight and the covers over them closed and locked.

She answered in a voice just above a whisper, as she stood in warm sun by the left wing. She wore a sand-color suit that must have been tailored for her, yet she looked ill at ease near my business-plane.

"Excuse me, wook?" I said. "I didn't quite hear you."

She cleared her throat. "I said that I've managed to get along without an airplane so far."

I put her briefcase in the back, slipped into the left seat, helped her into the right and closed the door from the inside, talking.

"First time I saw this panel, I said, 'Wow! Look at all the dials and switches and gauges and radios and things!' The Meyers does have more than its share of instruments, but you get used to it after a while and it's pretty simple."

"Good," she said in a tiny voice. She looked at the panel about the way I had looked at the movie-set the day she had taken me to MGM. Not quite that much awe, but I could tell she didn't do this often.

"PROP CLEAR!" I called, and she looked at me with big eyes, as though something was wrong, that I should be shouting. Not used to anything smaller than a jumbo-jet, I guessed.

"It's OK," I said. "We know there's no one near the airplane, but still we yell *Prop clear!* or *Look out for the propeller!* or something like that, so anyone hearing knows that our engine will be starting and get out of the way. An old aviation courtesy."

"Nice," she nodded.

Master switch on, mixture rich, throttle cracked a half-inch open, fuel pump on (I pointed to the fuel-pressure gauge so she could see we had fuel pressure), ignition switch on, starter button down.

The propeller spun; the engine fired at once, catching on four cylinders roughly, then five, then six, smoothing down into a lion's glad purr to be awake again. Now instrument-needles were moving all over the panel: oil pressure, vacuum gauge, ammeter, voltmeter, heading indicator, artificial horizon, navigation indicators. Lights came on to show radio frequencies; voices sounded in the speakers. A scene I had played some ten thousand times in one airplane or another since I was a kid out of high school, and I liked it as much now as I did then.

I got the airport takeoff information from the tower, chatted with ground control that we were a Meyers and not a baby Navion, released the brakes and we taxied half a mile to the runway. Leslie watched the instrument panel, the other airplanes taxiing, landing, taking off. She watched me.

"I can't understand a word they're saying," she said. Her hair was combed severely back, tucked under a beige tam-o'-shanter. I felt like a company pilot, with the beautiful president on board for the first time.

"It's air-language, sort of a code," I said. "We can understand it because we know exactly what's going to be said: airplane numbers, runway numbers, takeoff sequences, winds, traffic. Say something the control tower doesn't expect: 'This is Meyers Three Niner Mike, we're having cheese sandwiches please hold the mayo,' the tower-lady will come back, 'What? What? Say again?' *Cheese sandwich* is not a word in air-language."

So much of hearing, I thought, is listening to what we expect and tuning out the rest. I'm trained to hear air-talk; she's trained to hear music I can't even tell is there. Is it the same with seeing? Do we tune visions out of our eyes, and UFOs and ghosts? Do we tune out tastes, do we tune down our senses, until we discover that the physical world is what we expect it to be, and not a miracle more? What would our day look like if we saw in infrared and ultraviolet, or if we could train ourselves to see auras, futures unformed, pasts lingering?

She listened intently to the radio, puzzling out sudden bursts of tower-talk, and I thought for a second of the widening range of calm adventures I was having with her.

209

Anyone else this moment would see the trim lovely businesswoman, neatly on her way to discuss film-production finances, above-the-line costs and below-the-lines, shooting schedules and locations. Yet narrowing my eyes I could see her as she had been an hour earlier, clad only in warm air from two hair dryers after her shower, winking at me as I passed her door, laughing a second later when I ran into the wall.

What a shame, I thought, that such pleasures always lead to taking-for-granted, to frowns and arguments and all the wrecked shambles of marriage, married or not.

I pressed the microphone button on the control wheel. "Meyers Two Three Niner Mike's ready to go on Two-One."

"Three Nine Mike, you are cleared for takeoff, please expedite. Aircraft on final approach."

"Mike, Roger," I said. I reached across the company president to check her door latched and locked. "Ready?" I said.

"Yes," she said, looking straight ahead.

The Meyers' purr swept into a three-hundred horsepower wall of sound. We were pressed back into our seats as the airplane surged down the runway, already changing from asphalt and painted lines into a long blur, into Santa Monica falling away.

I moved the landing-gear lever to the UP position.

"The wheels are coming up now," I said to Leslie, "and now, the flaps . . . see them retract into the wing? Now we'll come back to climb power and it will get a little quieter in here. . . ." I spun the throttle down a few turns, then the propeller pitch knob, then the mixture control to bring the exhaust-gas temperature up where it belonged.

Three red lights were glowing on the panel . . . the wheels were streamlined out of the way, up and locked. Gear lever to neutral, to shut off the hydraulic pump. The airplane settled into her climb, going up something less than a thousand feet per minute. She did not climb like the T-33, but then she wasn't burning six hundred gallons per hour, either.

Shoreline moved below, hundreds of people on the beach. If the engine fails now, I thought, we've got enough altitude to turn back and land on the golf course, or now, back on the runway itself. We swung into a wide turn up over the airport, then locked onto the first heading for San Diego. That heading took us over Los Angeles International Airport, and Leslie pointed to a sparse line of jetliners on final approach to land.

"Are we in their way?"

"Nope," I said. "There's a corridor over the airport; we're in it now. Safest place for us to be is right over the runways, 'cause all the big jets come in from one side to land, they go out the other side to take off, see that? 'String of pearls,' the controllers call them. At night they're a string of diamonds, with their lights on."

I eased the power down to cruise, the engine going quieter still. She asked questions with her eyes when I changed things in the airplane, and I told her what was going on.

"Now we're all leveled off. See the airspeed needle moving? That will come up to right about here; it'll show about a hundred and ninety miles per hour. This dial is our altitude. The little hand shows thousands; the big one shows hundreds. What's our altitude?"

"Three thousand . . . five hundred?"

"Tell me without the question mark."

She leaned against me to see the altimeter straight-on. "Three thousand five hundred."

"Right!"

A Cessna 182 flew toward us in the corridor, a thousand feet above our altitude. "See there? She's flying at four thousand five hundred feet, going in the opposite direction. There are rules we follow to keep us from flying too close together. Even so, any airplane you see, even if you know I see it too, point it out to me. We always want to look around, see and be seen. We have strobe-lights on the tip of the tail and on the belly, to help other airplanes see us."

She nodded, looked for other airplanes. The air was smooth as a lake of cream—except for the hum of the engine, we could have been flying a low-speed space capsule in a pass along planet Earth. I reached down and adjusted the trim knob on the instrument panel. The faster the airplane flew, the more it wanted to be trimmed nose-down, else it would climb.

"Do you want to fly it?"

She edged away, as if she thought I was going to hand her the engine. "No thank you, wookie. I don't know how."

"The airplane flies itself. The pilot just shows it where to go. Gently, gently. Put your hand on the control wheel in front of you. Real lightly. Just a thumb and two fingers. That's OK. I promise I won't let you do anything bad."

She put her fingers gingerly on the wheel, as though it were a steel trap set to gnash her hand.

"All you do is press down, ever so soft, on the right side of the wheel."

She looked at me, questions.

"Go on. Believe me, the airplane loves it! Give it a little pressure on the right."

The wheel moved half an inch under her touch, and of course the Meyers tilted slowly right, starting to turn. She caught her breath.

"Now press down on the left side of the wheel." She did, as though she were performing an experiment in physics whose outcome was entirely unknown. The wings leveled, and she gave me a smile of delighted discovery.

"Now try pulling back, half an inch, on the wheel. . . ."

By the time the airport at San Diego rose on the horizon, she had finished her first flying lesson, pointed out airplanes the size of dust-particles, fifteen miles away. Her eyes were as sharp as they were beautiful; she was a pleasure to have alongside as we flew.

"You'll be a good pilot, if you ever want to take it up. You're gentle with the airplane. Most people first time, you say be gentle and they wind up clutching the controls way too tight and the poor plane starts bobbling and lurching . . . if I were an airplane, I'd love for you to fly me."

She gave me a sidelong glance, went back to looking for other aircraft as we slanted down toward San Diego.

Home again in Los Angeles that evening, after a flight as smooth as the morning's, she collapsed in bed.

"Let me tell you a secret, wookie," she said.

"I will let you. What's the secret?"

"I am terrified of flying! *TERRIFIED!!* Light planes especially. Until today, if somebody came along and put a gun to my head and said either you get into this little airplane or I am going to pull the trigger, I would say, 'Pull the trigger!' I can't believe what I did today. I was scared to death, and I did it!"

What? I thought. "Terrified? Why didn't you tell me? We

could have driven the Bantha. . . ." I couldn't believe. A woman I care about so much, she's *afraid of airplanes?*

"You would have hated me," she said.

"I wouldn't have hated you! I would have thought you were a silly goose, but I wouldn't have hated you. Lots of people don't enjoy flying."

"It's not that I don't enjoy it," she said, "I *can't stand* flying! Even a big airplane, a jet. I fly in the biggest airplane possible, only when I absolutely have to. I walk in, sit down and grab the armrests and try not to cry. And that's before they start the engines!"

I hugged her softly. "Poor little thing! And you didn't say a word. Far as you knew, those were the last few minutes of your life, getting into the Meyers, weren't they?"

She nodded in my shoulder. "What a brave, brave girl you are!"

More nodding.

"And now it's all over! All that fear flown away and everywhere we go from now on we'll fly and you'll learn to fly and get your own little airplane. . . ."

She had been nodding until "everywhere we go from now on," at which point she stopped, moved back from my hug to look at me in anguish, eyes huge, chin trembling as I went on. We both melted laughing.

"But Richard, really! I'm not kidding! I'm more scared of flying than anything in the world! Now you know how I feel about my friend Richard. . . ."

I led the way to the kitchen and opened the freezer, piled ice-cream and fudge on the counter.

"This calls for a celebration," I said, to cover my confusion over what she had said: "Now you know how I feel about my friend Richard." To overcome such a fear of flying would require a trust and affection as strong as love itself, and love is a passport to disaster.

Every time a woman said she loved me, we were on the road to the end of our friendship. Would my beautiful friend Leslie be lost to me in the firewind of jealous possession? She had never said that she loved me, and I'd never say that to her in a thousand years.

A hundred audiences I had warned: "Whenever somebody says they love you, look out!" No one had to take my word, anyone could see it in their own lives: parents battering children, shouting how they love them; wives and husbands who murder each other verbally, physically in knife-edge arguments, loving each other. The running putdowns, the eternal discounting of one person by another who claims to love. From such love, please, may the world be delivered. Why had such a promising word been crucified on the tree of obligation, thorned by duties, hanged by hypocrisy, smothered by custom? Next to "God," "love" is the word most mangled in every language. The highest form of regard between human beings is friendship, and when love enters, friendship dies.

I poured the hot fudge for her. Surely that is not what she meant. "Now you know how I feel" speaks of trust and respect, of those loftiest peaks that friends can climb. She couldn't have meant love. Please, no! How I would hate to lose her!

twenty-seven

*T*HE STARS are always and constant friends, I thought. A hatful of constellations, learned when I was ten; those and the visible planets and a few stars, friends today as though not a night had passed since we met.

Luminous soft greens twisted and curled in the wake of the sailboat through midnight ink, tiny bright whirlpools and tornadoes glowing for an instant, fading away.

Sailing alon: down the west coast of Florida, south from Sanibel to the Keys, I brought the boat a point starboard, to fit the constellation Corvus tight to the mast, a sail of stars. Too small a sail to add much speed.

Smooth black breeze, east-northeast.

Wonder if there are sharks in the water. Hate to fall overboard, I thought automatically, and then—would I really hate to fall overboard?

What's it like to drown? People who have been through

almost-drowning say it's not so bad; gets kind of peaceful after a while, they say. A lot of people have been near-dead and revived. Dying's the most beautiful moment in living, they tell us, and their fear of death is gone.

Do I need the running-lights on when I'm so alone out here? Wastes energy, runs the batteries down.

Thirty-one feet of boat is just about right. Bigger, you want a crew. Glad I don't need a crew.

Alone alone alone. How much of our lives is single-handing. Leslie's right. I distance her, she says.

> "I distance everybody, wook! It's not that it's you, it's that I don't let anyone get too close to me. I never want to get attached to anybody."
>
> "Why?" There had been annoyance in her voice. It was happening more often now. Without warning, the talks we had would jump the tracks and she'd be mad at me for the smallest thing. "What is so terrible about getting attached to someone?"
>
> Because I might make a huge investment of hope in one human being and then lose it all. I assume that I know who she is and then I find out that she's somebody else entirely and I have to go back to the drawingboard redesigning again and after a while I conclude there's no one I can fully know except myself and that's pretty iffy. The only thing I can trust anyone else to be is true to who they are and if they're going to explode into strange angers now and then the best thing to do is to stand back a bit so as not to get torn in the blast. Isn't that obvious, clear as yesterday?
>
> "Because then I'm not quite so independent as I want to be," I said.

217

She had tilted her head and looked at me carefully. "Are you telling me the highest truth you know?"

There are moments, I thought, when having a mind-reader for a best-friend is uncomfortable, indeed. "Maybe it's time for me to get away for a little while."

"That's it," she said. "Run away! You might as well. You're gone even when you're here. I miss you. You're right here and I miss you!"

"Leslie, I don't know what to do about that. I think it's time to get away. I have to move the boat down to Key West, anyway. Go back, see how things are getting along in Florida."

She frowned. "You could never stay with one woman for more than three days, you said; you'd go mad with boredom. We stayed together months and cried when we had to part! Happier than we've ever been, both of us! What's happened, what's changed?"

Corvus strayed from its place on the mast; a spoke of the wheel to port brought it back. But if I kept it there all night, I thought, I'd be somewhere off Yucatán by dawn, instead of on course for Key West. Navigate by the same star, unwilling to change, and you find yourself not only off-course but lost.

Damn it, Corvus, are you taking her side? I have carefully worked out this excellent system, this first-rate perfect-woman scheme, and it was running just fine until Leslie started messing with it, asking questions I dare not think about, less answer. Of course I want to love you, lady, but how can I know what you'd do if I did?

What would it feel like, to fall overboard now? There I'd be, a green-phosphor splash in the ocean; there's the boat huge above me one second and next second out of reach and next minute gone in the dark, the lights of her wake fading.

I'd swim for shore, that's what it would feel like. We're barely ten miles offshore, and if I can't swim ten miles in warm water I deserve to drown.

But what if I were a thousand miles offshore? What would it feel like then?

Someday, Richard, I thought, you are going to learn how to control your silly mind. It's like the boy said to the barnstormer landed in his hayfield:

"Mister, what would you do if the *engine quit?*"

"Why, I'd just glide down and land, my friend! The airplane's a good glider, doesn't need an engine to glide."

"But what would you do if the *wings fell off?*"

"If the wings fell off, I'd have to bail out, wouldn't I, and use the parachute."

"Yeah, but what if the *parachute didn't open?*"

"Then I'd try to fall in a haystack."

"But what if it was just *rocks everywhere?*"

Bunch of vultures, kids are. Same as I was. Same as I still am—"But what if I were a thousand miles offshore?" I'm so curious, the kid in me wants to run and find what's on the other side of dying right now. There'll be a time for that before too long. My mission is pretty well done, with the books written, but there may still be a lesson or two to learn, this side of dying.

How to love a woman, for instance. Richard, remember when you quit barnstorming to find your truelove, your soulmate, your ultimate friend across a million lifetimes? Seems so long ago. What are the chances that everything

I've learned about love is wrong, that there *is* one woman in all the world?

The wind picked up, the boat tilted starboard. I let Corvus go and steered by compass for Key West.

Why is it that so many airplane pilots also sail boats? Airplanes have freedom in space, sailboats have freedom in time. It's not the hardware, we want, it's the unshackledness that the hardware represents. Not a big airplane we like, but the speed and power that come from controlling its flight. Not a gaff-rigged ketch, but the wind, the adventure, the working purity of life that the sea demands, the sky demands. Unlatched from outside constraint. Sail for years nonstop in a boat, if you want to.

Boats, they own time. The longest an airplane's flown is a few hours; longer is a stunt. Someone ought to invent an airplane that has as much freedom in time as a boat.

I've got my freedom from all my other women-friends; why not from Leslie? They don't criticize me for being distant, for leaving when I want; why does she? Doesn't she know? Too long together, and even courtesy is gone . . . people are more courteous to strangers than they are to their own wives and husbands! Two people tied to each other like hungry dogs, fighting over every little scrap between them. Look at us, even us. You raised your voice to me! I didn't come into your life to make you angry. If you don't like me as I am, just say so and I'm gone! Together too long, and it's chains and duties and responsibilities, no delights no adventure no thank you!

Hours later through the night, the first faint glow of light on the horizon south. Not dawn but Key West street-light bouncing from mist way high in the sky.

Sailing is altogether too slow, I thought. You change your

220

mind, you don't want to be where you are, in an airplane you can do something about it; a short while takes you a long way. A sailboat, you change your mind, you can't even land the thing and get off! Can't glide if you're too high, climb if you're too low. Sailboat's always at the same altitude. No change. Boring. Change is adventure, whether it's sailboats or women. What other adventure is there, than change?

Leslie and I agreed to certain rules of friendship: total equality, freedom, courtesy, respect, nobody takes anybody for granted, a nonexclusive pact. If the rules are no longer all right with her, she ought to tell me. This whole affair is getting too serious.

Sure enough she'll say, Is there no room in your life Richard Bach for something more than rules?

Wish I could just say no and walk away from her.

Wish I could talk with her about it now.

Wish sailboats were a lot faster, wish they could fly.

Sorry state of the world. We put people on the moon, but we can't build a sailboat that can fly.

twenty-eight

"**R**EADY TO go, wookie?" she said.

I'm spending too much time with her again, I thought, altogether too much time. She's as organized as a microchip . . . everything she touches runs in order, honest and clear. So beautiful she blinds me still, she's funny and warm and loving. But the rules say I'll destroy myself if I spend too much time with one woman, and I'm spending too much time with her.

"Are you ready to go?" she asked again. She was dressed in a brush-of-amber suit, golden silk at her throat; her hair combed and pinned back for a long business meeting.

"Sure," I said.

Curious. She's the one hauling me from the sticky shards of empire, she's doing the job of all my fired employees.

Stan, calm to the end, said as he left that he was sorry I

had lost so much money. That's the way it happens sometimes, he said, the market turns against you.

Stan's tax lawyer apologized, sorry he had missed the IRS
deadline, said he thought they weren't being fair . . . he
was only two weeks late, filing his appeal, and they'd refused
to consider it. If it weren't for that, he said, he could have
proven that I didn't owe them a cent.

Harry the business manager smiled, said the IRS problem
was a shame; he didn't like it any more than I did, and he
had done his best to keep it from me as long as he could. By
the way, he'd appreciate it if I could come up with a
month's severance pay.

If it weren't for Leslie, I'd have left for Antarctica or
Botzwezoland, so disgusted was I with money, with taxes,
with accounts and ledgers. Any paper with numbers on it, I
wanted to shred.

" 'Bye," she said, as I got into the car.

" 'Bye?"

"You're gone again, Richard. 'Bye."

"Sorry," I said. "Think I ought to apply for Antarctican
citizenship?"

"Not yet," she said. "After this meeting, maybe. Unless
you can come up with a million dollars plus interest."

"I can't get over it! How could I owe that much in taxes?"

"Maybe you didn't," she said, "but the deadline was
missed; it's too late to argue it now. Damn, that makes me
mad! How I wish I could have been with you before it was
too late. They could at least have told you!"

"I knew on other levels, wook," I said. "I think part of
me wanted the whole thing wiped out. It wasn't working, it
wasn't making me happy."

"I'm surprised that you know that."

Richard! I thought. *You know nothing of the sort! Of course it was making you happy! Didn't you have all the airplanes . . . don't you still? And your perfect woman? Of course it made you happy!*

What a lie. The empire was a shambles, money plastered around like wallpaper stuck up by amateurs, myself the worst. I had a taste of empire life, and it was fluff, whipped cream, with a spoon of sweet-arsenic neglect for flavor. Now the poison was at work.

"That's not the way it had to be," she said. "You would have done so much better not to have hired anybody. Just gone on and been your same old self."

"I was my same old self. I had more toys, but I was still me. My same old self never could do bookkeeping."

"m," she said.

We settled around the desk of John Marquart, the attorney Leslie had hired when I was in Spain. Cups of hot chocolate were brought in, as though somebody knew it was going to be a long meeting. She opened her attaché case, set out her lists of notes, but the lawyer spoke to me.

"You filed a capital loss against ordinary income," he said. "Is that the problem, in a nutshell?"

"I think the problem is I hired a financial wizard who knew less about money than I did, which is less than zero," I told him. "The money he was investing, it wasn't numbers on paper, it was real money and it—pouf—disintegrated in the market. The IRS doesn't have a square on the tax-form for pouf. I think that's it, in a nutshell. To be honest, I don't know what the guy filed. I was sort of hoping you'd tell me answers instead of problems. It's me hiring you, after all, and this is supposed to be your specialty. . . ."

Marquart looked at me odder and odder, reached for his coffee, peered over the cup as though he hoped it might protect him from a raving client.

Leslie stepped in then, and I heard her voice in my mind, asking me please to sit there and be quiet, if possibly I could.

"As I understand it," she said, "the damage is done. Richard's tax attorney—the tax attorney his financial manager got for him—didn't answer the IRS in time, so the government won a judgment by default. Now it wants a million dollars. Richard doesn't have a million dollars in cash to pay them at once. So the question is, can he arrange to make payments? Can he give them a lump-sum down payment, and promise the rest as he liquidates his assets? Will they give him time to do it?"

The attorney turned to her with evident relief. "I don't see why not. That's fairly common in these cases; it's called an Offer in Compromise. Did you bring the figures I wanted?"

I watched her, marveled that she'd be so much at home in a law office.

She set labeled lists on his desk. "Here's Cash Available Now, this one is Assets To Be Liquidated, and here's his Income Projection Over The Next Five Years," she said. "Between these and new income, the figures show he can pay the full amount in two years, three at the most."

While I was sailing, I thought, Leslie was researching tax-payment schemes! I'm being wiped out, not getting rich—why does she care so much?

Soon the two of them were analyzing my problems as though I weren't in the room. I wasn't. I felt like a mosquito

225

in a bank vault . . . I could find no way to break through the utter heavy dullness of liens, assets, liquidations, payment schedules. The sun was shining outside. We could go for a walk, buy chocolate-chip cookies. . . .

"I'd rather structure the payout over the next five years, instead of three," Marquart was saying, "in case his income isn't quite what you project. If he can pay it sooner, that's fine, but he'll have a heavy current-tax burden with this kind of income, and we want to be sure we aren't making new problems for him down the road."

Leslie nodded, and they talked on, the two of them working out details. A calculator clucked numbers on the desk between them; Leslie's notes marched in order down a blue-lined tablet.

"I can see it from their point of view," she said at the end. "They don't care about the people Richard hired, or whether he knew or didn't know what was going on. They want their money. Now they'll get it, with interest, if they'll just wait a little. Do you think they'll wait?"

"It's a good offer," the attorney said. "I feel sure they'll accept it."

By the time we left, the disaster had been tamed. Once, I had found a million dollars in my account with a single telephone call; to come up with such a modest sum over five whole years, that would be simple. Sell the house in Florida, sell the airplanes, all but one or two of them, get the film produced . . . simple.

And now I have Leslie and a professional Los Angeles tax attorney to keep order in my life, no slender twigs to break under pressure.

There had been a storm at sea; I had fallen in way over

my head. This woman had jumped into the waves and pulled me out, saved my financial life.

We left the lawyer's office full of hope.

"Leslie?" I said, holding the door open for her as we left the building.

"Yes, Richard?" she said.

"Thank you."

"You're welcome, wookie," she said. "You're quite welcome!"

twenty-nine

"*C*AN YOU come over, wookie?" Her voice sounded weak, on the phone. "I'm afraid I need your help."

"I'm sorry, Leslie, I can't make it tonight."

Why was it so uncomfortable, to tell her? I know the rules. I made the rules. We couldn't have been friends without them. Still it was hard to say, even on the telephone.

"Wook, I'm feeling terrible," she said. "I'm dizzy and sick and I'd feel so much better if you were here. Won't you be my doctor, come heal me?"

The part of me that wished to rescue and heal I pushed into the closet and locked the door. "Can't make it. I have a date tonight. Tomorrow's fine, if you'd like."

"You have a *date?* You are going out with a date when I am sick and need you? Richard, I can't believe . . ."

Must I tell her again? Our friendship is nonpossessive, open, based on our mutual freedom to be away from each other whenever we wish, for any reason or for no reason. Now I was frightened. It had been so long since I had seen any other woman in Los Angeles, I felt us slipping into a taken-for-granted marriage, felt us forgetting that we needed our apart-times as well as together-times.

The date had to stand. If I felt obligated to be with Leslie just because I was in Los Angeles, something was wrong with our friendship. If I had lost my freedom to be with whomever I chose, our purpose together had ended. I prayed for her to understand.

"I can be with you till seven. . . ." I said.

"Till seven? Richard, don't you hear me? I *need* you. I need some help from you, this time!"

Why was she pressuring me? The very best thing for her to say would be that she'd get along just fine and that she hoped I'd have a good time. To do otherwise, doesn't she know? That's a fatal mistake! I will not be pressured, I will not be possessed by anyone, anywhere, under any conditions!

"I'm sorry. Wish I'd known earlier. Now it's too late to cancel. That won't work for me, I don't want to do that."

"Does she matter so much to you," she said, "whoever she is? What's her name?"

Leslie was jealous!

"Deborah."

"Does Deborah matter so much to you that you can't call her and say that your friend Leslie is ill and is it all right to postpone your hot date till tomorrow or next week or next year sometime? Is she so important to you that you can't call her and say that?"

There was anguish in her voice. But she was asking for

229

something that I couldn't give without destroying my independence. And her sarcasm wasn't helping, either.

"No," I said. "She's not that important. It's the principle she stands for—that we're free to be with whomever we choose. . . ."

She was crying. *"Damn* your freedom, Richard Bach! I work like hell to save your goddamn empire from being swept completely away, I can't sleep for worry there's some way I haven't thought of, nobody's thought of . . . to save you . . . because you matter so much . . . I'm so tired from it I can hardly stand up and you won't be with me when I need you because you have a date with some Deborah you've hardly seen, she stands for some goddamn *principle?"*

I spoke over walls a yard thick, solid steel. "That's right."

There was a long silence on the telephone.

Her voice changed. Jealousy gone, anguish gone, she was calm and quiet.

"Goodbye, Richard. Enjoy your date."

While I was saying thank you for understanding how important . . . she hung up.

thirty

SHE DIDN'T answer her phone the next day or the next. The day after that, this letter:

Wednesday evening 12/21

Dearest Richard,
It's so difficult to know how and where to begin. I've been thinking long and hard through many ideas trying to find a way. . . .
I finally struck one little thought, a musical metaphor, through which I have been able to think clearly and find understanding, if not satisfaction, and I want to share it with you. So please bear with me while we have yet another music lesson.
The most commonly used form for large classical works is sonata form. It is the basis of almost all symphonies and concertos. It consists of three main sections: the exposition

or opening, in which little ideas, themes, bits and pieces are set forth and introduced to each other; the development, in which these tiny ideas and motifs are explored to their fullest, expanded, often go from major (happy) to minor (unhappy) and back again, and are developed and woven together in greater complexity until at last there is: the recapitulation, in which there is a restatement, a glorious expression of the full, rich maturity to which the tiny ideas have grown through the development process.

How does this apply to us, you may ask, if you haven't already guessed.

I see us stuck in a never-ending opening. At first, it was the real thing, and sheer delight. It is the part of a relationship in which you are at your best: fun, charming, excited, exciting, interesting, interested. It is a time when you're most comfortable and most lovable because you do not feel the need to mobilize your defenses, so your partner gets to cuddle a warm human being instead of a giant cactus. It is a time of delight for both, and it's no wonder you like openings so much you strive to make your life a series of them.

But beginnings cannot be prolonged endlessly; they cannot simply state and restate and restate themselves. They must move on and develop—or die of boredom. Not so, you say. You must get away, have changes, other people, other places so you can come back to a relationship as if it were new, and have constant new beginnings.

We moved on to a protracted series of reopenings. Some were caused by business separations that were necessary, but unnecessarily harsh and severe for two so close as we.

Some were manufactured by you in order to provide still more opportunities to return to the newness you so desire.

Obviously, the development section is anathema to you. For it is where you may discover that all you have is a collection of severely limited ideas that won't work no matter how much creativity you bring to them or—even worse for you —that you have the makings of something glorious, a symphony, in which case there is work to be done: depths must be plumbed, and separate entities carefully woven together, the better to glorify themselves and each other. I suppose it is analagous to that moment in writing when a book idea must be/cannot be run from.

We have undoubtedly gone further than you ever intended to go. And we have stopped far short of what I saw as our next logical and lovely steps. I have seen development with you continually arrested, and have come to believe that we will never make more than sporadic attempts at all our learning potential, our amazing similarities of interest, no matter how many years we may have—because we will never have unbroken time together. So the growth we prize so highly and know is possible becomes impossible.

We have both had a vision of something wonderful that awaits us. Yet we cannot get there from here. I am faced with a solid wall of defenses and you have the need to build more and still more. I long for the richness and fullness of further development, and you will search for ways to avoid it as long as we're together. Both of us are frustrated; you unable to go back, I unable to go forward, in a constant state of struggle, with clouds and dark shadows over the limited time you allow us.

To feel your constant resistance to me, to the growth of this something wonderful, as if I and it were something horrible —to experience the various forms the resistance takes, some of them cruel—often causes me pain on one level or another.

I have a record of our time together, and have taken a long and honest look at it. It has saddened me, and even shocked me, but it has been helpful in facing the truth. I look back to the days in early July, and the seven weeks that followed, as our only truly happy period. That _was_ the opening, and it was beautiful. Then there were the separations with their fierce and, to me, inexplicable cutoffs—and the equally fierce avoidance-resistance on your returns.

Away and apart or together and apart, it is too unhappy. I am watching me become a creature who cries a lot, a creature who even _must_ cry a lot, for it almost seems that pity is necessary before kindness is possible. And I know I have not come this far in life to become pitiful.

To be told that canceling your date to help me when I was in a state of crisis "wouldn't work for you" brought the truth crushing down on me with the force of an avalanche. Facing facts as honestly as I can, I know I cannot continue, no matter how much I might wish to do so; I cannot bend further.

I hope you will not see this as the breaking of an agreement, but rather the continuation of the many, many endings you have begun. I think it is something we both know must be. I must accept that I have failed in my effort to let you know the joys of caring.

Richard, my precious friend, this is said softly, even tenderly and lovingly. And the soft tones do not camouflage an underlying anger: they are real. There are no accusations, no blames or faults. I am simply trying to understand, and to stop the pain. I am stating what I have been forced to accept: that you and I are never going to have a development, much less the glorious climactic expression of a relationship grown to full blossom.

I have felt if anything in my life deserved departure from previously established patterns, going beyond all known limitations, this relationship did. I suppose I might be justified in feeling humiliated about the lengths to which I have gone to make it work. Instead, I feel proud of myself and glad to know I recognized the rare and lovely opportunity we had while we had it, and gave all I could, in the purest and highest sense, to preserve it. I am comforted by this now. In this awful moment of ending, I can honestly say I do not know of one other thing I might do to get us to that beautiful future we could have had.

Despite the pain, I'm happy to have known you in this special way, and will always treasure the time we've had together. I have grown with you, and learned much from you, and I know I have made major positive contributions to you. We are both better people for having touched one another.

At this late juncture, it occurs to me that a chess metaphor might also be useful. Chess is a game in which each party has its own singular objective even as it engages the other; a mid-game in which a struggle develops and intensifies and bits and pieces of each side are lost, both sides diminished; an end-game in which one traps and paralyzes the other.

I think you see life as a chess game; I see it as a sonata. And because of these differences, both the king and the queen are lost, and the song is silenced.

I am still your friend, as I know you are mine. I send this with a heart full of the deep and tender love and high regard you know I have for you, as well as profound sorrow that an opportunity so filled with promise, so rare and so beautiful, had to go unfulfilled.

I stood looking out the window at nothing, noise roaring in my head.

She's wrong. Of course she's wrong. The woman doesn't understand who I am or how I think.

Too bad, I thought.

Then I crumpled her letter and threw it away.

thirty-one

*A*N HOUR later, nothing had changed outside the window.

Why do I lie to myself? I thought. She's right and I know she's right even if I never admit it, never think of her again.

Her story of the symphony, and of chess . . . why didn't I see those? I've always been so goddamned intelligent, except about taxes, so much more insightful than anybody who ever lived, how can she see these things when I can't? Am I not as bright as she? Yet if she's so smart, where's her system, her shield to keep her from pain? I've got my Perf . . .

DAMN your Perfect Woman! It's a half-ton peacock you've invented, flounced out weird colors fake feathers that will never fly! Your peacock might run around and flap its wings and screech instead of sing, but never never will it get off the ground. You, terrified of marriage, do you know you've married *that?*

The picture of it, a little me in a wedding photo with a twenty-foot peacock, it was true! I was married to an idea that was wrong.

But the restriction of my freedom! If I stay with Leslie, I'll get bored!

About that moment I split into two different people: the me who had run things for so long, and a newcomer out to destroy him.

Boredom is the least of your worries, you son-of-a-bitch, said the newcomer. Can't you see she's smarter than you are, she knows worlds you're afraid to touch with a stick? Go ahead, stuff my mouth full of cotton and wall me away like you do every other part of you that dares say your almighty theories are wrong! You're free to do that, Richard. And you're free to spend the rest of your life in superficial how-do-you-do's with women as scared of intimacy as you are. Like attracts like, bucko. Unless you've got a goddamn ounce of sense, which you do not stand a prayer of finding this lifetime, you belong with your gutless scared Perfect Woman fiction till you die of loneliness.

You're cruel as ice. You belong with your ice-cruel chessboard and your ice-cruel sky; you wrecked a glorious opportunity with that asinine empire of yours; now the whole thing's a bunch of splinters with a government—with of all things a *government* lien on it!

Leslie Parrish was an opportunity a thousand times more glorious than any empire, but you're scared to death of her because she's smarter than you will ever be so you're going to dump her, too. Or has she dumped you? It won't hurt her, pal, because she ain't a loser. She will feel sad and she will cry for a little while because she's not afraid to cry when something that might have been beautiful dies, but she'll get over it, she'll lift right on above it.

You'll get over it too, in about a minute and a half. Just pull your goddamn steel doors down shut, slam 'em tight and never think of her again. Instead of rising above, you'll go straight to the bottom, and before too long you'll be a brilliant success at your subliminal suicide-tries and wake up miserable that you were handed a fire-and-silver, a laser-diamond lifetime and you took your greasy damn hammer and smashed it to lard. You are looking at the biggest choice of your life and you know it. She's decided not to put up with your savage stupid fear, and she's happy this minute to be free of the dead weight of you.

Go ahead, do what you always do: run away. Run out to the airport, fire up the airplane and take off into the night. Fly, fly! Go find a nice girl with a cigarette in one hand and a rum-glass in the other and watch her use you for a stepping-stone to the something better that you're going to run away from tonight. Run, you stupid coward. Run to shut me up. Next time you see me is the day you die and then you can tell me how it felt after you burned the only bridge. . .

I slammed the doors down over the noise, and the room went still as calm at sea.

"My," I said aloud, "aren't we emotional!"

I retrieved the letter, started to read it again, let it fall back into the wastebasket.

If she doesn't like who I am, it's kind of her to say so. What a pity . . . if only she were different, we could have stayed friends. But I can't abide jealousy! Does she think I'm her personal property; does she decide who I spend my time with, and when? I told her clearly who I am and what I think and how she can trust me to live, even if that is not the I-love-you fakery she wants from me. No I-love-you's from me, Ms. Parrish. I will be true to myself, even though it costs me the joy-overflowing of every happy time we had together.

One thing I never did, dear Leslie—I never lied or cheated or deceived you; I lived what I believe exactly as I told you I would. If that now turns out to be unacceptable to you, that's the way it goes; I'm sorry and I wish you would have let me know a little sooner and saved us both the trouble.

I'll be off tomorrow sunrise, I thought. Throw my things in the plane and take off for someplace I've never been. Wyoming, maybe, Montana. Leave the plane for the IRS, if they can find it, and disappear. Borrow a biplane somewhere, vanish.

Change my name. Winnie-the-Pooh lived under the name of Sanders, so can I. That'll be fun. James Sanders. They can have the bank accounts and the airplanes and the whatever else it is they want. Nobody will ever know what happened to Richard Bach, and that will be a blessed relief.

Whatever I have to write again, if anything, I'll write with the new name. I can do that if I want. Drop everything. Maybe James Sanders will wander up to Canada, out to Australia. Maybe old Jim could knock around backwoods Alberta, or go way south to Sunbury, or Whittlesea, flying a Tiger Moth. He could learn Australian, hop a few passengers, enough to get along.

Then . . .

Then . . .

Then what, Mister Sanders? Is the government murdering

Richard Bach or are you? Do you want to kill him because Leslie cut him loose? Will his life be so empty without her that it won't matter to you if he dies?

I thought about it for a long time. It would be exciting to take off and change my name and run away. But: is that what I most want?

Is that your highest truth? she would have asked.

No.

I sat on the floor, leaned against the wall.

No, Leslie, that's not my highest truth.

My highest truth is I've got a long way to go to learn about loving another person. My highest truth is that my Perfect Woman at best is good for some talk, some sex— transient affairs, staving off loneliness. She's not the love that the kid at the gate had in mind, so long ago.

I knew what was right when I was the kid, and again when I quit barnstorming: find my lifemate foreversoul angel-become-woman to learn with and to love. One woman who will challenge the hell out of me, force me to change, to grow, to prevail, where otherwise I'd run away.

Leslie Parrish might be the wrong person. She may not be my soulmate come to find me on my way to find her. But she's the only one . . . she has Leslie's mind in Leslie's body, a woman I don't have to feel sorry for, I don't have to rescue, I don't have to explain to anyone, wherever I go. And she's so god-damn smart that the very worst thing that could happen is that I could learn a lot before she leaves me next.

If a person is cruel enough, I thought, anti-life enough, even his soulmate backs away, letting him alone, willing to wait another lifetime before a new hello.

But what if I *don't* run away? What's to lose but my

hundred tons of steel plate, supposed to protect me from hurt? Stretch my wings without armor and maybe I can fly well enough not to get shot down. *Next time* I can change my name to Sanders and take off for Port Darwin!

That impudent talk-back I had sealed away, he was right. I opened the doors, apologized, let him free; yet he said not one word more.

I *was* looking at the biggest choice of my life, he didn't have to say it again.

Could this be a test, planned by a hundred other aspects of me from different planets and times? Are they gathered now behind a one-way glass, watching me, hoping that I'll let go of the steel, or are they praying that I'll hold on? Are they taking bets on what I'm going to do?

If they were, they were awfully quiet, behind their glass. No sound. Even the roaring in my head was still.

The road split two directions, in front of me.

The two futures were two different lifetimes: Leslie Parrish, or my so-safe Perfect Woman?

Choose, Richard. Now. It's turning night outside. Which one?

thirty-two

"**_H_**ELLO?" HER voice was out of breath, nearly drowned in guitars and drums.

"Leslie? It's me, Richard. I know it's late, but could you have time to talk?"

No answer. The music smashed, beat on while I waited for the click of her telephone hanging up. All that struggling with choices, I thought, and the choice has already been made; Leslie was no longer interested in the likes of me.

"Yes," she said at last. "Let me turn down the music. I've been dancing."

The phone went quiet, and in a moment she was back. "Hi."

"Hi. I got your letter."

"Good."

I held the phone and paced, left and right, not knowing I

moved. "Do you really want to stop everything, just like that?"

"Not everything," she said. "I hope we'll still work together on the film. I'd like to think of you as my friend, if that's OK with you. The only thing I want to stop is the hurting."

"I never wanted to hurt you." It's not possible for me to hurt you, I thought. You can't be hurt unless you first *perceive yourself hurt.* . . .

"Well, it hurt anyhow," she said. "I guess I'm no good at open relationships. At first it was OK, but later we were so *happy* together! We had such warm delight, the two of us! Why keep ripping it apart for people who didn't matter, or for abstract principles? It just didn't work."

"Why didn't it work?"

"I used to have a cat," she said. "Amber. Big fluffy Persian cat. Amber and I, every minute I was home, we'd spend together. She'd have her dinner when I did, we'd sit and listen to music together, she'd sleep on my shoulder at night; each of us knew what each other was thinking. Then Amber had kittens. Cute as could be. They took her time and love, and they took my time and love. Amber and I weren't alone together anymore, we had to take care of the kits, we had to spread our love around. I was never as close to her after the kittens came, and she was never as close to me, not until the day she died."

"The depth of intimacy we feel toward another is inversely proportional to the number of others in our lives?" I asked. Then, afraid she'd see it as mockery, "Do you think you and I should have been exclusive to each other?"

"Yes. I accepted your many girlfriends, at first. What you did when you were gone was your business. But when Deborah came along, the principle of Deborah, as you would say, I suddenly realized that you were moving your harem west, and planned to make me part of it. I don't want that, Richard.

"Do you know what I learned from you? I learned what is *possible,* and now I must hold out for what I thought we had. I want to be very close to someone I respect and admire and love, somebody who feels the same way about me. That or nothing. I realized that what I'm looking for is not what you're looking for. You don't want what I want."

I stopped pacing, sat on the arm of the couch. Dark slanted in the windows around me.

"What do you think I want?" I asked.

"Exactly what you have. Many women that you know a little and don't care very much about. Superficial flirtations, mutual use, no chance of love. That's my idea of hell. Hell is a place, a time, a consciousness, Richard, in which there is no love. Horrible! Leave me out of it."

She spoke as if her mind were made up and as if mine were, too. As if there were no hope of change. She was asking for nothing; she was telling me her highest truth, knowing I'd never agree.

"I've had the greatest respect and admiration for you," she said. "I thought you were the most wonderful person I ever knew. Now I'm beginning to see things about you that I don't want to see. I'd like to end it thinking you're wonderful."

"What I was scared of, Leslie, is that we were starting to own each other. My freedom is as important to me as . . ."

"Your freedom to do what?" she shot back. "Your freedom not to be intimate? Your freedom not to love? Your freedom to seek relief from joy in restlessness and boredom?

245

You're right . . . if we had stayed together, I wouldn't have wanted you to have those freedoms."

Well said! I thought, as though her words had been a chessmove.

"You've pretty well shown . . ." I said. "I understand what you're saying, and I didn't understand before. Thank you."

"You're welcome," she said.

I shifted the telephone. Someday a wizard will design a telephone that stays comfortable more than a minute. "I think there's a lot to say. Is there any way we could get together and talk for a while?"

A pause, and then, "I'd rather not. I don't mind talking on the phone, but I don't want to see you in person, for a while. I hope you understand."

"Sure. No problem," I said. "Do you have to go now?"

"No. I can stay on the phone."

"Is there any way you can see, that you and I could still be close? I've never met anybody like you, and your idea of friendship I think means a cordial letter and handshake at the end of every fiscal year."

She laughed. "Oh, it's not that bad. A handshake semiannually. Quarterly, since we've been such good friends. Just because our love-affair didn't last, Richard, doesn't mean it failed. We learned from it what we needed to learn, I guess."

"Maybe the freedom I was talking about," I said, "a big part of it, maybe it's the freedom to change, to be different next week from what I am today. And if two people are changing in different directions . . ."

"If we change in different directions," she said, "then we don't have any future anyway, do we? I think it's possible for two people to change together, to grow together and

246

enrich instead of diminish each other. The sum of one and one, if they're the right ones, can be infinity! But so often one person drags the other down; one person wants to go up like a balloon and the other's a dead weight. I've always wondered what it would be like if both people, if a woman and a man both wanted to go up like balloons!"

"Do you know couples like that?"

"Few," she said.

"Any?"

"Two. Three."

"I don't know any," I told her. "Well . . . I know one. Of all the people I know, one happy marriage. The rest are . . . either the woman's a joy and the man's a weight, or the other way around, or they're both weights. Two balloons are pretty rare."

"I thought we could have been that way," she said.

"That would have been nice."

"Yes."

"What do you think it might take," I said, "what could possibly get us back together the way we were?"

I sensed that she wanted to say, "Nothing," but wasn't saying it because it would have been too glib. She was thinking about it, so I didn't prod her, didn't hurry her.

"The way we were, I don't think anything could get us back that way. I don't want that. I tried hard as I could to change, I even tried going out with other men when you were gone, to see if I could balance your Perfect Woman with my Perfect Man. It didn't work. Dull, dull, dull. Stupid waste of time.

"I'm not one of your party girls, Richard," she went on slowly. "I've changed as much as I'm willing to change. If you want to be close to me, it's your turn to change."

I stiffened. "What kind of change would you offer for my consideration?" The worst thing she could say would be something that I couldn't accept, I thought, and that's no worse than we've got right now.

She thought for a while. "I'd suggest that we consider an exclusive love-affair, you and me only. A chance to see if we're two balloons."

"I would not be free . . . I'd all at once stop seeing my friends who are women?"

"Yes. All the women you sleep with. No other love-affairs."

Now it was my turn to be silent, and hers to let the quiet stay on the line. I felt like a rabbit cornered by hunters. The men I knew who had agreed to those terms had been sorry for it. Holes had been shot in them and they'd managed to stay alive, but barely.

And yet, how different I was, with Leslie! Only with her could I be the kind of person I most liked to be. I wasn't shy with her, or awkward. I admired her, learned from her. If she wanted to teach me to love, I could at least give it a try.

"We're such different people, Leslie, you and me."

"We're different, we're the same. You thought you'd never find a word to say to a woman who didn't fly airplanes. I couldn't imagine myself spending time with a man who didn't love music. Could it be it's not as important to be alike as it is to be curious? Because we're different, we can have the fun of exchanging worlds, giving our loves and excitements to each other. You can learn music, I can learn flying. And that's only the beginning. I think it would go on for us as long as we live."

"Let's think about it," I said. "Let's think about it. We've both had marriages and almost-marriages, we both have scars, promised we won't make mistakes again. You don't see any other way for us to be together than to try . . . than to try being married?"

"Give me some suggestions," she said.

"I was pretty happy the way it was, Leslie."

"Pretty happy is not good enough. I can be happier than that by myself, and I can do it without listening to you find excuses to run away, to put me off, to build walls against me. I'll be your only lover, or I won't be your lover at all. I've tried your halfway thing and it doesn't work—not for me."

"It's so hard, marriage has such limitations. . . ."

"I hate marriage as much as you do, Richard, when it makes people turn dull, when it makes them deceivers or shuts them in cages. I've avoided it longer than you have; it's sixteen years since my divorce. But I'm different from you this way—I think there's another kind of marriage that sets us freer than we can ever be alone. There's very little chance you'll see that, but I think you and I could have been that way. An hour ago, I would have said there was *no* chance. I wouldn't have thought you'd call."

"Oh, come on. You knew I'd call."

"Nope," she said. "What I knew you'd do is throw my letter away and fly off to somewhere in your airplane."

Mind-reader, I thought. I put myself into that picture again, running away to Montana. Plenty of action, new sights, new women. But it was boring, even thinking about it. I've done that, I thought, and I know what it's like and it's every bit of it on the surface; it doesn't move me or change me or matter. It's action that doesn't mean anything. So I fly away . . . so what?

249

"I wouldn't fly off without a word. I wouldn't leave with you mad at me."

"I'm not mad at you."

"Hm," I said. "Just mad enough to stop the nicest friendship I've ever had."

"Listen, Richard, really: I'm not mad at you. I was furious the other night, and disgusted. Then I was sad, and I cried. But after a while I stopped crying and I thought about you a lot, and I finally understood that you're being the very best person you know how to be; that you have to live with that until you change and no one is going to make that happen except you. How can I be mad at you for doing your best?"

I felt a wave of heat in my face. What a difficult, loving thought! For her to understand, in the midst of that moment, that I was doing the best I knew how! Who else in the world would have understood that? The burst of respect for her triggered a suspicion of myself.

"Well, what if I'm not doing my best?"

"Then I'm mad at you."

She nearly laughed when she said it, and I relaxed a little, on the couch. If she could laugh, it wasn't the end of the world, not quite yet.

"Could we write a contract, come to a very clear and careful agreement of exactly what changes we want?"

"I don't know, Richard. It sounds like you're playing games, and it's too important for that. Games, and your litany of old phrases, your old defenses. I don't want them anymore. If you have to defend yourself against me, if I have to keep proving over and over that I'm your friend, that I love you and I'm not going to hurt you or destroy you or bore you to death, that's too much. I think you know me well enough, and you know how you feel about me. If you're afraid, you're afraid. I've let you go, and I feel good about it, I really do. Let's leave it at that. We're friends, OK?"

I thought about what she said. I was so used to being right, so used to prevailing in any debate. But here, try as I did to find threads broken in her thinking, I couldn't. Her argument collapsed only if she were lying to me, only if she were out to hurt me or cheat me or destroy me. And that I could not believe. What she could do to anyone else, I knew, she could one day do to me, and I had never seen her cheat or wish pain to anyone, even people who had been cruel to her. She had forgiven them, every one, no bad feelings.

Had I allowed myself the word, that moment, I would have told her that I was in love with her.

"You're doing your best, too, aren't you?" I said.

"Yes, I am."

"Doesn't it strike you as strange that we would be the exception, you and me, when nearly no one can make intimacy work? Without shouting and slamming doors, losing respect, taking for granted, boredom?"

"Don't you think you're an exceptional person?" she said. "Don't you think I am?"

"We're like nobody I've ever met," I said.

"If I get mad at you, I don't think there's anything wrong with shouting and slamming doors. Throwing things, if I get mad enough. But that doesn't mean I don't love you. And that doesn't make any sense to you, does it?"

"None. There's no problem we can't solve with calm, rational discussion. When we disagree, what's wrong with saying, 'Leslie, I disagree, and these are my reasons'? And then you say, 'Quite so, Richard. Your reasons have convinced me that yours is the better way.' And there's the end of it. No crockery to sweep up, no doors to repair."

"Don't you wish," she said. "The shouting comes when I get frightened, when I think you aren't hearing me. Maybe you're hearing my words, but you're not *understanding*, and I'm scared you're going to do something that will hurt us both and we'll be sorry and I see a way to avoid it and if you're not hearing I have to say it loud enough so you will!"

"You're telling me that if I listen to you, you won't have to shout?"

"Yes. I probably won't have to shout," she said. "Even if I do, it's over in a few minutes. I get it out of my system and I calm down."

"Meanwhile I'm a quivering ball clinging up at the top of the curtains. . . ."

"If you don't want anger, Richard, then don't make me mad! I've grown into a fairly calm and well-adjusted person. I'm not hair-trigger set to blow up at the smallest thing, but you are one of the most selfish people I have ever known! I've needed my anger to keep you from trampling right over me, to let both of us know when enough is enough."

"I *told* you I was selfish, a long time ago," I said. "I promised you that I'd always act in what I thought was my own best interest, and I hoped you'd do the same. . . ."

"Spare me your definitions, please!" she said. "It is by *not* always thinking of yourself, if you can manage it, that you might someday be happy. Until you make room in your life for someone as important to you as yourself, you will always be lonely and searching and lost. . . ."

We talked on for hours, as though our love were a terrified fugitive, leaning wide-eyed on a twelfth-floor ledge, set to jump the instant we stopped trying to save it.

Keep talking, I thought. If we keep talking, it won't push off the cornice and plunge screaming to the pavement. Yet neither of us wanted the fugitive to live unless it turned sane and strong. Each comment, every idea we shared was a wind blown at the ledge—sometimes our future together teetered out over the streets, others it was trembled back against the wall.

How much would die if it fell! The warm hours separated from time, when we so mattered to each other, when I breathlessly delighted in who this woman is; they all will have led to nothing, worse than nothing: to this terrible loss.

The secret of finding someone to love, she had told me once, is first finding someone to like. We had been the best of friends long before we became lovers. I liked her and admired her and trusted her, *trusted* her! Now so much good tilted in the balance.

If our fugitive slipped, the wookies would be killed in the fall, Hoggie clutching a sundae, the sorceress, the sex-goddess; the Bantha would die, chess and films and sunsets would disappear forever. Her fingers flashing over the keyboard. I'd never listen to Johann Sebastian's music again, never hear his secret harmonies because I had learned them from her, never another composer-quiz, never see flowers without thinking of her, never anyone again so close to me. Build more walls, bolt spikes on top, and then build walls inside those, and more spikes. . . .

"You don't *need your walls,* Richard!" she cried. "If we never see each other again, can't you know that walls don't protect? They *isolate* you!"

She's trying to help, I thought. In the last minutes we pull ourselves apart, this woman wants me to learn. How can we leave each other?

"And Hoggie . . ." she said, ". . . Hoggie doesn't . . . he doesn't have to die. . . . Every July eleventh, I promise . . . I'll make a chocolate-chip hot-fudge sund . . . hot-fudge sundae . . . and remem . . . my dearest Hoggie. . . ."

Her voice broke; I heard her press the phone into a pillow. Oh Leslie no, I thought, listening to the choking silence of the feathers. Does it have to disappear, our enchanted city of two, a mirage come once in a lifetime only to vanish into smog and the everyday world? Who is it that's killing us?

If some outsider broke upon us, tried to pull us apart, we'd turn to claws and tear him to hell. This now, it's an inside job, the outsider is me!

What if we're soulmates, I thought while she sobbed. What if we're the ones we've been looking for our whole lives long. We've touched and we've shared this quick taste of what love on earth can be, and now, because of my fears, are we going to separate and never meet again? Will I go on the rest of my days looking for the one I've already found, and was too frightened to love?

The impossible coincidences! I thought, that led us to meet at a time when neither of us was married or committed to marry, when neither of us was devoted every-waking-second to causes, when neither of us was too busy with acting or writing or traveling or adventuring or otherwise too blindly involved. We met on the same planet in the same era, we met at the same age, grown up in the same culture. Had we met years earlier, it wouldn't have happened . . . we *did* meet years earlier, and we went sailing past in an elevator—the time wasn't right. And it will never be right again.

I paced quietly forth and back, a half-circle on the tether of the telephone cord. If I decide in ten years or twenty that I shouldn't have let her go, where will she be then? What if I come back in ten years to say Leslie I'm sorry! and find she's Mrs. Leslie Parrish-Somebody? What if she's not to be found, her house empty, she's moved, left no address? What if she's dead, killed by something that never would have killed her had I not flown away tomorrow?

"I'm sorry," she said, back on the phone again, tears wiped away. "I'm a silly goose. I wish I had your control, sometimes. You handle goodbyes so well, as if they don't matter."

"It's all in deciding who's in charge," I explained, glad for a change of subject. "If we let our emotions run things, then times like these aren't much fun."

"No," she sniffed. "They're not much fun."

"When you pre-live it, pretend it's tomorrow now, or next month, how do you feel?" I said. "I try that, and I don't feel better, without you. I imagine what it's like alone, no one to talk with nine hours on the telephone, run up a hundred-dollar bill on a local call. I'll miss you so much!"

"I'll miss you, too," she said. "Richard, how do you get someone to look around a corner when he hasn't reached it yet? The only life worth living is the magical one, and this is magic! I'd give anything if you could see what's there for us. . . ." She paused for a moment, casting for what more to say. "But if it's out of sight for you, I guess it doesn't exist, does it? Even if I'm looking at it, it's not really there." She sounded tired, resigned. She was about to hang up the telephone.

Whether it was because I was tired or scared or both, I'll

never know. No warning; something snapped, something broke loose inside my head and it was not happy.

RICHARD! it screamed. WHAT ARE YOU DOING? *ARE YOU CRAZY GONE OUT OF YOUR MIND?* That's not some metaphor swaying on the ledge, that is YOU! That is your future, and if it falls you are a ZOMBIE, you are living dead, marking time till you kill yourself right! You've been playing games with her for nine hours on the telephone, WHAT DO YOU THINK YOU'RE ON THIS PLANET FOR, TO FLY AIRPLANES? You're here, you arrogant bastard, to learn about LOVE! She's your teacher, and in twenty-five seconds she is going to hang up and you will never see her again! Don't sit there, you idiot son-of-a-bitch! You've got ten seconds and she's gone! Two seconds! *SPEAK!*

"Leslie," I said. "You're right. I'm wrong. I want to change. We've tried it my way and it didn't work. Let's try it your way. No Perfect Woman, no walls against you. Just you and me. Let's see what happens."

There was silence on the line.

"Are you sure?" she said. "Are you sure, or are you just saying that? Because if you're just saying that, it's going to make it worse. You know that, don't you?"

"I know it. I'm sure. Can we talk about it?"

Another silence.

"Of course we can, wookie. Why don't you hang up the phone and come over here and we'll have breakfast."

"OK, sweet," I said. " 'Bye."

After she hung up I said to the empty phone, "I love you, Leslie Parrish."

In absolute privacy, no one to hear, the words that I had so despised, that I never used, were true as light.

I put the phone down in its cradle. "DONE!" I shouted to the empty room. "IT'S DONE!" Our fugitive was in our arms again, safely down from the ledge. I felt light as a mountain-summer sailplane launched for the stratosphere.

There's an alternate me this moment, I thought, veering sharp away, turned left out the fork in the road where I turned right. This moment in a different time, Richard-then hung up on Leslie-then after an hour or ten, or he didn't call her in the first place. He dropped her letter in the wastebasket, caught a cab to the airport, took off and climbed northeast, he levelled at nine-thousand-five and he ran to Montana. After that, when I looked for him, everything went dark.

thirty-three

"*I* CAN'T do it," she said. "I try, Richie; I'm scared to death, but I try. I start the spin, we're diving straight down and spinning, and then I black out! The next thing I know we're level again and Sue is saying, 'Leslie! Are you all right'?" She looked at me, dejected, hopeless. "How can she teach me—how can I learn spins if I black out?"

Hollywood disappeared four hundred miles over the horizon west, my Florida house sold, we lived in a trailer parked in ten thousand square miles of Arizona sagebrush and mountains, on the fringe of an airport for gliders. Estrella Sailport. Sunset like clouds soaked in jet-fuel and lit afire on a noiseless match. Sailplanes parked smooth seamless sponges for the light, dripping crimsons and melted-gold into pools on the sand.

"Dear little wook," I told her. "You know it, I know it, it is useless for us to fight what is true: there is nothing that

Leslie Parrish cannot do when she sets her mind to do it. And against that, a simple little thing like learning spins in a glider, it doesn't have a chance. You are *in control* of that flying-machine!"

"But I faint," she said sullenly. "It's hard to be in control when you're unconscious."

I went to the trailer's micro-closet, found our little broom, brought it to her where she sat on the edge of the bed. "Here's your control stick, the handle of this broom," I said. "Let's do it together, we'll do spins right here on the ground till you get bored."

"I'm not bored, I'm terrified!"

"You won't be. The broom is your control-stick, your feet are on the rudder pedals, pretend. Now here you are way up in the sky, flying along straight and level, and now you ease the stick back slowly, slowly, and the glider's nose comes up and it's going to shudder now, it's going to stall the way you want it to, and keep the stick back and the nose drops and NOW you stomp on full right rudder, that's right, hold the stick back and count the spins: one . . . two . . . three . . . count every time Montezuma Peak turns around the nose. Three, and stomp on the left rudder, at the same time move that stick forward, just forward of neutral, the spin's already stopped, and you lightly ease the nose back up to level flight. That's all there is to it. Was that so hard?"

"Not here in the trailer."

"Do it some more and it'll get easy in the airplane, too, I promise. I went through the same thing and I know what I am talking about. I was terrified of spins, too. Now again. Here we are in level flight, and you ease the stick back . . ."

Spins, the most frightening lesson in basic flying. So

frightening that the government dropped the requirement for spin instruction years ago . . . students reached spin-training and they quit flying. But Laszlo Horvath, the national soaring champion who owns Estrella, Horvath insisted that every student learn spin-recoveries before solo. How many pilots had been killed because they fell into a spin and didn't know how to recover? Too many, he thought, and it wasn't going to happen at his sailport.

"You *want* the bottom to drop out right here," I told her, "that's what's *supposed* to happen. You *want* the nose to point straight down and the world to go whirling round and round! If it doesn't do that, you're doing it wrong! Again . . ."

It was Leslie's test to confront that fear, vault over it and learn to fly an airplane that didn't even have an engine to keep it up.

My test was a different fear. I promised that I'd learn from her how to love, to drop my frozen Perfect Woman and let Leslie as close to me as she would let me to her. Each trusted the other to be gentle, no barbs or daggers in that quiet place.

The trailer in the desert had been my idea. If this experiment in exclusivity could blow up, I wanted it to explode quickly and get it over with. What better test than to live two of us in a tiny room under a plastic roof, without a private corner for escape? How better challenge people intensely private? If we could find delight in that, month after month, we had found a miracle.

Instead of snarling, pressed together so, we thrived.

We ran with each other at sunrise, hiked in the desert with flower-handbooks and field-guides in our pockets, flew sailplanes, had two-day talks, four-day talks, studied Spanish, breathed clean air, photographed sunsets, began a lifetime's training to understand one and only one other human being besides ourselves: where did we come from, what had we learned, how might we build a different world if it were up to us to build it?

We wore our premiere best for dinner, desert-flowers in a vase on our candle-lit table; we talked and listened to music till the candles melted out.

"Boredom between two people," she said one evening, "doesn't come from being together, physically. It comes from being apart, mentally and spiritually." Obvious to her, it was such a startling thought to me that I wrote it down. So far, I thought, we don't have to worry about boredom. But one can never promise for the future. . . .

The day came, I stood on the ground and watched her meet her dragon, stood in the rumbling blast of a towplane pulling her trainer aloft for spin-practice. In minutes the white cross of the glider released from the towline way overhead, alone and quiet. It slowed, stopped in the air and Whush! the nose dropped and wings swirled, a cotton-color maple-seed falling, falling—and smoothly recovered, eased out of its dive, to slow, to stop in the air and spin again.

Leslie Parrish, not so long ago a prisoner of her fear of light-planes, today in control of the lightest plane of any, bidding it do its worst: spins left, spins right, half-turns and recover, three turns and recover; all the way down to minimum altitude, then floated into the pattern and landed.

The glider touched down, rolled smoothly on its single wheel toward a stripe limed white on the dirt runway, stopped within feet of it. The left wing gradually tilted down to touch the ground and her test was done.

I ran toward her on the runway, heard a cry of triumph

across the distance from inside the cockpit, her instructor rejoicing. "You did it! You spun it by yourself, Leslie! Hurray!"

Then the canopy swung open and there she was, a smile on her mouth, looking shyly out to see what I might say. I kissed her smile. "Perfect flying, wook, perfect spins! How proud I am of you!"

The next day, she soloed.

What a delighted fascination it is, to stand aside and watch our dearest friend perform on stage without us! A different mind had stepped into her body and used it to destroy a fear-beast that had lurked and threatened for decades, and the mind showed now in her face. Within the seablue eyes were golden sparkles, electricity dancing in a powerplant. Power, she is, I thought. Richard, never you forget: this is no ordinary lady you are looking at, this is not a conventional human being and never you forget it!

I was not so successful with my tests as she was with hers.

From time to time, for no reason, I'd be cold to her, silent, push her away without knowing why.

Those times she was hurt and she said so. "You were rude to me today! You were talking to Jack when I landed and I ran over to join you and *you turned your back on me*, as if I weren't there! As if I were there and you wished I weren't!"

"Leslie, please! I didn't know you were there. We were talking. Must everything stop for you?"

I *did* know she was there, but didn't act, as though she were a leaf fallen, or a breeze passing by. Why was I annoyed when she minded?

It happened again, between the walks and musics and flying and candlelight—from habit, I built new walls, hid cold behind them, used old shields against her. She was not so angry, then, as she was sad.

"Oh, Richard! Are you cursed with a demon that so hates love? You promised to *lift* barriers, not dump new ones between us!"

She left the trailer, walked back and forth, alone, the length of the glider-runway in the dark. Back and forth, for miles.

I'm not cursed with a demon, I thought. One thoughtless moment, and she says I'm cursed with a demon. Why must she overreact?

Unspeaking, deep in thought when she returned, she wrote for hours in her journal.

It was practice-week for the sailplane race we had entered; I was pilot and Leslie was ground-crew. Up at five A.M. to wash and polish and tape the plane before the morning temperature rose past a hundred degrees, push it to its place in line on the runway, fill the wings with water-ballast. She kept ice packed around my neck in towels till takeoff-time, while she stood in the sun.

After my takeoff, she stayed in contact on the truck radio as she went to town for groceries and water, ready to come collect me and the plane should we be forced to land a hundred miles away. She was there with cold root-beer when I landed, helped push the glider back to its tiedown for the night. Then transformed into Mary Moviestar, she served candlelight dinner and listened to my day's adventures.

She had told me once that she was sensitive to heat, but now she gave no sign of it. Like a sand-trooper she worked, without letup, five days in a row. We were chalking up excellent times in our practice, and much of the credit was hers. She was as perfect a ground-crew as she was everything else she chose to be.

Why did I pick that time to distance her? Shortly after she met my landing, there were my walls again; I got to talking with some other pilots, didn't notice she was gone. I had to put the sailplane away by myself, no small job in the sun, but made easier by my anger at her walkout.

When I entered the trailer, she was lying on the floor, faking exhaustion.

"Hi," I said, tired from work. "Thanks a lot for the help."

No response.

"Just what I needed, after a really tough flight."

Nothing. She lay on the floor, refusing to say a word.

Probably noticed I was a little distant, reading my mind again, and got mad.

Silence-games are silly, I thought. If something's bothering her, if she doesn't like what I'm doing, why doesn't she just come out and say so? She won't talk, I won't talk.

I stepped over her body on the floor, turned on the air-conditioner. Then I stretched out on the couch, opened a soaring book and read, thinking that there is not much future for us if she insists on acting this way.

After a time she stirred. Still later she rose, infinite weariness, dragged herself to the bathroom. I heard the pumps running water. She was wasting the water because she knew I had to haul every drop of it from town, fill the trailer tanks myself. She wanted to make work for me.

The water stopped.

I put down the book. The wonder of her, and of our life together in the desert, was it corroding in acids from my past? Can't I learn to forgive her thorns? She misunderstood, and she was hurt. I can be big enough to forgive, can't I?

No sound from the bathroom; the poor thing is probably sobbing.

I walked to the little door, knocked twice.

"I'm sorry, wookie," I said. "I forgive you. . . ."

"*RRREEEEEAAAAAARGHH!!!* A beast exploded, inside. Bottles disintegrated against the wood; jars, brushes, hair-dryers hurled at walls.

"YOU GODDAMN (SMASH!) SON OF A BITCH! I (VLAMSHATTR!) HATE YOU! I NEVER WANT TO SEE YOU EVER AGAIN! I'M (THAKL!) LYING ON THE FLOOR PASSED OUT GODDAMNED NEARLY DEAD FROM HEAT-STROKE WORKING ON YOUR DAMNED GLIDER AND YOU LET ME LIE THERE WHILE YOU *READ A BOOK* I COULD HAVE *DIED* YOU DON'T CARE! (VASH-TINKL-THOK!) WELL I DON'T CARE EITHER RICHARD GODDAMN BACH!! GET OUT GET THE HELL OUT OF HERE AND LEAVE ME ALONE, YOU SELFISH . . . PIG!" (SVASH!)

Never; had anyone; in my life; talked that way; to me. Nor had I seen anyone act like that. She was *breaking* things, in there!

Disgusted, furious, I slammed from the trailer, ran to the Meyers, parked in the sun. The heat was relentless as ants swarming; I barely noticed. What is the matter with her? For her sake I've given up my Perfect Woman! What a fool I've been!

When I was barnstorming, my cure for crowdophobia was simple: get away from crowds at once, fly off and be

265

alone. So effective a fix was it that I began using it for persophobia, which it cured equally well. Anyone I didn't like, I'd leave, nor thereafter a word or thought of them.

Most of the time it works perfectly—leaving is an instant cure for whomever ails you. Except, of course, on the one-in-two-billion chance that the whomever that ails you happens to be your soulmate.

It felt like I was locked on a rack and stretched. I wanted to run, run, run. Jump in the plane start the engine don't check the weather don't check nothing just take off point the nose any direction, firewall that throttle and GO! Land somewhere, anywhere, fuel, start the engine, take off and GO!

Nobody has the right to shout at me! One time, you shout at me. And you never get another chance because I am permanently and forever *gone*. Slam-clank done and finished and through!

Yet there I stayed, fingers on the blistering handle of the airplane door.

My mind, this time, didn't allow running.

My mind nodded, OK, OK . . . so she's mad at me. She's got a right to be mad at me. I've done something thoughtless again.

I set off walking into the desert, walking to cool my rage, my hurt.

This is one of my tests. I'll prove I'm learning if I don't run away. We have no real problem. She's just a little . . . more expressive, than I am.

I walked for a while, till I remembered from survival training that people can die, out too long in this sun.

Had SHE been too long in the sun? Had she collapsed not from spite but from *heat?*

Temper and hurt vanished. Leslie had fainted from the *heat*, and I had called it faking! Richard, can you be that much a fool?

I hurried toward the trailer. On the way I saw a desert flower unlike any we'd seen, quickly dug it from the sand, wrapped it in a page from my notebook.

When I entered, she was lying on the bed, sobbing.

"I'm sorry, wookie," I said quietly, stroking her hair. "I'm very sorry. I didn't know . . ."

She didn't respond.

"I found a flower . . . I brought you a flower from the desert. Do you think it wants water?"

She sat up, wiped her tears, examined the little plant gravely.

"Yes. It wants water."

I brought a cup for the plant to be in, and a glass of water for it to drink.

"Thank you for the flower," she said after a minute. "Thank you for the apology. And Richard, try to remember: Anyone you want to keep in your life—*never* take them for granted!"

Friday afternoon late, she came down happy from a flight, bright and lovely; she had stayed in the air more than three hours, landed not because she couldn't find lift, but because another pilot needed the plane. She kissed me, glad and hungry, telling me what she had learned.

I tossed a salad, listening to her, stirred it in the air over its bowl, dished it into two parts.

"I watched your landing again," I said. "Like Mary

Moviestar for the camera. Your touchdown was light as a sparrow!"

"Don't I wish," she said. "I had full spoilers all the way down final approach or I would have rolled on into the sagebrush. Bad judgment!"

She was proud of her touchdown, though, I could tell. When she was praised, she often switched the subject to something alongside not quite perfect to spread the shock of the compliment, make it easier to accept.

This is the time, I thought, to tell her. "Wook, I think I'm going to take off for a while."

She knew at once what I was saying, looked at me frightened, gave me a door to change my mind last minute by speaking two levels at once:

"Don't bother taking off now. The thermals are all cold."

Instead of turning back, I plunged ahead. "I don't mean take off in a sailplane. I mean leave. After the race tomorrow; how does that sound? I need to be alone for a while. You do, too, don't you?"

She put down her fork, sat back on the couch. "Where are you going?"

"I'm not sure. Doesn't matter. Anywhere. Just need to be alone for a week or two, I think." Please wish me well, I thought. Please say you understand, that you need to be alone, yourself, maybe go back and shoot a TV thing in Los Angeles?

She looked at me, her face a question. "Except for a few problems, we've been having the happiest time in our lives, we're happier than we've ever been, and you suddenly want to run off to anywhere and be alone? Is it alone, or do you need to be with one of your women so you can start over new with me?"

"That's not fair, Leslie! I promised changes, I've made changes. I promised no other women, there aren't any other women. If our test wasn't working out, if I wanted to see somebody else, I'd tell you. You know I'm cruel enough to tell you."

"Yes, I do." There was no expression in the lovely planes and shadows of her face . . . her mind was sorting, sorting, fast as light: reasons, suggestions, options, alternatives.

I thought she should have expected this, sooner or later. My cynical destroyer, that viper in my mind, doubted our experiment would last longer than two weeks, and we'd been living in the trailer six months tomorrow, not a day apart. Since my divorce, I thought, never had I stayed six days with one woman. Even so, time for a break.

"Leslie, please. What is so wrong about getting away from each other once in a while? That's the murderous thing that happens in marriage . . ."

"Oh, God, he's getting on his soapbox. If I have to listen to that litany of reasons you've got for not loving . . ." she held up her hand to stop me, ". . . I know you hate the word love it's had all the meaning mangled out of it you have told me a hundred times you never want to use it but I'm using it right now! . . . litany of reasons you've got for not loving anyone but the sky or your airplane, if I have to listen I am going to scream!"

I sat quietly, trying to put myself in her mind and failing. What could be wrong with a vacation from each other? Why should the idea of being out of touch for a while be so threatening to her?

"To scream would be to raise your voice," I said with a smile, by way of saying if I can poke fun at my own sacred rules then it can't be a terribly bad time we're in for.

She refused to smile. "You and your damn rules! How long—oh God!—how long are you going to drag those things around with you?"

A bolt of anger tensed me. "If they weren't true, I wouldn't bother you with them. Don't you see? These things matter to me; they're true for me; I happen to live by this stuff! And please watch your language in front of me."

"Now you're telling me how to talk! I'll goddamn well say what I goddamn well please!"

"You're free to say it, Leslie, but I don't have to listen. . . ."

"Oh, you and your stupid pride!"

"If there's one thing I can't stand, it's being treated without respect!"

"And if there's one thing I can't stand, it's being ABANDONED!" She buried her face in her hands, her hair cascading, a golden curtain, to cover her misery.

"Abandoned?" I said. "Wook, I'm not going to abandon you! All I said . . ."

"You are! And I can't stand . . . being abandoned. . . ." The words choked out in sobs through her hands, through the gold.

I moved the table, sat with her on the couch, pulled the rigid curled ball of her body to lean against me. She didn't uncurl; she didn't stop sobbing.

She was transformed that moment to the once-was never-gone little girl who had felt abandoned and abandoned and abandoned after her parents' divorce. She had since rejoined and loved them both, but the scars from her childhood would never disappear.

Leslie had fought her way to where she was by herself, lived her life alone, she had been happy alone. Now she had

270

let herself think that because we spent so many happy months together, she was for the first time free from that part of her independence that meant alone. She had her own walls, and I was inside them right now.

"I'm here, wook," I said. "I'm here."

She's right about my pride, I thought. I get so carried away protecting me at the first hint of storm, I forget she's the one who's been through hell. Strong as she is, and smart, she's still scared.

In Hollywood, she had been the center of a lot more attention than I ever had to face. The day after our nine-hour telephone call, she had left her friends, her agent, studios, politics; left them all without goodbye, without explanation, without knowing if she'd be back soon or never. She simply left. Looking west, I could see question marks over the town she'd put behind her: *Whatever happened to Leslie Parrish?*

She's the center of a lot of desert, now. Instead of her dear old cat, peacefully died, there's not-so-peaceful rattlesnakes and scorpions and sand and rocks for comfort, her nearest world the softly violent one of flight. She's gambling everything, letting Hollywood fall away. She's trusting me in this harsh land, with nothing to shield her but the warm power that surrounds the two of us when we're happy together.

The sobs came slower, but still she was curled tense as oak against me.

I don't want her to cry, but it's her own fault! We agreed this was an experiment, spending so much time together. It was not part of our agreement that we couldn't have a few weeks alone. When she clings to me, denies my freedom to go where I please and when, she's becoming a reason herself for me to go. She's so smart, why can't she understand this simple fact? As soon as we become jailors, our prisoners want escape.

"Oh, Richard," she said, bleak and tired. "I want it to work, being together. Do you want it to work?"

"Yes, I do." I do, if you'll let me be who I am, I thought. I'll never stand between you and anything you wish; why can't you say the same for me?

She uncurled and sat away from me at the far end of the couch, silent. No more tears, but there was the weight in the air of so much disagreement between us, such a distance between our two islands.

And then a strange thing: I knew that this instant had happened before. The sky turning to blood in the west, silhouette of a gnarled tree looming just outside the window, Leslie downcast under the load of difference between us; it had happened exactly this way in a different time. I had wanted to leave and she had argued with me. She had cried, and then was silent and then had said, Do you want it to work? and I had said, Yes I do, and now the very next thing she's going to say is. *Are you sure?* She said those words before, and now she's going to say

She lifted her head and looked at me. "Are you sure?"

My breathing stopped.

Word for word, I knew my answer. My answer to that had been, "No. To be honest with you, I'm *not* sure . . ." And then it faded out: the words, the sunset, the tree, they all faded. With that swift view into a different now came a massive sadness, a sorrow so heavy I couldn't see for tears.

"You're better," she said slowly. "I know you're changing from who you were in December. You're sweet, most of the time, it's such a good life we have together. I see a future so beautiful, Richard! Why do you want to run away? Do you

272

see that future and not want it, or after all this time do you just not see it?"

It was nearly dark in the trailer, but neither of us moved to put on the light.

"Leslie, I saw something else, just now. Has this happened before?"

"You mean this minute happened before?" she said. "Déjà vu?"

"Yes. Where you know every word I'm going to say. Did you just have that feeling?"

"No."

"I did. I knew exactly what you were going to say, and you said it."

"What happened then?"

"I don't know, it faded out. But I was terribly awfully sad."

She stretched out her arm, touched my shoulder; I caught the ghost of a smile in the dark. "Serves you right."

"Let me chase it. Give me ten minutes. . . ."

She didn't protest. I lay down on the carpet, closed my eyes. One deep breath.

My body is completely relaxed. . . .

Another deep breath.

My mind is completely relaxed. . . .

Another.

I am standing at a door, and the door is opening into a different time. . . .

The trailer. Sunset. Leslie curled in a defensive shell on the far side of the couch, real as a three-dimension film.

"Oh, Richard," she said, bleak and tired. "I want it to work, being together. Do you want it to work?"

273

"Yes, I do." I do if you'll let me be who I am, I thought. I'll never stand between you and anything you wish; why can't you say the same for me?

She uncurled and sat at the far end of the little couch, silent. No more tears, but there was the weight in the air of so much disagreement between us, such a distance between our two islands.

"Are you sure? Are you sure you want it to work?"

"No! To be honest with you, I'm not sure. I don't think I can put up with these ropes, I feel like I'm caught in a rope-storm! Move this way and you don't like it, move that way and you shout at me. We're so different, you scare me. I've given this experiment a fair try, but if you can't let me go off and be alone for a couple of weeks, I'm not sure I do want it to work. I can't see much future."

She sighed. Even in the dark, I could see her walls going up, me on the outside. "I can't see any future either, Richard. You told me you were selfish, and I didn't listen. We tried, and it didn't work. Everything had to be your way, exactly your way, didn't it?"

" 'Fraid so, Leslie." I almost called her wookie, and when I didn't, I knew that the last time I had used the word had been the last time ever. "I can't live without the freedom . . ."

"Not your freedoms again, please. No more soapboxes. I should never have let you talk me into one more try together. I give up. You are who you are."

I tried to lift some of the weight. "You did solo the glider. You'll never again be afraid to fly."

"That's right. Thank you for helping me do that." She stood, turned on the light, looked at her watch. "There's

274

a late plane back to Los Angeles tonight, isn't there? Can you drive me to Phoenix to catch the late plane?"

"If that's what you want. Or we can fly back ourselves, in the Meyers."

"No, thanks. The late plane will be fine."

She packed her clothes in ten minutes, crammed everything in two piles, shut lids over them.

Not a word between us.

I set the suitcases in the truck, waited for her in the desert night. There was a slim quarter-moon, low in the west. *A baby moon, laughing sideways,* she had written. Now the same moon, just a few turns later, dim and mourning.

I remembered our nine-hour phone call, when we barely saved our life together. What am I doing? *She is the dearest, wisest, most beautiful woman ever to touch my life,* and I'm driving her away!

But the ropes, Richard. You have given it a fair try.

I felt a lifetime of happiness and wonder, learning and joy with this woman break away, shift and fill like a giant silver sail under the moon, flutter once, fill again, and fade, and fade, and fade. . . .

"Do you want to lock the trailer?" she said. The trailer was my place now, not hers.

"Doesn't matter."

She left it unlocked.

"Shall I drive?" she said. Never had she liked my driving; it was too distracted for her, unwatchful.

"It doesn't matter," I said. "I'm sitting in front of the steering-wheel, I might as well drive."

We rode together without speaking, forty miles through the night to the Phoenix airport. I parked the truck,

275

waited quietly with her to check her baggage, wishing for something to say that hadn't been said, walked with her toward the gate.

"Don't bother," she said. "I can take it from here. Thank you. We'll be friends, OK?"

"OK."

" 'Bye, Richard. Drive . . ." . . . carefully, she would have said, drive carefully. Not now. Now I could drive any way I wanted. " 'Bye."

"Goodbye." I leaned to kiss her, but she turned her head.

My mind was a slow grey blur. I was doing something irrevocable, like diving out the door of a jump-plane two miles up.

Now I was in reach of her; I could touch her arm if I wanted.

She walked away.

Now it was too late.

A thoughtful person considers, makes a decision, acts on it. Never is it wise to go back and change. She had done that once with me, and she had been wrong. To do it again was not worth another word between us.

But Leslie, I thought, I know you too well for you to leave! I know you better than anyone in the world, and you know me. You are my best friend of this lifetime; how can you leave? Don't you know I love you? I've never loved anyone and I love you!

Why hadn't I been able to say that to her? She was still walking away and she wasn't looking back. Then she was through the gate, and she was gone.

There was that sound like wind once more in my ears,

a propeller turning slow, patient, waiting for me to climb back aboard and finish out my life.

I watched the gate for a long time, stood there and watched it as though she might suddenly come running back through it and say oh Richard how foolish we both are, what silly geese to do such a thing to each other!

She didn't, and I didn't run through the gate to catch her.

The fact is that we are alone on this planet, I thought, each of us is totally alone and the sooner we accept that, the better it is for us.

Lots of people live alone: married and single, searchers without finding, at last forgetting they ever had searched. That had been my way before, and so it will be again. But never, Richard, never let anyone come so close to you as that one came.

I walked out of the airport, no hurry, to the truck, drove no hurry away from the terminal.

There, a DC-8 lifting off westward, was she aboard?

A Boeing 727 followed, then another. Deck-angles tilting high as they took off, so high; wheels coming up, flaps coming up, turning on course. That was my sky she was flying, this moment, how can she leave me on the ground?

Out of your mind with it. Put it out of your mind, think of it later. Later.

My launch-time next day put me the eighteenth sailplane in line for takeoff. Full water-ballast in the wings, survival kit aboard, canopy marked and turn-point cameras checked.

How empty the trailer had been all the sleepless night, how completely still!

Is it true she's gone? Somehow I can't believe . . .

I lay back in the contoured pilot's seat, checked the flight controls, nodded OK to the crew outside, didn't even know his name, rocked the rudder-pedals left-right-left: Let's go, towplane, let's go.

Like an aircraft-carrier catapult-launch, in slow motion. A great thrashing and roaring from the towplane out ahead on its rope, we creep forward for a few feet, then faster, faster. Speed gives power to the ailerons, to the rudder, to the elevators, and now we lift a foot off the ground and wait, runway blurring below, while the towplane finishes its takeoff and begins to climb.

Last night I made a spectacular mistake, to say what I said, to let her go. Is it too late to ask her to come back?

Five minutes later, a climb on the end of the tow-rope, a dive to loosen the tension, and I pull the handle for an easy release.

There is one good thermal near the airport, and it is thick with sailplanes. First plane off finds the lift, and the rest of us like lemmings follow in a great swirl of sleek white fiberglass, a gaggle of gliders going round and round, higher and higher in the warm rising air.

Careful, Richard, look around! Enter the thermal at the bottom, circling same direction as everyone else. A midair collision, some like to mutter, it can spoil your whole day.

All the flying I've done, still I'm nervous, jumpy as a duck when I slide into this small airspace with so many airplanes.

Tight turn. Fast turn. Catch the core of the lift and it's an express elevator on the way to the top . . . five hundred feet per minute, seven hundred, nine hundred. Not Arizona's best thermal, but good enough, for the first lift of the day.

Would she answer the phone if I called, and if she did, what would I say?

Leslie, I am terribly sorry?

Let's go back to where we were?

I've said those before, I've used up I'm-sorry.

Across the thermal from me is an AS-W 19, mirror of my own sailplane, race-number CZ painted on the wing and tail. Below, three more gliders enter the thermal together; above, a dozen at least. Looking up is looking up through the eye of a cyclone just hit an airplane factory, a swirling dream of noiseless flying sculpture.

Did I want to drive her away? Was I've-got-to-be-alone a pill I knew she'd never swallow; was it a coward's way of quitting? Is it possible for soulmates to meet and then to separate forever?

Very gradually I climb past CZ in the thermal, a sign I'm flying well, tired as I am. Our race is a 145-mile triangle above the ferocious broil of desolation that is the desert. It looks like death on the ground, but there's enough lift to hold a sailplane up all afternoon long, at high speed.

Look sharp, Richard! And careful. Next above me is a Libelle, then a Cirrus and a Schweizer 1-35. I can outclimb the Schweizer, maybe the Cirrus, not the Libelle. Before long we'll be at the top, get headed on-course, it won't be quite so tight.

Then what? The rest of my life alone, racing

sailplanes? How does an expert retreater run away from being without the woman he was born to meet? Leslie! I'm so sorry!

No warning, a sun-bright strobe fired in my eyes. A flash, a spray of flying plexiglass, the cockpit juddering sideways, windblast in my face, bright red light.

I'm slammed against the shoulder harness, then smashed into the seat, G-force trying to throw me out, then trying to crush me flat.

The cockpit tumbles like shrapnel flying. Time creeps.

Richard, you've been hit! And there is not much left of your airplane and if you want to live you've got to kick out of this thing and pull a ripcord.

I feel wreckage lurch, tear apart, tumble faster.

In a red haze there's sky whirling to rocks whirling to sky. Pieces of wing in a ragged torn cloud around me. Sky-ground-sky. . . . Can't seem to get my hands to the safety-belt release.

Not much improved with experience.
Slow to evaluate problem.

Oh, hi, pal! Give me a hand, will you. They're gonna say I was pinned in the wreckage. I'm not pinned. It's just the G's are so heavy . . . I can't . . .

Says "<u>can't</u>" when means "<u>won't</u>."

I <u>will</u> . . . pull that release. . . .

Listens to observer in last seconds.
Curious end to lifetime.

THERE!

The instant I pull the release, the cockpit is gone. I grab the parachute ripcord, pull it, roll over to see the ground before the parachute opens . . . too late. Wook, I am sorry. So . . .

black

On the floor of the trailer, my eyes blinked open into dark.

"Leslie . . ."

I lay on the floor, breathing deep, my face wet with tears. She was still there, on the couch.

"Are you OK?" she said. "Wookie, are you all right?"

I got up from the floor, curled close as I could beside her, held her tightly.

"I don't want to leave you, little wookie, I never want to leave you," I said. "I love you."

There was the faintest ripple through her in the night, silence for a moment that felt like forever.

"You what?" she said.

thirty-four

*A*LONG ABOUT two in the morning, discord forgotten, twined on our bed together in the midst of a talk about flowers, about inventions, about what a perfect life for us might be, I sighed.

"Remember my old definition?" I said. "That a soulmate is someone who meets all our needs, all of the time?"

"Yes."

"Then I don't guess we're soulmates."

"Why not?" she said.

"I don't have a need to argue," I said. "I don't have a need to fight."

"How do you know?" she said softly. "How do you know that's not the only way some lessons can get through to you? If you didn't need to fight in order to learn, you wouldn't create so many problems! There are times I don't understand you till you're angry . . . aren't there times you don't know what I mean until I scream? Is there a rule that we can't learn except in sweet words and kisses?"

I blinked, startled. "I thought being soulmates was supposed to be every moment perfect, so *how can soulmates fight?* Are you saying, wookie, that it *is* perfect? Are you saying even when we clash, it's magic? When a clash materializes understanding between us that hasn't been there before?"

"Ah," she said in the golden dark, "life with a philosopher . . ."

thirty-five

OUR LAUNCH-time for the race next day put me twenty-third sailplane in line for takeoff, second from last. Full water-ballast in the wings, survival-kit aboard, canopy marked and turn-point cameras checked. Leslie handed me maps and radio codes, kissed me good luck, eased the canopy down. I locked it from the inside. I lay back in the contoured pilot's seat, checked the flight controls, nodded OK, blew her one last kiss, rocked the rudder-pedals side to side: Let's go, towplane, let's go.

Every launch is different, but every one is the same air-craft-carrier catapult-launch in slow motion. A great thrashing and roaring from the towplane out ahead on its towline, we creep forward for a few feet, then faster, faster. Speed gives power to the ailerons, to the rudder, to the elevators, and now we lift a foot off the ground and wait while the towplane finishes its takeoff and begins to climb.

Leslie had been mischievous this morning, generously cooling me with ice-water at moments I least expected. She was happy and so was I. What a spectacular mistake it would have been, to have insisted on leaving her!

Five minutes later, a climb on the end of the line, a dive to loosen the tension, and I pulled the handle for an easy release.

There was one good thermal near the airport, thick with sailplanes. I shivered in the heat of the cockpit. A cyclone of sailplanes, it was. But I was almost last one out and couldn't spend all day looking for lift. I was ginger on the stick, careful. Look around, I thought, watch out!

Tight turn. Fast turn. I caught the core of the lift, an express elevator on the way to the top . . . five hundred feet per minute, seven hundred. Look around.

My neck was sore from twisting fast left, fast right, looking, counting. A Schweizer slid in below me, turning hard.

She's right. I do create problems. We've had our bad times, but hasn't everybody? The good times are glorious, they just . . . LOOKOUT!

The Cirrus above tightened its turn too steeply, sank toward me thirty feet, its wing a giant's blade slashing toward my head. I jammed the stick forward, fell away, in the same instant dodging the glider below.

"You gonna fly like that," I choked, "you gonna get plenty room from me!"

I swung back into the cyclone, looked up the center of the half-mile cylinder of climbing aircraft. Not many pilots, I thought, ever see anything like this.

The moment I looked, an odd movement, way above. It was a sailplane, *spinning!* down through the center of the other planes! I saw, and could not believe . . . what a *stu-*

pid, dangerous thing, to SPIN! in the midst of so many other airplanes!

I squinted against the sun. The glider was not spinning for sport, it was spinning because it had lost a wing.

Look! Not one plane spinning—two! Two sailplanes tumbling out of control, falling straight down toward my cockpit.

I snatched the stick to the left, floored the left rudder and shot away, out from under.

High behind my right wing whipped and tumbled the two broken aircraft. In their trails floated a cloud of broken pieces, lazy autumn leaves swirling down.

The radio, that had been quiet static for minutes, shouted, "MIDAIR! *There's been a mid-air!*"

"*BAIL OUT! BAIL OUT!*"

What possible good can it do, I thought, to tell them on the radio to bail out? When your airplane is reduced to pieces, doesn't the idea of a parachute come right quickly to mind?

One of the glider-parts in the midst of the cloud was a man's body, tumbling. It fell for a long time, then nylon streamed behind it, into the wind. He was alive; he had pulled the ripcord. Good work, fella!

The chute opened and drifted without a sound toward the rocks.

"There's two parachutes!" said the radio. "Contest Ground, there's two parachutes! Going down three miles north. Can you get a jeep out there?"

I couldn't see the other chute. The one I watched collapsed as the pilot hit the ground.

Still fluttered the parts of the demolished gliders, one section with half a wing attached, pinwheeling slow-motion round and round and round.

Never had I seen a midair collision. At a distance, it was gentle and silent. It could have been a new sport invented by a bored pilot, except for the shreds of airplane sparkling down. No pilot would invent a sport that shredded airplanes for fun.

The radio crackled on. "Anyone have the pilots in sight?"

"Affirmative. Got 'em both in sight."

"How are they? Can you tell if they're OK?"

"Yeah. They're both OK, seem to be. Both on the ground, waving."

"Thank God!"

"OK, chaps, let's look alive up here. We got a lot of airplanes in a little space. . . ."

Four of the pilots in this race, I thought, are women. How would it feel to be a woman, flying up here, and be called a "chap"?

All at once I froze in the heat. *I saw this yesterday!* What are the odds against it . . . the only mid-air I've ever seen, coming the day after I lay on the floor of the trailer and watched it in advance!

No, I hadn't watched, it had been *me,* hit by the wing! It might have been me, down there in the desert, and not so lucky as the two climbing into the jeep with exciting stories to tell.

Had Leslie left me last night, had I been tired and sad today instead of rested and cool before the race, it could have been me.

I turned on course, in a sky oddly deserted. Once they get started, contest sailplanes don't stay much in clumps if the leaders can help it.

Nose down, my quiet racer hushed top-speed toward a mountain ridge. Rocks close below, we burst into a new thermal, spiralled steeply up in the lift.

The vision, I thought, had it saved me?

I'm being protected now, for a reason.

Having made the decision to love, had I chosen life instead of death?

thirty-six

*I*T WAS coiled in the sand of the jeep-trail, coiled and ready to strike at the pickup truck bumping toward it ten miles per hour. I stopped the truck short and reached for the CB microphone.

"Hi, wook, can you hear me?"

There was a moment's silence, and she answered from the radio in the trailer.

"Yes. Why are you stopped?"

"There's a snake, blocking the way. Could you get the snake books? I'll give you a description."

"Just a minute, sweetie."

I eased the truck ahead, turned to draw alongside the creature. It licked the air with its black tongue, frowning. When I ran the engine up, it blurred the rattles of its tail, a dry-gourd hiss: *I'm warning you . . .*

What a brave snake! If I had that courage, I'd stand with

289

my fists against a tank three blocks tall six blocks wide, frown Don't you roll ahead, I'm warning you . . .

"Got the snake books," she said on the radio. "Be careful, now. Stay inside and don't open the door, OK?"

Yeah, the snake said. You listen to her and you be careful. This is my desert. You mess around with me, I'll kill your truck. I don't want to do it, but if you force me, I got no choice. The yellow eyes looked at me unblinking, the tongue tasted the air again.

Leslie couldn't contain her curiosity. "I'm coming out to see."

"No! Better you stay right there. Might be a whole nest of these in the sand. OK?"

Silence.

"Leslie?"

Silence.

In the rear-view mirror I saw a figure step from the trailer and start toward me. One thing you don't get with these modern man-woman relationships, I thought, is obedience.

"Excuse me," I said to the snake. "We'll be right back."

I reversed down the road, stopped for her. She got in the right side with the books: *A Field Guide to North American Reptiles and Amphibians* and *A Sierra Club Naturalist's Guide—The Desert Southwest.*

"Where's the snake?"

"Waiting for us," I said. "Now, I want you to stay inside. I don't want you popping out of the truck, do you hear?"

"I won't if you won't." There was adventure in the air.

The snake hadn't moved, hissed the truck to a stop.

Back again? Well, that's as far as you're going, not one inch farther than last time.

Leslie leaned over against me to see. "Hel-lo!" she said, bright and vivacious, "hello, snakey! How are you today?"

No answer. What do you say when you are a rugged wily tough poison desert rattler and a sweet pretty little-girl voice asks you a question like that: "How are you today?" You don't know what to say. You blink your eyes, but you say nothing.

Leslie sat back and opened the first book. "What color, would you say?"

"OK," I said. "He's a green sand color, dusty pale olive. Black jelly-bean ovals down his back, darker olive inside the jelly-beans, almost white just outside them. He's got a wide flat triangle head, short nose."

Pages turned. "My, there are some tough customers in here!" she said. "How big is she?"

I smiled. Either one of us turned sexist, these days, the other corrected, subtly or not, as required. She was being subtle.

"She isn't a little snake," I said. "If she were all stretched out . . . four feet, maybe?"

"Would you say *oval markings tend to narrow into inconspicuous crossbands near tail?*"

"Sort of. No. Black and white bands around the tail. Narrow black, wide white."

The snake uncoiled, moved to the sage at the side of the road. I touched the accelerator to race the engine and immediately she sprang back into her coil, eyes blazing, tail blurred. I warned you and I was not kidding! You want a dead truck you're going to get one! Stand back, stand clear or so help me . . .

"*Scales keeled, in twenty-five rows?*" asked Leslie. "Ah!

Black and white rings encircle tail! Try this: *Light stripe behind eye extends backward above angle of mouth."*

See this light stripe behind eye? the snake said. What more do I have to tell you? Just leave your hands where I can see 'em and back away slow. . . .

"Right you are!" I said. "That's her! What is she?"

"Mojave Rattlesnake," she read. *"Crotalus scutellatus.* See her picture?"

The snake in the photograph was not smiling.

She opened the *Naturalist's Guide,* turned pages. *"Dr. Lowe states that the Mojave has a 'unique' venom with neurotoxic elements for which no specific antivenin has been developed and that the bite of the Mojave is potentially much more serious than that of a Western Diamondback, a species with which it is sometimes confused."*

Silence. There being no Western Diamondbacks near, this snake was not confused.

We looked at each other, Leslie and me. "Maybe we'd better stay in the truck," she said.

"I have not been feeling too strong an urge to get out, if that's what you're worried about."

Yeah, hissed the Mojave, proud and fierce. You don't want to do nothin' fast. . . .

Leslie peeked again. "What's she doing?"

"She's telling me I don't want to do nothin' fast."

After a time the snake uncoiled, watching our eyes, ready for any tricks from us. There were none.

If it bit me, I thought, would I die? Of course not. I could pull psychic shields down, turn venom to water or root-beer, not give power to a world's belief-system that snakes kill. I could do it, I thought. But there's no need to test myself right now.

We watched the snake, admiring it.

Yes, I sighed to myself, I had felt the stupid boring predictable response: kill it. What if it breaks into the trailer and starts biting everybody; better take a shovel now and smash it flat before that can happen it's the most deadly snake in the desert get the gun and blast it before it kills Leslie!

Oh, Richard, what a disappointment that there's part of you thinks so ugly, so cruel. Kill. When will you advance to a level that is not somehow *afraid?*

I accuse me wrong! The kill-thought was a stray scared ignorant insane suggestion. I'm not responsible for the suggestion, only for my action, my final choice. My final choice is to value this snake. She's an expression of life just as true and just as false as this one that sees itself a two-legged tool-using truck-driving semiviolent learning creature. In that moment, I would have turned a shovel against anyone dared attack our brave Mojave Rattlesnake.

"Let's play her some music on the radio." Leslie touched the switch, found a classical-music station in the midst of something Rachmaninevsque and turned the volume as far as the knob would go. "SNAKES AREN'T SUPPOSED TO HEAR TOO WELL," she explained.

After a moment the rattler mellowed and relaxed; a single loop of the coiled wall remained. In a few minutes she licked one last time toward us. Well done. You passed your test. Congratulations. Your music is too loud.

"There she goes, wook! See?"

Goodbye.

And away poured Ms. M. R. Snake, rippling smooth to disappear in the sage.

" 'Bye!" called Leslie, and waved, almost sadly.

I released the brake, backed the truck to the trailer again, disembarked my dear passenger and her snake-books.

"What do you think?" I said. "Did we imagine everything she said? Think she could have been a passing spirit, took the form of a snake for an hour to find what control we had over our fear, to kill or not to kill? An angel in a snake costume, there in the road, checking up on us?"

"I'm not going to say no," said Leslie, "but in case not, from now on let's make a lot of noise when we come out of the trailer so we don't surprise her, OK?"

thirty-seven

*C*HANGE OUR thought, and the world around us changes. Arizona in summer turned a little on the warm side for us, it was time for a different view. Better something northward, cooler? How about Nevada, take the trailer and the sailplane to Nevada?

It was cooler, sure enough. Instead of 115 degrees outside, it was 110. Instead of small mountains on the horizon, big ones.

The generator failed, in the trailer . . . three days of constant troubleshooting, tinkering, and it ran again. Soon as the generator was fixed, the water-pumps failed. Luckily the prospect of living waterless in the middle of a million acres of sand and cattle-bones helped us rebuild the pumps with a pocketknife and cardboard.

Back from a sixty-mile drive for water and mail, she stood in the kitchen and read aloud the letter from Los Angeles.

Living in the wilderness, our senses had changed. Megalopolis had grown so unreal that it was difficult for us to imagine it still there, people still living in cities. The letter reminded us.

"Dear Richard: I am sorry that I must tell you that the Internal Revenue Service has rejected your offer, and it is demanding payment of the one million dollars at once. As you know, it has a lien on all of your property and has legal right to seize whenever it wishes. I suggest we meet at the earliest possible time. Sincerely, John Marquart."

"Why did they reject the offer?" I said. "I offered to pay them in full!"

"There's a misunderstanding somewhere," Leslie said. "We'd better go find out what it is."

We drove across the desert to a gas-station pay-phone, set a meeting for nine the next morning, threw some clothes in the Meyers, blazed high-speed crosscountry, landed in Los Angeles by sundown.

"The offer is not the problem," said Marquart, next morning. "The problem is, you're famous."

"What? The problem is what?"

"This will be hard for you to believe, and I've never heard it before, myself. The IRS now has a policy not to accept Offers in Compromise from famous people."

"What . . . makes them think I'm famous?"

He swiveled his chair. "I asked that, too. The agent told me he went down the corridor outside his office, asked people at random if they had heard of Richard Bach. More of them had, than hadn't."

Total silence in the room. I couldn't believe what I was hearing.

"Let me get this straight," Leslie said at last. "The Internal Revenue Service; won't accept Richard's offer; because people in some hallway; have heard of him. Are you serious?"

The attorney spread his hands, helpless to change what had happened. "They'll accept a single payment in full. They won't accept a payout over time from a famous person."

"If he were Barry Businessman they'd accept the offer," she said, "but since he's Richard Bach they won't?"

"That's right," he said.

"But that's discrimination!"

"You could charge that, in court. You'd probably win. It would take about ten years."

"Come on! Who's this guy's boss?" I said. "There has got to be somebody there . . ."

"The fellow who's handling your case at the moment, he *is* the boss. He's the one who wrote the Famous rule."

I looked at Leslie.

"What can we do now?" she said to Marquart. "Richard's got all this money to give them, we've sold nearly everything he owns to make the down payment! He could write them a check for nearly half of it today, if they'd accept it without seizing what's left. I think he could pay the balance in a year, especially if he could get back to work. But he can't go ahead on the film, he can't even write if these people are going to swoop down and seize the work off his desk. . . ."

An idea lifted out of my resentment.

"Another agent," I said. "Surely there is some way to have this case transferred to another agent?"

He ruffled papers on his desk. "Let's see. You've had seven already: agents Bulleigh, Paroseit, Ghoone, Saydyst,

Blutzucker, Fradequat and Beeste. None of them wants to take responsibility, none of them wants to deal with it."

Leslie's patience broke. *"Are they crazy?* Don't they want the money? Do they understand this man is trying to *pay* them, he isn't trying to run away or make a deal for thirty cents on the dollar, he's trying to *pay them in full! WHAT KIND OF STUPID GODDAMN IDIOTS ARE THEY?"* She was yelling, tears of frustration in her eyes.

Marquart remained as calm as though he had played this scene many times.

"Leslie. Leslie? *Leslie!* Listen. This is important for you to understand. The Internal Revenue Service is staffed by some of the least intelligent, some of the most frightened, vicious, vindictive people ever to hide behind a government office. I know. Three years, I worked there. Every young tax attorney works for the government first, to learn the enemy. If you haven't worked for the IRS, you can't function very well in tax law; you can't believe what you're dealing with."

I felt myself going pale, as he went on.

"Unless IRS thinks you're going to skip the country, it doesn't answer letters, it doesn't return telephone calls, we can't get through for months at a time. Nobody there wants to be responsible for dealing with a matter of this kind, this amount. A mistake, and they're criticized in the press: 'You evict little old ladies from their shacks, but you let Richard Bach get off with time payments'!"

"Then why don't they seize, right now? Take everything I've got?"

"That could be a mistake, too: 'Richard Bach offered to pay in full if you'd let him, but you seized, and his property wasn't worth half of what you could have gotten. . . .'

Don't you see? How much better no decision than a wrong decision?

"That's why we've gone through so many agents," he said. "Every new agent throws the hot potato in the air, hoping for a transfer or a still newer agent to come along before they have to catch the thing and deal with it."

"But certainly at the top," said Leslie, "the area director, if we went to him. . . ?"

Marquart nodded. "I used to work with him. I called him first thing, finally got through. He says no exceptions, you have to move through the ranks in an orderly fashion. He says we have to deal with the agent who's assigned, and then with the next one, and the next."

Leslie attacked the problem like a chess-position. "They won't accept his offer, yet he can't pay a million dollars at once. If they seize, he can't work. If they won't decide, he still can't work, because they *might* seize tomorrow and the work is lost. If he can't work, he can't earn the money to pay them the rest. We've been in limbo for almost a year, now! Does this drag on till the end of the world?"

For the first time in the meeting, the attorney brightened. "In a way, time is on Richard's side. If his case drags on for three years with no resolution, he'll be eligible to dissolve the debt in bankruptcy."

I felt as if we were having tea with the Mad Hatter. "But if I go broke, they won't get paid! Don't they know that?"

"Of course they do. But I think they want to wait the time, I think they want you to go bankrupt."

"WHY?" I said. "What kind of insane . . . they'd get a million dollars if they'd let me make the payments."

He looked at me sadly. "You keep forgetting, Richard. If you go bankrupt it will not be an IRS decision, it will be *your* decision—*there will be no blame for the government!* No one has to take responsibility. No one can be criticized. The debt will be legally discharged. Till then, it's not all bad. Unless they make a decision on your case, you're free to spend the money. Why don't you take a world tour, stay in the finest hotels, give me a call once in a while from Paris, Rome, Tokyo?"

"Three years?" said Leslie. "Bankruptcy?" She looked to me, pity for us both in her eyes, and then resolve. "No! That is not going to happen! We are going to settle this!" Her eyes blazed. "Famous or not, up the ante and try another offer. Make this one so good they can't turn it down. And for God's sake, find somebody there with the guts to take it!"

Marquart sighed that it was not a matter of offers, but he agreed to try.

An accountant was called in, other lawyers for consultation. More columns marched through calculators, more papers shushed across the desk, plans proposed and plans trashed, new appointments set for tomorrow as we searched for an offer so risk-free that the government couldn't turn it down.

I stared out the window into the sky as they worked. Like the pilot of a crippled plane, I was certain of the crash but not frightened of it. We'd walk away from it; we'd start over. It would be a relief to have it done.

"Remember the Mojave Rattlesnake?" Leslie said, after the meeting adjourned and we rode the elevator to the parking lot.

"Sure. *Croandelphilis scootamorphulus.* No known antidote to the venom," I said. "Of course I remember. One brave snake, she is."

"Makes you realize, after days like this trying to deal with those slugs in the IRS, how good it is to sit in the desert and deal with a real honest straightforward rattlesnake!"

We flew back to Nevada exhausted, arrived at last in the desert to find the trailer ransacked: door pried open, bookshelves cleared, drawers emptied; everything we had left in our little house-on-wheels was gone.

thirty-eight

*L*ESLIE WAS stunned. She went through the place looking for the friendly tools we had lived with, her dear companions, as though they would suddenly appear in their places. Books, clothes, wooden kitchen-spoons that meant home to her, even her hairbrushes: gone.

"No problem, wook," I soothed. "They're only things, we lost. As long as the IRS won't make up its mind, there's plenty of money to spend. One trip into town and we've bought it all back."

She barely heard, looking up from the empty desk drawer. "Richard, they even took our ball of *string*. . . ."

I was desperate to cheer her. "And we thought we were the last string-savers in the world! Think how happy we've made someone . . . a whole *ball* of string, they got! And burnt wooden spoons! And plates with chips in them!"

"Our plates didn't have chips in them," she said. "We bought those plates together, don't you remember?"

"Well, we'll buy some more plates. How about we get some nice orange and yellow pottery ones, this time? And bigger cups than we had. We can go wild in the bookstore, and we'll need new clothes. . . ."

"It's not the things, Richie, it's the meaning of the things. Doesn't it hurt you that strangers broke into our home and took meanings out of our life?"

"It hurts only if we let it," I said. "There's not much we can do about it now; it's happened and it's done and the sooner we move past it the better. If it'd help to feel bad about it, I'd feel bad. What'll help will be to get our minds off it and buy some new things and put some time between us and today. So they take the whole trailer, so what? It's us that matters, isn't it? Better us together in a desert and happy than us apart in palaces full of plates and string!"

She dried a tear. "Oh, you're right," she said. "But I think I'm changing. I used to say if someone broke into my house, they could steal whatever they wanted, I'd never take a chance harming someone to protect my property, or myself. But this is it. I've been robbed three times before, and we've been robbed today, and I've just decided that I have had all the robbing I'm going to have. If we're going to live in the wilderness, it's not fair for you to be the only one to protect us. I'm going to do my part. I'm going to buy a gun!"

Two days later, there was one less fear in her life. All of a sudden she who couldn't stand the sight of a gun now loaded firearms with the ease of a Desert Rat on patrol.

She practiced diligently, hour after hour; the desert sounded like the last battle for El Alamein. I threw tin cans into the sagebrush and she hit the things once out of five with a .357 Magnum revolver, then three of five, then four of five.

While she loaded the Winchester rifle I set a row of empty shell-casings in the sand for targets, then stood back and watched while she aimed and squeezed the trigger. Now gunfire barely blinked her eye, her targets disappeared one after another, left to right, in sharp-hiss booms and brass-glittering sprays of lead and sand.

It was hard for me to understand what had happened to her because of that robbery.

"Do you mean," I said, "that if someone broke into the trailer, you would . . ."

"Somebody breaks in wherever I am, they're going to be sorry! If they don't want to get shot, robbing us is the wrong business to get into!" She laughed at the expression on my face. "Don't look at me that way! You say the same thing, you know you do."

"I do not! I say it different."

"How do you say it?"

"I say it's not possible for anybody to die. 'Thou Shalt Not Kill' isn't a commandment, it's a promise: Thou couldn't kill if thee tried, because life is indestructible. But thou're free to *believe* in dying, if thou insisteth.

"If we try to rob the house of somebody waiting for us with a loaded gun," I said, "why, we're telling that person that we're tired of the belief of life on this belief of a planet, we're asking her to do us the favor of shifting our conscious-ness from this level to a different one, courtesy of a bullet in self-defense. That's how I say it. Isn't it true, don't you think?"

She laughed, levered a fresh cartridge into the chamber of

her rifle. "I don't know which of us is more cold-blooded, Richard, you or me."

With that she held her breath, aimed, and squeezed the trigger. In the desert, another casing screamed and disappeared.

After the robbery, and the generator failure, and the water failure, after the refrigerator broke down and the gas-line to the stove cracked, filling the trailer with explosive gas, there came the dust-devil.

Dust-devils are baby tornadoes in the desert. They wander around in summertime, sniff a sand-dune here, a bunch of sagebrush there, send them a thousand feet into the sky . . . dust-devils can go wherever they feel like going and do whatever they want to do.

With the generator running again, Leslie finished cleaning the trailer, put down the vacuum cleaner, glanced out the window. "Wookie, come see the huge dust-devil!"

I unfolded from under the water-heater, which was refusing to heat water. "My, that *is* a big one!"

"Hand me the camera, please, I want a picture."

"Camera was stolen," I said. "Sorry."

"The little new camera, on the bottom shelf. Quick, before it's gone!"

I handed her the camera and she snapped a picture from the trailer window. "It's getting bigger!"

"Not really bigger," I said. "It seems bigger, because it's getting closer."

"Is it going to hit us?"

"Leslie, the odds against that dust-devil, which has got the entire Nevada desert to move around in, the odds against that dust-devil hitting this tiny trailer parked in the middle of nowhere are on the order of several hundred thousand to one. . . ."

Then the world shook, the sun went out, our awning ripped its struts from the ground and exploded thrashing on the roof, the door burst open, windows howled. Sand, powdered dirt like a mine-collapse, billowed down our hallway. Curtains stood straight out inside the room, the house rocked, set to fly. It was familiar, a plane-crash without the view.

Then the sun blinked on, the howling stopped, the awning fell in a ragged heap, strewn on the side of the trailer.

". . . make that," I gasped, "that the chances . . . of hitting us . . . are on the order . . . of two to one in favor!"

Leslie was not amused. "I just finished cleaning, finished *dusting*, this whole place!" If she could have gotten her hands around the neck of that tornado, she would have taught it about thrashings.

As it was, the devil had a full ten seconds to work on the trailer, so it stuffed forty pounds of sand through the screens and windows and doors. That much earth in so few square feet—we could plant potatoes on the kitchen counters.

"Wookie," she said hopelessly, "do you ever get the feeling that we are not meant to live here? That it is time for us to move on?"

I put down the wrench I had clutched through the storm, my heart filled with warm agreement. "I was just about to ask you the same thing. I'm so tired of living in a little box on wheels! It's been more than a year! Can we stop? Can we find a house, a real house somewhere that isn't made of plastic?"

306

She looked at me strangely. "Do I hear Richard Bach talking about settling down, a permanent place?"

"Yes."

She cleared a spot in the sand on the chair and sat quietly.

"No," she said. "I don't want to put my heart into getting a house and fixing it up and then stop in the middle of it if you decide you're restless and the experiment didn't work. If you're still convinced the boredom will get us, sooner or later, we're not ready for a house, are we?"

I thought about it. "I don't know."

Leslie thought we were finding inner horizons, frontiers of the mind; she knew we were on our way to discovering pleasures that neither she nor I could find alone. Was she right, or merely hopeful?

We've been married more than a year, ceremony or not. Do I still bow to the old fears? Did I sell my biplane and go searching for a soulmate to learn how to be afraid? Have I not been changed by what we've done together, have I learned *nothing*?

She sat without moving, thinking her own thoughts.

I remembered the days in Florida, when I had looked at my life and it was dead in the river—lots of money and airplanes and women, zero progress living. Now there's not nearly so much money, and before long there may be none. The airplanes are most of them sold. There's been one woman, only one. And my life is moving swift as a racing-boat, so much I've changed and grown with her.

Each other's company our sole education and entertainment, our life together had grown like summer clouds. Ask a woman and a man sailing their boat over oceans, aren't you bored? how *do* you pass the time? They smile. Not enough hours in the year to do what needs be done!

Same for us. Delighted we had been, laughed sometimes till we could not stand, scared now and then, tender, desperate, joyous, discovering, passionate . . . but not one second bored.

What a story that would make! How many men and women go through the same rivers, menaced by the same sharp clichés, the same jagged dangers that had threatened us! If that idea stands up, I thought, it would be worth uncovering the typewriter! How Richard-years-ago would have wanted to know: What happens when we set off searching for a soulmate who doesn't exist, *and find her?*

" 'I don't know' isn't right, wook," I said after a while. "I do know. I want us to get a house where we can be still and quiet and alone together for a long time."

She turned to me once more. "Are you talking about commitment?"

"Yes."

She left her chair, sat down with me in the inch of desert settled on our floor, kissed me softly.

After a long time, she spoke. "Any particular place in mind?"

I nodded. "Unless you feel strongly otherwise, wook, I'd hope we might find a place with a lot more water and a lot less sand."

thirty-nine

*I*T TOOK three months' soaking in a torrent of real-estate catalogs, maps and out-of-town newspapers; it took weeks of flying, looking down from the Meyers for the perfect place to live, towns with names like Sweet Home and Happy Camp and Rhododendron. But the day came at last when the trailer windows that had framed sagebrush and rocks and a seared crust of desert now looked out on flower-spangled spring-color meadows, steep green forests, a river of water.

The Little Applegate Valley, Oregon. From the top of our hill we could see twenty miles around, and scarcely another house in sight. Houses there were, hidden by trees and slopes, but here we felt alone and blessed quiet; here we would build our home.

A little home, first; one room with loft, while the IRS negotiations continued. Later, with the problem solved,

309

we'd build our permanent house alongside and call the little one a guesthouse.

The Revenue Service growled to itself, trying to unravel my new offer, while months slid into years. It was an offer a child might make, nothing denied. I felt like a visitor in a foreign country, unfamiliar with the money. I owed a bill, didn't know how to pay, so held out everything I owned and asked IRS to take whatever it wanted.

My offer passed to the desk of yet another agent in Los Angeles, who asked for a current financial statement. He got one. We heard nothing for months. The case was transferred. The new agent asked for an updated financial statement. She got one. More months passed. Another agent, another financial statement. Agents went by like leaves of a calendar, turning.

In the trailer, Leslie looked up sadly from the latest request for a new financial statement. I heard the same little voice that I had heard long-distance in Madrid, two and a half years before. "Oh, Richie, if only I had known you before you got into this mess! It wouldn't have happened. . . ."

"We met as early as we could have met," I said. "Earlier than that, you know it—I would have destroyed you or run away from you or you wouldn't have had the patience, you would have walked out on me, with good reason. It never would have worked; I had to learn my way through that mess. I'd never do it again, but I'm not that person anymore."

"Thank the Maker," she said. "Well, I'm here now. If we survive this, I promise you, our future is going to look nothing like your past!"

The clock ticked; the IRS neither noticed nor cared that our lives were stalled.

Bankruptcy, the attorney had said. Perhaps John Marquart's bizarre theory was right, after all. Not a pretty ending, I thought, but better than stalemate, better than making these same moves over and over through eternity.

We tried to consider it, but in the end we couldn't. Bankruptcy. Such a desperate thing to do. Never!

Instead of a tour through Paris and Rome and Tokyo, we began construction at the top of the hill.

The day after the foundation was poured, buying groceries in town, my eye was caught by a new business on the mall: *Custom Computer.*

I walked inside.

"Leslie, I know that you are going to call me a silly goose," I said when I got back to the trailer.

She was covered with dirt, from back-filling water-pipe trenches for the solar panels on the hilltop, from running her Bobcat earth-mover mixing topsoils, carving gardens, from lavishing care and love into this final place we'd chosen to live.

So beautiful, I thought, as if the makeup department had streaked dust to accent her cheekbones. She didn't care. She was going to take her shower anyway.

"I know I went to town to buy us a loaf of bread," I said, "and to get milk and lettuce and tomatoes if I could find any good tomatoes. But do you know what I got instead?"

She sat down before she spoke. "Oh, no. Richard, you are not going to tell me you got . . . magic beans?"

"A gift for my darling!" I said.

"Richard, please! What did you get? We don't have *room!* Is there time to take it back?"

"We can take it back if you don't like it. But you will not not like it, you will love it. I predict: YOUR mind, and THIS machine . . ."

"You bought a machine? At the grocery-store? How big is it?"

"It's sort of a grocery. It's an Apple."

"Richard, your thought is very sweet but are you sure I need—an apple—at this time?"

"By the time you pop out of the shower, wook, you are going to see a miracle, right here in our trailer. I promise."

"We have so much to do, already, and there isn't enough space. . . . Is it big?" But I said not another word, and at last she laughed and went for her shower.

I hefted boxes down the narrow hallway, moved the type-writer off the shelf-turned-desk, put books on the floor, then lifted the computer from its foam packing and set it where the typewriter had been. I put the toaster and the blender in the broom closet to make room for the printer on the kitchen counter. In minutes, two disk drives were con-nected, the video-screen glowed softly.

Word-processing program inserted into one drive, I turned the machine on. The disk whirred, made whisking breathing sounds for a minute, then went still. I typed a message, scrolled it out of sight, till only a small square of light remained on the screen, blinking.

She came out of the bathroom fresh and clean, her hair gathered under a towel-turban to dry.

"OK, Richie, I can't stand the suspense! Where is it?"

I unveiled the computer from under the dish-towel. "Ta-da!"

"Richard?" she said. "What is it?"

"Your very own . . . COMPUTER!"

She looked at me, wordless.

"Sit you down right here," I urged, "and then press the key marked 'Control' and at the same time press the 'B.' That's called 'Control-B.' "

"Like this?" she said.

The light-square vanished, and in its place the screen filled with words:

GOOD AFTERNOON, LESLIE!
I AM YOUR NEW COMPUTER.
I AM DELIGHTED TO HAVE THIS OPPORTU-
NITY TO MEET YOU AND TO SERVE YOU.
YOU ARE GOING TO LOVE ME I THINK.
YOUR NEW,

APPLE.

WON'T YOU TRY WRITING SOMETHING
IN THE SPACE THAT FOLLOWS?

"Isn't that sweet," she said.

She typed a tentative line: NOW IS THE TIME FOR ALL GOOD PERSONS TO CAME TO THE

"I made a mistake."

"Move the cursor to the right of the mistake, then type Left-Arrow." She did, and the mistake disappeared.

"Does it have instructions?"

"It teaches you itself. Press the Escape key twice, then the *M* key a few times, and follow what the screen tells you. . . ."

That was the last I spoke with Leslie for the next ten hours. She sat tranced in front of the machine, learning the system. Then she typed things-to-remember files into it, building schedules, idea-lists; attacked correspondence.

The computer used no paper till the writing was finished and ready to print; no trees had to die to become paper thrown away for typing errors.

"Wookie," she said, after midnight, "I apologize to you. I am sorry."

"That's all right," I said. "What are you sorry for?"

"I thought you were being a silly gosling, I thought here's just what we need, a big electric toy in the trailer to put us right out in the rain, but I didn't say anything because it was your sweet gift. I was *wrong!* It's so . . ." She looked up at me, searched the word and came down on it center-square: ". . . *organized!* It's going to change our *lives!*"

So enchanted was she with the powers of the computer that more than once in the days that followed I had to ask very courteously if it might be possible for me to have a few minutes at the keyboard. I wanted to learn, too.

"Poor dear," she said absently, as she typed. "Of course you want to learn. Just a few minutes more. . . ."

Minutes turned to hours, to days; interrupt her I refused to do. Soon I was back once again from the Apple store, a second computer in tow. For this one we had to set a drafting-table in the least-crowded corner of the trailer, making it the most-crowded corner.

Curiosities, the computers were, but they were compasses, too, through a forest of ideas and schedules and strategies demanding attention. In addition, they could whip out financial statements faster than the IRS could blink; pressing one key, we could bury them in financial statements.

By the time the little house was finished, we were both comfortably expert in driving our smart little machines. We smoothed them to our personal design, switches set just so, extra memory-boards installed, electronics to link them by telephone to giant computers long-distance.

A week after we moved to the hilltop, the computers were running six hours a day, side by side on their desk in the bedroom-corner-turned office.

Our vocabulary changed.

"I booted straight into a hang, wookie!" She showed me a screen full of frozen-ant lines. "Has that ever happened to you?"

I nodded in sympathy. "Yep. It's your disk or your drive," I said. "No. It's your 80-character board. Control-reset if you can, or re-boot on my disk. If it works on mine, it's not the board, it's your disk. Maybe your drive speed's off and it ate your disk I hope to God not but we can fix it."

"It wouldn't be the disk, or I would have gotten an I/O error," she said, full of frowns. "I have to be so careful about things that cause the whole program to blow up, or my computer to self-destruct. Like touching it, for instance . . ."

Then we heard an impossible sound, the crunch of tires on gravel outside. Up our long steep forbidding drive, through five *No Trespassing Keep Away At All Costs This Means You* signs, had driven an automobile.

Out stepped a woman carrying a sheaf of papers, daring to invade our precious privacy.

I stormed from my computer out the door and met her before she had taken five steps.

"Good morning," she said politely, in a fine British accent. "I hope I'm not interrupting . . ."

"You are," I barked. "Did you happen to notice the *signs!* The NO TRESPASSING signs?"

She froze like a doe looking point-blank into the barrel of a hunting-rifle.

"I just wanted to tell you—*they're going to cut all the trees and they'll never grow back!*" She bolted for the safety of her car.

Leslie ran from the house to keep her from going.

"They're . . . who's *they?*" she said. "Who's going to cut all the trees?"

"The government," the lady said, looking nervously over Leslie's shoulder at me, "the Bureau of Land Management. It's illegal, but they're going to do it because nobody's going to stop them!"

"Come in," Leslie said to her, nodding a wordless *Down, King,* to me, as though I were the family attack-dog. "Please come in, and let's talk about it."

That was the way, hackles raised, I met Community Action—a meeting I had resisted since approximately the hour I had learned to walk.

forty

*D*ENISE FINDLAYSON left us with a stack of documents, a dwindling drift of dust over the driveway and a dark sense of oppression. Did I not have enough troubles with the government that now it had to destroy the very land around us?

I stuffed pillows around me in bed, read the first few pages of the timber-sale Environmental Assessment Report and sighed. "This looks very official, wookie; seems like we chose the wrong place to build a house. What say we sell and move farther north. Idaho, maybe? Montana?"

"Isn't Idaho where they do the strip-mining?" she said, barely looking up from the document in her hand. "Isn't Montana where they have the uranium mines and the radioactive wildflowers?"

"I sense that you are trying to tell me something," I said.

"Why don't we put our cards right here on the bed and say what's on our mind?"

She set down the page of government microprint. "Let's not run away, unless you absolutely have to, before we find out what's going on. Have you never considered fighting injustice?"

"Never! You know that. I don't believe in injustice. We bring to ourselves every event, every . . . don't you agree?"

"Maybe," she said. "Why did you bring this one to you, do you suppose, the government cutting down the forest the day after we move in? To have something to run away from? Or something to learn from?"

A lover who is very smart, I thought, is a joy and sometimes she is a burr.

"What's to be learned?"

"If we want to, we can change things," she said, "how powerful we might be, how much good we might do, together."

My mind sank. She had been willing to die in order to change things, to end a war, right the wrongs she had seen around her. And that which she had set out to change, had changed.

"Aren't you burned out with Social Activism? Haven't you said *Nevermore?*"

"I have," she said. "I think I've paid my dues to society for the next ten lifetimes, and after the KVST takeover I swore to stay out of causes for the rest of this one. But there are moments . . ."

I sensed she didn't want to say what she was saying, that she was looking for words to suggest the once-unsuggestible.

"I can share with you what I've learned," she said, "but

not what I *know*. If you'd like to find out about your power for good, instead of retreating, I might come out of retirement. I don't have the smallest doubt: if we want to stop the government from cutting timber that won't grow back, we can stop it. If it's illegal, we can stop it. If it isn't illegal, we can always move to Idaho."

Nothing was less interesting to me than convincing a government to change. People squander lives, trying. At the end, if we win, what we win is the bureaucracy doesn't do what it shouldn't have tried to do in the first place. Aren't there more positive things to be done than keeping officials inside the law?

"Before we move," I said, "it might be worth a quick check to see that they're doing things right. Turn the computers loose on it. But, my little deer, I'm sure we won't find the United States Government breaking its own laws!"

Was her smile sweet or bitter? "I'm sure," she said.

That afternoon our computers in the woods flickered questions, fast as light, to a computer in Ohio, which flashed them to a computer in San Francisco, which fired answers into our screens: *Federal law prohibits the sale and logging of nonregenerable timber from public lands.* Summaries of eighty-two related cases followed.

Moving to the frail forest of southern Oregon, were we chancing into an alley last-minute before an attack of rape and murder?

I looked at Leslie, agreed with her unspoken conclusion. There was no ignoring the crime about to happen.

"When you have a minute," I said the next day as we watched our glowing screens. It was our computer-operator's code; asking for attention and in the same breath saying please don't answer if a wrong key-stroke is going to scramble your whole morning's work.

A moment later she looked up from her screen. "OK."

"Do you think the forest itself called us here?" I said. "Do you think it was psychically crying for help, tree-devas and plant-spirits and wild-animal guides changing a hundred coincidences to bring us here to fight for them?"

"That's very poetic," she said. "It's probably true." She turned back to work.

An hour later, I couldn't stay quiet. "When you have a minute . . ."

In a few seconds her computer's disk-drive whirred, saving data.

"OK."

"How can they do this?" I said. "The BLM is destroying the very land it's required by law to protect! It's like . . . Smokey the Bear, *he's murdering trees!*"

"One thing I bet you're going to learn, wookie," she said. "Governments have almost zero foresight and an almost infinite capacity for stupidity, violence and destruction. Not quite, but almost infinite capacity. The not-quite is when people get mad enough to stand in the way."

"I don't want to learn that," I said. "Please, I want to learn that government is wise and wonderful and that citizens do not have to take their own private time to protect themselves from elected leaders."

"Don't we wish . . . ," she said, her mind far down the road ahead of me. Then she turned to confront me. "This is not going to be easy. That's not a forest out there, it's big money, big power."

She laid a Federal document on my desk. "BLM gets a lot

of its money from the timber companies. The bureau gets paid to *sell* trees, not to save them. So don't think we're going to walk up to the district director, point to broken laws, and he's going to say, 'Gee, we're sorry and we sure won't do *that* anymore!' This is going to be a long, tough fight. Sixteen-hour days and seven-day weeks, that's what it's going to take to win. But let's not start any action that we don't intend to win. If you want to quit, let's quit now."

"We can't lose, anyway," I said, loading a new data-disk into my machine. "As long as the IRS can swoop down and seize a first-draft manuscript out of my computer, there's no point in writing manuscripts. But I can write one hell of a timber-sale protest! The government won't have to seize what I write . . . we'll mail it to 'em direct. *The Clash of the Bureaus,* I can see it now: before IRS can decide whether to take my money, I'll spend it fighting BLM!"

She laughed. "Sometimes I believe you. Maybe there is no such thing as injustice."

Our priorities changed. Other work stopped while we studied. On our desks, on the kitchen counter, piled on the bed were thousands of pages about forest management, sustained-yield practices, erodible soils, fragile-lands regeneration, watershed protection, climatic evolution, endangered species, the socioeconomics of timber management versus the benefits of anadromous fisheries on marginal sites, riparian-zone protection, heat-transfer coefficients in granitic soils, and laws, laws, laws. Books of laws. The National Environmental Protection Act, the Federal Land Policy and Management Act, the Endangered Species Act, NHPA, FWPCA, AA, CWA, DOI 516M. Laws leaped from

321

pages, through our fingers, into our computers; written in electrons, coded and cross-referenced, filed in disk after disk, duplicated in bank-vaults, lest something happen to us or the house where we worked.

When there was enough information to change minds, we began meeting with neighbors. Joining with Denise Findlayson and Chant Thomas, who had fought mostly alone before we came, we pressed for help from others.

Most of the people of the valley were reluctant to get involved . . . how I understood their thinking!

"Nobody's ever stopped a government timber sale," they said. "There's no way to keep the BLM from logging whatever it wants to log."

Yet when they learned what we had learned, that turning forests into deserts was breaking the law, we found ourselves with a Save-the-Forest membership of more than seven hundred people. Our private hideaway in the wilderness became a headquarters, our little mountain an anthill as fellow workers came and went all hours to pour findings into the computers.

I met a Leslie I had never seen: total focused business-at-hand; no smiles, no personal asides, one-track one-rail single-minded concentration.

Time and again, she told us. "Emotional appeals won't work: 'Please don't cut the pretty trees, don't ruin the landscape, don't let the animals die.' That means nothing to the Bureau of Land Management. And not violence either: 'We'll spike the trees, we'll shoot you if you try to kill the forest.' That means they'll do their logging with the Army to protect them. The only thing that will stop the government is legal action. When we know the law better than they do, when they know we can take them to court and win, when we can prove that they're violating Federal regulations, the logging will stop."

We tried negotiating with the BLM. "Do not expect cooperation," she said. "Expect double-talk, defensiveness, we-don't-do-it-that-way-anymore. But talking with them is a step we have to take." She was right, every word.

"Leslie, I can't believe this transcript! Have you read? The Director of the Medford BLM sat there and told us, on tape! Listen:"

> RICHARD: Is what you're telling us that you need to have a lot of people make an outcry about this, against the logging, or that it would make no difference what people say?
>
> DIRECTOR: If you are asking me a personal question, very likely it would not.
>
> RICHARD: Whether you get four hundred signatures or four thousand . . .
>
> DIRECTOR: We get petitions like that. No, it wouldn't make a difference.
>
> RICHARD: If there were *forty thousand* signatures, if the entire population of Medford, Oregon, protested the sale, would that make a difference?
>
> DIRECTOR: Not to me.
>
> RICHARD: If there were professional foresters who were objecting, would you listen to that?
>
> DIRECTOR: No. I am not concerned about public outcry.
>
> RICHARD: We would like to see what has made you so certain that this is worth going ahead in spite of so much public outcry.
>
> DIRECTOR: Well, we are doing it.

RICHARD: Have you ever changed a timber sale because of a protest by the people?
DIRECTOR: No. Never.

She scarcely blinked, watching her computer-screen.
"Good. Load that under *Lack of Good Faith.* It's disk
Twenty-two, after *Sale Violates National Environmental
Protection Act.*"

Rarely did she show anger at our adversary. She documented evidence, entered it into the files, built her case for
court.

"What if we were psychics," I said to her once, "and we
knew how and when the director is going to die? If we knew
he's got two days to live—day after tomorrow, a ton of logs
is going to roll from a truck and smash him? Does that
make any difference, how we think about him now?"

"No," she said.

The money that IRS refused to accept turned into com-
missioned studies: *A Preliminary Water Quality Survey of the
Grouse Creek, Waters Gulch, Mule Creek and Hanley Gulch
Drainages of the Little Applegate River and Beaver Creek
Watersheds of Jackson County, Oregon; A Report on the An-
ticipated Effects of the Scheduled Timber Harvest Activities
Within the Proposed Grouse Creek Timber Sale Area on
Anadromous Fish and Habitat; Economic Review of the
Grouse Creek Timber Sale.* Eight others, with equally catchy
titles.

Once in a while we'd stand on our little hilltop and look
at the forest. Unkillable as the mountains, we used to think.
Now we saw it as a fragile family of plants and animals

living together in blended harmony, balanced on a chain-saw-blade, tilting toward extinction from foolish logging.

"Hang on, trees," we'd shout to the forest. "Hang on! Don't worry! We're going to stop them, we promise!"

Other times, when the going was hard, we'd just glance out the window from our computers. "We're doing our best, trees," we'd mumble.

The Apples were to us as Colts to gunfighters. The BLM allows the public thirty days to prepare a timber-sale protest before the wheels turn and a forest is destroyed. It expects to receive between two and ten impassioned pages from citizens pleading for environmental mercy. From us, from our organization and its home computers it got six hundred pages of fact documented up one side down the other, incidents and examples for proof, bound in three volumes. Copies to senators and representatives and the press.

It was constant, full-time battle for twenty months, fighting the Bureau of Land Management.

All my airplanes were sold. For the first time in my adult life, weeks passed, then months without a single airplane flight, without once being off the ground. Instead of looking down from the lovely free machines, I was looking up at them, remembering how much it had meant to me, to fly. So this is what it feels like to be a groundling, I thought. Grf!

Then one Wednesday, to Leslie's grim certainty and to my utter astonishment, the government withdrew the timber sale.

"The sale involves enough improprieties in BLM rules and procedures that it can't be legally awarded," the assistant state director of the Oregon BLM told the press. "In order to comply with our own procedures we had no choice but to withdraw the sale and reject all bids."

The local BLM director was not crushed to death under logs. He and his area manager were transferred out of state, to other parts of the bureaucracy.

Our victory celebration was two sentences long.

"Please don't forget this," Leslie told me, her computer cooling for the first time since the struggle began. *"You can't fight City Hall* is government propaganda. When the people decide to fight City Hall, just a few little people against something huge that's wrong, there's nothing—*nothing!*—can stop them from winning!"

Then she fell on the bed and slept three days.

forty-one

SOMEWHERE IN the midst of the BLM fight, the IRS clock struck midnight unheard. Internal Revenue had languished nearly four years without a decision, a year past the time I'd had the option to dissolve the million-dollar debt in bankruptcy.

While the BLM battle raged, we couldn't spare a moment to consider bankruptcy; when it was done, we could think of little else.

"It wouldn't be fun, little wook," I said, plowing manfully into my fourth attempt to bake a lemon pie the way her mother did. "Everything would be gone. I'd be starting over from nothing."

She set the table for dinner. "No you wouldn't," she said. "The bankruptcy book says they let you have 'tools required for your trade.' And there's a bare minimum you can keep, so you don't starve too fast."

"Really? Keep the house? A place to live?" I rolled the piedough thin, draped it over the pan, calling on the pie-crust-deva for help.

"Not the house. Not even the trailer."

"We could go live in the trees."

"It wouldn't be that bad. Mary Moviestar has her savings, don't forget; *she* wouldn't go broke. But how would you feel —the rights to your *books!*—you'd lose them! How would you feel, somebody buying the rights and not caring, somebody making junk-films out of your beautiful books?"

I slipped the crust into the oven. "I'd survive."

"You didn't answer my question," she said. "Don't bother. No matter what you say, I know how you'd feel. We'd have to live very carefully, save every cent and hope we could buy them back."

The loss of the book rights haunted us both, like putting our children up for auction to the highest bidder. Yet lost they would be, and auction there would be, if I filed for bankruptcy.

"If I file, the government gets thirty or forty cents for every dollar I owed it, when it could have been paid in full. The BLM trying to push through outlaw timber sales, failing at it, that cost the government another fortune. If this is happening to us, wookie, if we're just seeing our little part of it, how many millions are they wasting everywhere else? How can government be so successful at doing so much so wrong?"

"I've wondered that too," she said, "for a long time I've thought about that. I finally came up with the only possible answer."

"What's that?"

"Practice," she said. "Tireless, unrelenting practice."

We flew to Los Angeles, met with attorneys and accountants in a last-ditch attempt at settlement.

"I'm sorry," said John Marquart, "we can't get past their computer. There's not a human being we can reach to answer letters, return a phone call. The computer sends forms. Not long ago, we got a notice that a new agent has the case, a Ms. Faumpire. She's the twelfth. Want to bet she's going to ask for a financial statement?"

So clear, I thought. They are forcing me into bankruptcy. Still, I'm sure there's no such thing as injustice; I know lifetimes are for our learning and entertainment. We bring our problems to us to test our powers on them . . . if I didn't have these problems, there would have been others equally challenging. Nobody gets through school without tests. But tests often have unexpected answers, and once in a while an extreme answer is the only right choice there is.

One of the consultants frowned. "I worked for IRS in Washington when the law you want to use, when the bill about discharging Federal tax debts in bankruptcy came up for a vote in Congress," he said. "IRS hated that bill, and when it passed into law we swore that if anybody tried to use it, we'd make them sorry!"

"But if it's the law," Leslie said, "how can they keep people from using . . ."

He shook his head. "I'm giving you fair warning. Law or no law, the IRS is going to be after you; they're going to harass you every chance they get."

"But they *want* me to go bankrupt," I said, "so there's no blame for any of them!"

"That's probably true."

329

I looked at Leslie, at the strain showing in her face. "To hell with the IRS," I said.

She nodded. "Four wasted years is enough. Let's get our lives back."

To the bankruptcy attorney we brought lists of everything I owned: house, truck and trailer, bank accounts, computer, clothes, car—copyrights to every book I had written. I would lose them all.

The attorney read the list in silence, then said, "The court will not be interested in how many socks he has, Leslie."

"My bankruptcy book said to list everything," she said.

"It didn't mean list socks," he said.

Strung in limbo by the turgid Cyclops of the IRS on one hand, attacked on the other by the saw-swinging Bureau of Land Management, we had fought one monster or both-at-once for four years, nonstop.

No stories, no books, no screenplays, no films, no television, no acting, no production—nothing of the lives we'd lived before battle-with-government became our full-time occupation.

Through it all, through the most stressful difficult times either of us had known, the oddest thing . . . we kept growing happier than ever with each other.

Having survived the test of the trailer, we had lived easily together in the little house we had built on the hill. Not once were we separated for more than the time it took to drive to town for groceries.

I knew she knew, but I found myself telling her more and

more that I loved her. We walked arm in arm like sweet-hearts along town sidewalks, hand and hand in the forest. Would I have believed, years before, that I'd be unhappy to walk with her without touching?

It was as if our marriage were working in reverse—instead of becoming cooler and more distant, we were growing closer and warmer.

"You promised ennui," she'd pout, from time to time.

"Where's my loss-of-respect?" I demanded.

"Soon the boredom will set in," we told each other. What once were solemn fears had turned into silly jokes that tickled us till we laughed.

Day by day we knew each other more, and our wonder and joy at being together grew.

We had been morally married since our experiment in exclusivity began, four years before, when we gambled that we were soulmates.

Legally, however, we were single adults. No legal marriage until you settle with the IRS, Marquart had warned us. No marriage, please. Keep Leslie clear, or she'll be caught with you in the quicksand.

Bankruptcy filed, IRS cut away, we were free to be married legally at last.

The wedding-office I found listed in the telephone book between *Weaving* and *Welding,* and the event took its place on our To Do list for one last Saturday in Los Angeles:

9:00: Pack and check out
10:00: Drugstore—sunglasses, notebooks, pencils
10:30: Wedding

In a seedy storefront, we answered questions the minister asked. When she heard Leslie's name, she looked up, squinted.

"Leslie Parrish. That's a familiar name. Are you some-body?"

"No," said Leslie.

The lady squinted again, shrugged, typed the name onto a form.

To the carriage of her hand-powered typewriter was taped a sign: *Christians aren't perfect, just forgiven.* Nailed to the wall, another sign: THIS IS A SMOKING AREA. The office reeked of cigarettes, ashes spilled on the desk and floor.

I glanced at Leslie, then quickly to the ceiling and sighed. There was no warning on the phone, I told her, not using words, that the place would be quite this tacky.

"Now, we have the plain marriage certificate," said the minister; "that's three dollars. Or the special, with the gold lettering that's six dollars. Or the deluxe, with gold letters and the sparkly stuff on it that's twelve dollars which do you want." There was a sample of each, pinned to a cork bulle-tin-board.

We looked at each other, and instead of folding up laugh-ing we nodded solemnly. This was a legally important step we were taking.

We mouthed the word to each other at the same instant: PLAIN.

"The plain will be fine," I said. The woman didn't care. She rolled the humble certificate into the typewriter, bashed away at the keys, signed it, shouted across the hall for wit-nesses, turned to us.

"Now if you two will sign right here . . ."

We signed.

"The photographer will be fifteen dollars. . . ."

"We can skip that," I said. "We don't need photographs."

"The chapel fee is fifteen dollars. . . ."

"We'd just as soon not have a ceremony. Of any kind."

"No ceremony?" She looked questions at us, which we didn't answer, and she shrugged. "OK. I pronounce you man and wife."

She added figures under her breath. "Witness fee . . . fee for the county . . . registration fee . . . comes to thirty-eight dollars, Mister Bach. And here's an envelope for any donation you'd like to make."

Leslie took the cash from her purse, thirty-eight dollars and five dollars for the envelope. She gave it to me and I handed it to the marriage-lady. Signings finished, certificate in hand, my wife and I, we got out of there as fast as we could.

In city traffic, we handed each other wedding rings, opened the windows to blow the smoke from our clothes. There was laughter for the first minute-and-a-half of our formal married life.

Her first words as my legal wife: "You sure know how to sweep a girl off her feet!"

"Look at it this way, Ms. Parrish-Bach," I said. "It was memorable, wasn't it? Are we likely to forget our wedding-day?"

"Unfortunately, no," she laughed. "Oh, Richard, you are the most romantic . . ."

"Forty-three dollars does not buy romance, my dear. Romance you get with the deluxe; that's the sparkly stuff you have to pay extra for. You know we have to watch our pennies."

I looked at her for a second as I drove. "Does it feel any different to you now? Do you feel any more married?"

"No. Do you?"

333

"A little. Something's different. What we did in that smoke-house a minute ago, that is what our society recognizes as the Real Thing. What we've been doing till now hasn't made any difference, the joys and tears together, it's *signing the paper* that matters! Maybe it feels to me as if there is one area less where government can mess with us. You know what? The more I learn, wook, the less I like governments. Or is it just our government?"

"Join the crowd, my sweetie. I used to get tears in my eyes at the sight of the Flag, I loved my country so. I'm lucky to live here, I thought, I mustn't take it for granted, I must do something—work in elections, participate in the democratic process!

"I studied a lot and slowly came to realize that things were not quite the way we learned them in school: Americans were not always the good guys; our government wasn't always on the side of liberty and justice!

"The Vietnam War was just heating up, and the more I studied—I couldn't believe . . . the United States, suppressing elections in someone else's country because we knew we wouldn't like the outcome; America supporting a puppet dictator; an American president on record that we were there not because we wanted justice in Vietnam, but because we wanted its *tin and tungsten!*

"I'm free to protest, I thought. So I joined a peace march, a legal, nonviolent demonstration. We weren't crazies, we weren't looters throwing firebombs, we were the super-straights of Los Angeles: lawyers, doctors, parents, teachers, business-people.

"The police came after us like we were mad dogs, they clubbed us bloody. I saw them beat mothers holding babies, I saw them knock a man out of his wheelchair with those clubs, blood running on the sidewalk! And this is Century City, Los Angeles!

"I kept thinking, this can't be happening! We're *Americans,* and we're being attacked by *our own police!* I was running away when they hit me, and I don't remember much else. Some friends took me home."

Glad I wasn't there, I thought. The violent me, so carefully under guard within, would have gone blind with fury.

"I used to think, whenever I saw a picture in the newspaper of someone taking a beating from the police, that they'd done something terrible to deserve it," she said. "That evening I learned that, even here, the only terrible thing you need to do is to disagree with the government. They wanted the war, we didn't. So they beat the hell out of us!"

I was tense and trembling, I could feel it in my hands on the wheel. "You were a huge threat to them," I said, "thousands of law-abiding citizens saying no to a war."

"War. We spend *so much money* on killing and destruction! We justify it by calling it Defense, by spreading fear and hatred of other people, countries we don't like. If they try a government we don't approve of, and if they're weak enough, we smash them. Self-determination's for *us,* not them.

"What kind of example is that? How much do we reach out in kindness and understanding to other people? How much do we spend on peace?"

"Half of what we spend on war?" I said.

"Don't we wish! It's our sanctimonious God-and-Country mentality that gets in the way. It's the *obstacle* to peace in the world. It sets people against each other! God-and-Country, Law-and-Order is what clubbed us in Century City. If there were any other country in the world to go to, I used to

335

think, I'd go," she said. "But, bully that it is, scared as it is, it's the best country I know. I decided to stay to try to help it grow up."

And you love it still, I wanted to say.

"Do you know what I miss most?" she said.

"What?"

"Looking at the flag and being proud of it."

She slid over next to me on the seat of the car, determined to change the subject.

"Now that we have government out of the way, what else do you want to talk about on your wedding day, Mister Bach?"

"Anything," I said. "I want to be with you." But part of me would never forget. They had *clubbed* this lovely woman, *when she was running away!*

Legal marriage was another long step away from the person I used to be. The Richard who hated obligations was legally obligated. The one who despised the bonds of matrimony was legally bound.

I tried those labels on myself, labels that four years ago would have fit like a collar of spikes and a hat of ashes. You are a *Husband*, Richard. You are *Married*. You will spend the rest of your life with one woman only, this one at your side. No longer can you live your life exactly as you please. You have given up your independence. You have given up your freedom. You are legally Married. How does that feel?

Any one of those would have been a holly-stake in my heart, any one a steel arrow point-blank through my armor. Beginning today, they were true, every one, and it felt like an attack of sweet butter-creams.

We drove to my parents' house in the suburbs, the place I had lived from the time I was a kid until the day I ran away to fly. I slowed, parked the car on the one driveway that was familiar to me-thens as far back as I could remember.

Here the same dusk-green cloud of eucalyptus overhead; here the lawn I used to mow as little as humanly possible. Here the flat-topped garage where I set my first homemade telescope toward the moon, here the ivy on the wall around the yard, here the same white smoothwooden gate, with its eyeholes bored for a dog long dead.

"Won't they be surprised!" Leslie reached forward, her fingers touched the gate.

In that instant I froze, time stopped. Her hand on the wood, new ring gleaming gold, the sight of it burst down through my mind, vaporized thirty years in the blink of an eye.

The kid, had known! The kid I was had stood at this gate and known that the woman that he was born to love would one day be here. Not a gate in space, that moment, the white wood was a gate in time. For the flash of an instant I saw him, standing in the dark of that deep past, standing open-mouthed at the sight of Leslie radiant in the sunlight. The kid had known!

My wife pushed the gate open, ran to hug my dad and stepmother.

The boy went transparent and vanished, eyes goggling wonder, mouth still open, and the moment was gone.

Don't forget! I shouted wordless, across decades. *Never forget this moment!*

forty-two

*A*s we undressed that night in our hotel room, I told her about the gate, about how my life had been shaken those years ago by her lightest of touches on that wood. She listened, smoothing her blouse neatly to a hanger.

"Why did you have to hold me away for so long?" she said. "What were you afraid of?"

I laid my shirt on a chair for a moment, nearly forgetting to be as neat as she, then reached for a hanger. "Afraid I'd change, of course. I was protecting my known, my almost-right routine."

"And so the armor?" she said.

"Well, the defenses, yes."

"Defenses. Nearly every man I knew, buried in defenses," she said. "That's why even the beautiful ones were so damned unattractive!"

"They drove you away. I did, too."

"You didn't," she said, and when I protested with facts, admitted. "You almost drove me away. But I knew the cold thing I saw wasn't you."

I drew her into bed, breathed her golden hair.

"What a lovely body! You're so . . . impossibly lovely, and you're my *wife!* How can those fit together?"

I kissed the corner of her mouth, ever so lightly. "Goodbye, hypothesis!"

"Goodbye?"

"I had an hypothesis, almost a theory, well on its way before you stopped my research: *beautiful women, they don't much care for sex.*"

She laughed in surprise. "Oh, Richard, you're not serious! Really?"

"Really." I was caught in contrary pressures. I wanted to tell her, and I wanted to touch her, too. Time for both, I thought, time for both.

"Do you know what's wrong with your hypothesis?" she said.

"Nothing, I don't think. There are exceptions and you're one, thank the Maker, but generally it's true: beautiful women get so tired of being seen as sex-things, when they know they matter so much more than that, their switches turn off."

"Nice, but no," she said.

"Why not?"

"Sexist goose. Turn it around. 'I have a theory, Richard, that handsome men don't much care for sex.' "

"Nonsense! What are you getting at?"

"Listen: 'I'm defended like a fortress against handsome men, I'm cold to them, I keep them at arm's-length, don't

339

let them be a part of my life, and somehow it doesn't seem as if they *enjoy* sex as much as I want them to. . . .' "

"No wonder," I said, and in a flying shatter of broken conjecture knew what she was saying. "No wonder! If you weren't so cold to them, wookness, if you'd open up a little, let them know how you feel, what you think—none of us really handsome men wants to be treated as a sex-machine, after all! Now, if a woman shows us a little human warmth, there's a different story!"

She moved her body very close to mine. "Class?" she said. "What's the moral of this story? Richard?"

"Where intimacy is not, is not the finest sex," I said. "Is that the moral, teacher?"

"What a wise philosopher you are becoming!"

"And if one learned that, if one found someone whom one loved and admired and respected and for whom one had spent one's life looking, might one find the warmest bed of all? And even if the one that one found was a very beautiful woman, would one find that she might care a very great deal for sex with one, and might enjoy sweet carnality as much as one might, oneself?"

"Fully as much as one might, oneself," she laughed. "Could be, more!"

"Teacher!" I said. "No!"

"If you could be a woman, you might be surprised."

We newlyweds touched and talked through a night that made crumbling walls, collapsing empires, clashing with government and plunging into bankruptcy—that made those insignificant. One night of many, lifting from the past, arching through the present, shimmering into the future.

What matters most in every lifetime we choose? I thought. Can it be so simple as intimacy with one we love?

Except for the hours when we had been furious with each other in the desert, or collapsing in fatigue over the computers, there hummed a soft glimmering aura of sex over everything we did. The brief flash of an eye, a quick smile, a touch in passing, those were welcome events between us every day long.

One reason I had sought out beginnings, years before, was that I hated endings, hated the vanishment of the subtle electrics of sex. To my delight, with this one woman, voltages didn't fade. Gradually my wife became more beautiful, became ever more lovely to see and touch.

"It's all subjective, isn't it?" I said, lost in curves and golden light.

"Yes it is," she said, knowing what I thought. There was no technique to our telepathy, it just happened, often, that we knew each other's mind.

"Somebody else could look at us and say we hadn't changed," she said, "that we're still the same. But there is something about you that gets more and more attractive, to me!"

Exactly, I thought. If we weren't changing, to each other, we *would* get bored!

"Have we ended our beginning?" I said. "Or does it go on like this always?"

"Remember in your book, what the seagull said? Could be that's where you are: *Now you're ready to fly up and begin to know the meaning of kindness and of love.*"

"He didn't say that. It was said to him."

She smiled. "Now it's being said to you."

forty-three

*T*HE BANKRUPTCY court allowed us to stay
in our little house as caretakers for a time, while we looked
for a place to rent. Someplace farther north, someplace
cheap. Then it was time to leave the Little Applegate Valley.

We walked inside, outside, saying goodbye together.
Goodbye desk and timber-sale protest. Goodbye bed under
skylight, where we watched the stars before we slept. Goodbye fireplace of stones we had carried one by one. Goodbye
warm little house. Goodbye gardens that Leslie had imagined into flowered reality, that she had mixed and dug and
planted and protected. Goodbye forests and animals we
loved, and fought to save. Goodbye, we said.

When it came time to leave, she buried her face in my
chest, her courage dissolved in tears.

"Our garden!" she sobbed. "I love our garden! And I love
our little house and our wildplants and our deer-family and

the sun coming up over the forest. . . ." She cried as though she would never stop.

I held her, smoothed her hair. "It's all right, wookie," I murmured, "It's all right. It's just a house. The home is us. Wherever we go . . . someday we'll build another house better than this one, and your gardens will be everywhere, fruit trees and tomato trees and flowers more than we ever dreamed of here. And we'll get to meet new wildplants and a new deer-family will come live near us. The place we're going will be even more beautiful, I promise!"

"But Richie, I love *this* place!"

She sobbed deeper and deeper within herself, till I helped her into the car and we drove away. The valley where we had lived dropped behind us, out of sight.

I didn't cry, for we had an unspoken agreement—only one of us goes off-duty at a time, one of us at a time exhausted or ill or injured, grief-stricken, dependent. I drove the car in silence, and at last Leslie cried herself to sleep against my shoulder.

We're free at last, I thought, turning north on the Interstate. We can start over, and not from nothing. We can start over, knowing everything we've learned along the way! Principles of love and guidance and support and healing, those are working for us, even now.

Bankruptcy, losing the rights to the books, it may look like unjust disaster, Richard, but we know better than to believe appearances, don't we? Now's our chance to hold strong to what is, in spite of what seems.

Clean slate, no ties, no anchors—I've just been handed a chance to prove the power of my so-trusted Unseen! It's

Cosmic Law, I thought, unbreakable: *Life never abandons life.*

Lifting from the ruins of wealth is like lifting out of a dungeon in a light-balloon. Rough dark walls dropped from around us both; the most challenging, testing, difficult iron-bound years were falling away. Yet within those walls had grown the gold-and-rainbow answer to the barnstormer's search . . . I had found the one person who mattered more to me than any other in the world, the restless search of decades had stopped at last.

This is the moment, right here as the hills of Oregon disappear in twilight, that any good writer would whisper, "The End."

forty-four

WE MOVED farther away north, started over in a house rented with Mary Moviestar's money, which Leslie now insisted was *our* money. How strange it felt, not to have a dime of my own!

She was as prudent and careful as I had been profligate. Prudence, thrift—qualities nowhere to be found on my list of requirements for a soulmate, yet such is the foresight I expect of the universe: one of a charmed pair must always supply what the other might lack.

What I had missed, from the moment of first attack by a heavyweight income, was simplicity. Unless one is ready in advance for the shock, sudden wealth buries one in complistiquesque multibranch crosswebulated tangleworks weight-freighted toward intricationary ponderositives. Simplicity, like quicksilver, disappears when it's squeezed.

Now simplicity shyly knocked on the jamb where the

door used to be. "Hi, Richard. Couldn't help notice your money's gone. Have you seen the sky, lately! Have a look at them clouds! Regard what happens when Leslie plants flowers, even in a rented garden! And isn't it beautiful to watch your wife come to work at her computer?"

Beautiful it was. On warm days, Leslie dressed in the simplest clothes: white sailcloth pants, a gossamer blouse to work next to me in our little office. It was lustful pleasure just to turn and ask her the right way to spell compatable. How I loved simplicity!

Not all pressures were gone, however. The time came at last when the trustee in bankruptcy, charged to liquidate all my former assets, sent us notice that he was ready to receive bids for the copyrights of my books. They were for sale, seven of them. Like anyone else, we could make a bid if we wished.

Our roles reversed. I was the cautious; Leslie, after months of waiting, the sudden spendthrift.

"Let's not offer much," I said. "Three of the books are out of print. Who's going to offer good money for that?"

"I don't know," she said. "I don't want to take any chances. I think we should offer every penny we have."

I caught my breath. "Every penny? How are we going to pay the rent; how are we going to live?"

"My parents said they'd lend us money," she said, "till we're on our feet again." Leslie was ferociously determined.

"Not borrow money, please. I can go back to work, now. There's a new book to write, I think."

She smiled. "I think so, too. Remember when you said your mission was done? Remember when you told me you could die anytime because you had said everything you had come to say?"

346

"I was a silly goose. I didn't have anything else to live for, then."

"Now you do?"

"Yes."

"Make sure you do," she said. "If you die, there are going to be two bodies on the floor! I'm not going to stay around here if you go."

"Well, there are going to be two bodies right quick if you spend our grocery-money buying old copyrights!"

"We'll manage. We can't let seven of your books go without even trying to save them!"

Around midnight, we compromised. We'd offer every penny we had, and borrow money from Leslie's parents to live on. The next morning before I could convince her it was too much, she sent the bid to the trustee.

The trustee sent notices to other prospects: Can you top this offer, for these copyrights?

The suspense, in our rented house, you could have cut it with an axe.

Weeks later, a telephone call.

She ran breathless up the stairs. *"Wookie!"* she cried. "We got 'em! *We got 'em!* The books, they're ours again!"

I hugged the air out of her, we screeched and shouted and jumped and laughed. I hadn't known it would matter so much to me, that our paper children had come home.

"What was the next closest bid?" I said.

She looked sheepish. "There were no other bids."

"Nobody else even BID? Ever?"

"No."

"Not even close! Hurray!"

"Not hurray," she said.

"Not hurray?"

347

"You were right! We shouldn't have bid so high. I've squandered our grocery money for the next hundred years!"

I hugged her again. "Not at all, little wookie. Your offer was so intimidating, nobody else even dared to bid, that's what happened! Had you bid lower, they would have moved right in and topped you by a nickel!"

At this she brightened, and so did a strange light over our future.

forty-five

*I*N THOSE months aviation was bursting with the revolution of low-cost aircraft, and the first story I wrote on my clean slate was one that earned just enough money to buy us some food and an ultralight airplane kit, a flying machine from a company called Pterodactyl, Ltd. Soon as I heard its name, I liked the company, but it turned out Pterodactyl made the best ultralight for what I wanted to do: fly once more from hayfields and pastures, look down on clouds from the open air, for the fun of it.

What a delight to work with my hands again, building that machine! Aluminum tube and steel cable, bolts and rivets and fabric, an engine one-quarter the size of the Fleet's old Kinner. I finished it in a month, reading the instruction book step by step, following the photos and drawings in the box from the factory.

"What a cute little thing," Leslie had said when she first saw pictures of the Pterodactyl.

She said it again, in bigger letters, when ours stood completed on the grass, a giant edition of a child's model airplane, teetering like a silk-and-metal dragonfly on its lilypad.

It's so simple, I thought, why wasn't this machine invented forty years ago? No matter. It had been invented now, just in time for people shy of money and eager to get off the ground again.

With great respect for the unknown thing, and after much practice taxiing and many a ten-second flight skimming a borrowed pasture, I finally pushed full throttle and the power-kite launched up out of the grass, colors like a flame-and-sunshine Spirit of Flight, going home. Pterodactyl's president gave me a snowmobile suit to match the airplane . . . that season of year, without a cockpit, it was cold indeed.

There in the sky, the air! Wind and calm, mountains and valleys, grass and earth and rain and sweet ice air through me for the first time ever once again! I had stopped counting flying-hours at 8,000, stopped keeping record of the airplane-types I had flown at 125, yet this one gave me a pure pleasure of being in the air like no other I had flown.

It did require special cautions—by no means was it for flying in heavy weather, for instance—but in a calm there was nothing that could match it for delight. Flying done for the day, the Pterodactyl folded its wings, slipped into a long bag lifted on top of the car, came home to sleep in the yard.

The only thing wrong with the machine was that it carried one person only; I couldn't share the flying with Leslie.

"It's OK," she said. "I'm up there, too, when you fly. I can look down and see me waving when you fly over!"

She sat in the framework cockpit, ran its engine, tucked her hair into a crash-helmet and taxied the little kite around the pasture for fun, promising to fly it when she had time to learn.

It must have been the exhilaration of that first month's flying, but a night came not long after with a most unusual dream.

I flew the Pterodactyl, which had two seats instead of one, high over a misty silver bridge to land on a meadow-green slope by some huge meeting-place, an open-air auditorium. Wandered inside, still wearing the bright coveralls, sat down and waited, chin on my knees. I've never had a dream, I thought, in which I show up early for something that's not quite ready to happen. In a minute or two there was a sound behind me.

I turned, recognized him at once. Recognized me. An earlier me, looking lost, a me from five years gone, shelled around with yearnings turned to shields, wondering what this place could be.

An odd pleasure to see the man, I was swept with love for him. Yet I felt sorry for him at once; he was desperately alone and it showed. He wanted so much to ask and he dared so little to know. I stood up and smiled at him, remembering. He was a terror about time-contracts, never was he late.

"Hi, Richard," I said, off-handed as I could. "Not only punctual, you're early, aren't you?"

He was ill at ease, trying to place me. If you're not sure, I thought, why don't you ask?

I led him outside, knowing he'd be more at home near the airplane.

Every answer to his questions I had, answers to his pain and isolation, corrections for his mistakes. Yet the tools that worked enchantments in my hands, they'd be white-hot irons in his. What could I say?

I showed him the airplane, told him about the controls. Funny, I thought. Me telling him about flying, when I'm the one who hasn't flown anything beside the ultralight in years. He may be lonely, but he's a lot better airplane pilot than I am.

When he was settled in his seat, I called the propeller clear and started the engine. It was so quiet and different that for a moment he forgot why he had chosen to meet me, forgot the airplane was the background and not the focus of our dream.

"Ready?" I said, set for takeoff.

"Go."

How would I describe him? Game, I thought. The guy's going through the deceitful torture of sudden money, what it does to an innocent and his friends, and now the whole thing is blowing up around him, his world is coming apart. Yet this minute he's a kid with a toy, he likes airplanes so much. How easy it is to be compassionate, I thought, when it's ourselves we see in trouble.

Airborne a thousand feet, I took my hands from the controls. "You've got it."

He flew with ease, cautious and smooth in a machine the likes of which he hadn't imagined.

I knew this was somehow my show, this dream, that he was waiting for me to tell him something. Still, the man was so sure that he had learned the last there was for him to learn! I could feel him spring-loaded to reject the very knowledge that would set him free.

"Can we shut the engine down?" he asked over the wind.

For answer I touched the kill-switch on the throttle. The propeller slowed and stopped and we turned into a glider.

Airplane-lessons he didn't resist.

"What a perfect little airplane!" he said. "How can I get one?"

A few minutes flying and he was ready to run out and buy a Pterodactyl. He had the money to do it; he could have bought a hundred Pterodactyls, except of course that in his time it was an invisible idea, not even a sketch on paper.

Buying wasn't the way he would get this one, and that was the avenue, there was my opening to talk through his defenses against change.

I asked him to tell me what he knew, what this airplane was and who was this guy in the snowmobile suit, flying it. I wasn't surprised when he told me, he just needed to be asked.

After a while, mixed in with the flying, I told him straight out that I had the answers he was looking for, and that I knew he wouldn't listen to what they were.

"You <u>sure</u> I won't listen?" he said.

"Will you?"

"Who can I trust more than you?"

Leslie, I thought, but he'd laugh at that, we'd get nowhere.

"This is what you came here to learn. This is what you

353

are going to do," I told him. "The answer you're looking for is to give up your Freedom and your Independence and to marry Leslie Parrish. What you'll find in return is a different kind of freedom, so beautiful you can't imagine. . . ."

He didn't catch anything after marry Leslie; he nearly fell from the plane, he was so startled.

Such a long way he has to go, I thought, while he choked and gasped. And he'll go it in only five years. A stubborn closed son-of-a-bitch, but basically I like the guy. He'll make it, all right, I thought . . . or will he? Might this one become the voice from the sailplane crash, or from the other turn to Montana? Is this one facing a future that failed?

His very loneliness, so well defended, turned out to be my hope. When I talked about Leslie, he listened sharp, even swallowed and took some truth about his future. Knowing about her could make surviving easier for him, I thought, even if he forgets words and scenes. I turned the plane north.

She was waiting when we landed, dressed as she did for private days at home. He jolted at the sight of her; the vision of her vaporized a ton of iron in less than a second. Such a power is beauty!

She had something personal to say to him, so I stirred in my sleep, faded back, and woke up years later than he would wake from the same dream.

Soon as I opened my eyes, the story evaporated, misted away like steam on air. A flying dream, I thought. How lucky am I to have so many flying dreams! Something special about this one, though . . . what was it? I was investing in uncut diamonds, was that it, was I flying somewhere with a box of diamonds or seeds or something, and they almost fell from the plane? An investment dream. Some part of my subconscious thinks it still has money? Maybe it knows something I don't.

On a night-pad I put a note: *Why not self-induced dreams, to travel and see and learn whatever we want to learn?*

I lay quiet, watching Leslie sleep, dawn glowing in that golden hair splashed careless about her pillow. For a moment, she was so still—*what if she's dead?* She breathes so lightly, I can't tell. Is she breathing? *She's not!*

I knew I was kidding myself, but what relief, what sudden joy, when she moved softly in her sleep that instant, smiled the smallest of dream-smiles!

I've spent my life looking for this woman, I thought. Told myself here's my mission, to be together with her again.

I was wrong. Finding her wasn't the object of my life, it was an imperative incident. Finding her allowed my life to begin.

The object is: Now What? What are you two going to learn about love? I've changed so much, I thought, and it's barely begun.

Real lovestories never have endings. The only way to find what happens in happily-ever-after with a perfect mate is to live it for ourselves. There's romance, of course, and the sensual delight of lust fallen in love.

And then what?

Then days and months of talking nonstop, catching up again after being centuries apart—what did you do then, what did you think, what have you learned, how are you changing?

And then what?

What are your most private hopes dreams wishes, your most desperate if-onlys to bring true? What's the most impossibly beautiful lifetime you can imagine, and here's mine, and the two of them fit like sun and moon in our sky, and we together can bring them true!

And then what?

So much to learn together! So much to share! Languages and acting, poetry and drama and computer-programming and physics and metaphysics, and parapsychology and electronics and gardening and bankruptcy and mythology and geography and cooking and history and painting and economics and woodworking and music and music-history, flying, sailing and the history of sail, political action and geology, courage and comfort and wildplants and native animals, dying and death, archaeology and paleontology and astronomy and cosmology, anger and remorse, writing and metallurgy and sharpshooting and photography and solar design, house construction and investing and printing and giving and receiving and wind-surfing and befriending children, aging and earth-saving and warstopping, spiritual healing and psychic healing and cultural exchange and film-making, photovoltaics, microscopy and alternate energy, how to play, how to argue and make up, how to surprise and delight and dress and cry, to play the piano and the flute and the guitar, to see beyond appearances, remember other lifetimes, past and future, unlock answers, research and study, collect and analyze and synthesize, serve and contribute, lecture and listen, see and touch, travel cross-time and meet the other we, to create worlds from dreams and dwell there, changing.

Leslie, in her dream, smiled.

And then what? I thought. And then more, always more

for life-hogs to learn. To learn, to practice, to give back to other life-hogs, to remind them we're not alone.

And then what, after we've lived our dreams, when we're tired of time?

And then . . . Life, *Is!*

Remember? Remember *I AM! AND YOU ARE! AND LOVE; IS ALL; THAT MATTERS!*

That's and-then-what!

That's why lovestories don't have endings! They don't have endings because love doesn't end!

Then in the morning all at once, for the space of a hundred seconds, I knew how simply Everything-That-Is is put together. I grabbed the bedside notebook, slashed those seconds down felt-tip black, huge excited letters:

The only real, is Life!

Life sets consciousness free to choose no-form or infinite multiple trillions of forms, any form it can imagine.

My hand trembled and flashed, words tumbled over the blue-ruled lines of the paper.

Consciousness can forget itself, if it wants to forget. It can invent limits, begin fictions; it can pretend galaxies and universes and multiverses, black-holes white-holes big-bangs and steady-states, suns and planets, astral planes and physical. Whatever it imagines, it sees: war and peace, sickness and health, cruelty and kindness.

Consciousness can shape itself three-dimension into a waitress turned prophet of God; it can be a daisy, a spirit-guide, a biplane in a meadow; it can be an aviator just wakened from a dream, loving the smile of his wife asleep; it can be the kitten Dolly in mid-spring to the bed impatient where PLEASE is the catfood this morning?

And any instant it wants, it can remember who it is, it can remember reality, it can remember Love. In that instant, everything changes. . . .

Fluff-ball Dolly crouched, unseen blue eyes behind dust-chocolate mask, sprang, stunned that mouse-tail line of ink from my pen racing along, knocked it off the page.

"Dolly, no!" I whispered ferociously.

You don't feed me catfood? I'll eat your pen. . . .

"Dolly! No! Go on! Get!"

Not your pen? she glittered. I'll eat your HAND!

"Dolly!"

"What's going on, you two?" Leslie, wakened to the commotion, moved her fingers under the blanket. A hundredth of a second and the little creature whirled to attack, needle-teeth twenty claws rapidfire on the new threat to kittens.

"Dolly The Kittalorium is suggesting that we start the day," I sighed over the storm of battle.

Most of what I suddenly knew was safe in ink.

"Are you awake, yet, wook?" I said. "I had the most remarkable idea just now, and if you're awake I want to tell you . . ."

"Tell me." She fluffed a pillow under her head, avoiding a trouncing for that from Dolly on the sheer chance that Angel The Other Kitten walked innocent into the room at that moment, a new target for Dolly to stalk and pounce.

I read from the notebook just as I had written, the sentences bounding over each other, gazelles over high fences. In a minute I finished and looked up to her from the paper. "Years ago, I tried writing a letter to a younger me, *Things I Wish I Knew When I Was You.* If only we could hand THIS to the kids we were!"

"Wouldn't it be fun to sit on a cloud," she said, "and

358

watch them find a notebook from us, everything we've learned?"

"Be sad, in a way," I said.

"Why sad?"

"So much good, waiting to happen, and they can't find each other till now, or till five years ago. . . ."

"Let's tell them!" she said. "Put in the notebook, 'Now, Dick, you call Leslie Maria Parrish, she's just moved to Los Angeles, under contract to Twentieth Century-Fox, and her telephone number is CRestview six, two nine nine three. . . .'"

"And what?" I said. "And tell him to say, 'This is your soulmate, calling'? Leslie was a little star already! Men saw her pictures and fell in love with her! Is she going to invite him to lunch, a kid about to run away from his only year in college?"

"If she's smart, she'll say let's get out of Hollywood fast!"

I sighed. "It would never work. He's got to join the Air Force and fly fighter planes, get married and divorced, unfold who he's starting to be and what he's starting to know. She's got to get her own marriage over and done, learn for herself about business and politics and power."

"Then let's get a letter off to her," she said. " 'Dear Leslie you'll be getting a call from Dick Bach, he's your soulmate so be nice to him, love him always. . . .'"

" 'Always,' wook? Always is . . ."

I looked at her in mid-answer and froze, knowing.

Pictures from forgotten dreams, fragments from lifetimes lost in pasts and futures shone like color slides behind my eyes, -clik, -clik, -clik. . . .

The woman on the bed this moment, this person whom I could right now reach a hand to, touch her face, she's the one killed with me in the massacre in colonial Pennsylvania, *the same woman,* she's the dear mortal to whom I've been spirit-guide a dozen times, and who's been guide for me; she's the willow-tree whose branches twined into mine; she the fox and I the vixen, fangs bared, snapping lashing out-numbered, saving the kits from wolves; she the gull who led me higher; she the living light on the road to Alexandria; she the silver lifeform of Bellatrix Five; the starship engineering officer I'd love in my distant future; the flower-deva from my distant past.

-clik and -clik and -clik; frame and frame and frame.

Why my weakness for, my joy in the singular turn of this one mind, in the singular curve of this face and breast, in the singular merry light in her eyes when she laughs?

Because those unique curves and sparkles, Richard, *we carry them with us,* lifetime to lifetime, they're our *trademarks,* stamped deep in what each of us believes, and without knowing, we *remember them!* when we meet again!

She looked at my face, alarmed. "What's wrong, Richard? What's wrong?"

"OK," I said, thunderstruck. "I'm all right, I'm fine. . . ."

I grabbed for paper, dashed words down. What a morning!

Time and again and again we had drawn ourselves to each other, because we had most to learn together, hard learnings and happy ones, too.

How is it that I know, why am I so utterly convinced that dying does not separate us from the one we love?

Because this one I love today . . . because she and I have died a million times before, and we're this second, minute, hour lifetogether again! We're no more separated by death than we're separated by life! Deep within us, every one of us knows the laws, and one of the laws is this: we shall forever return to the arms of those we love, whether our parting be overnight or over-death.

"Just a minute, wook. Got to get this down. . . ."

The only thing that lasts, is love!

The words ripped out fast as ink could dash.

At the start of the universe . . . Before the Big Bang, was us!

Before all the Big Bangs in all of time, and after the echo of the last has faded, is us. We, dancers in every form, reflecting everywhere, we're the reason for space, the builders of time.

We're the bridge across forever, arching above the sea, adventuring for our pleasure, living mysteries for the fun of it, choosing disasters triumphs challenges impossible odds, testing ourselves over and again, learning love and love and LOVE!

I lifted the pen, sat out of breath on the bed, looking at my wife.

"You're alive!" I said.

Her eyes sparkled. "We're alive together."

It was quiet for a while, till she spoke once more. "I had stopped looking for you," she said. "I was happy by myself in Los Angeles, with my garden and my music, my causes and my friends. I liked living alone. I thought I'd do that for the rest of my life."

"And I would have been happily strangled on my freedom," I said. "It wouldn't have been bad, it would have been the best that each of us knew. How could we miss what we never had?"

"But we did miss it, Richie! Once in a while, when you

were alone, whether or not there were people around, did you ever feel so sad you could cry, as if you were the only one of your kind in the world?" She reached to touch my face.

"Did you ever feel," she said, "that you were missing someone you had never met?"

forty-six

W<small>E</small> HAD stayed up late, the two of us. Leslie was submerged on page 300-something of *The Passive Solar Energy Book: Expanded Professional Edition.*

I closed *A History of the Colt Revolver,* put it on the Finished stack and took the top volume from my To-Read-Next pile.

How our books describe us, I thought. At Leslie's bedside: *Complete Poems of E.E. Cummings, The Global 2000 Report to the President, Muddling Toward Frugality, Carl Sandburg's Abraham Lincoln, Unicorns I Have Known, This Timeless Moment, The Lean Years, Baryshnikov At Work, American Film Directors, 2081.*

At mine: *The Dancing Wu Li Masters, The Stories of Ray Bradbury, Airman's Odyssey, The Aquarian Conspiracy, The Many-Worlds Interpretation of Quantum Mechanics, Western Edible Wildplants, The Trimtab Factor.* When I want to understand someone swiftly, I need only look at their book-shelf.

The sound of the book change caught her at the end of a calculation. "How was Mister Colt?" she said, moving her solar charts into better light.

"Oh, he's doin' just fine. Do you know that without the Colt Revolver there would be forty-six states in this country today, instead of fifty?"

"We stole four states at gunpoint?"

"That's pretty crass, Leslie. Not stole. Defended some, liberated others. And not we. You and I had nothing to do with it. But a hundred-some years ago, to those people then, the Colt was a fearsome weapon. A repeating handgun faster than any rifle and straighter-shooting than most. I've always wanted an 1851 Navy Colt. Silly, isn't it? Originals are expensive, but Colt does make a replica."

"What would you want with something like that?"

She didn't mean to be sexy that moment, but even a winter nightgown couldn't hide that lovely outline. When will I outgrow my simple-minded fascination with the form she had happened to choose for her body? Never, I thought.

"Something like what?" I said absently.

"Animal," she growled. "Why would you want an old pistol?"

"Oh. The Colt. Funny feeling about it, as long as I can remember. When I realize I don't own one, I feel sort of undressed, vulnerable. It's a habit to be within arm's-reach of one, but I've never even touched a Colt. Isn't that odd?"

"If you want one, we can start saving for it. If it's that important to you."

How often we're led back to our other pasts by bits and pieces of hardware, old machines, buildings, lands that we passionately love or fiercely hate without knowing why. Does anyone live who hasn't felt magnetic yearnings toward other places, an easy at-home-ness with other times? One of my pasts, I knew, held the brass-and-blue-iron of a Colt's Patent Revolver. Be fun to track that one down, someday.

"I guess not, wookie. Silly thought."

"What are you going to read now?" she said, turning her book sideways to study the next chart.

"It's called *Life at Death*. Looks like some pretty careful research, interviews with people who nearly died, what it felt like, what they saw. How's your book coming along?"

Angel T. Cat jumped onto the bed, six pounds of white longhair Persian, walked heavily as six tons to Leslie, collapsed on the pages in front of her, purred.

"Fine. This chapter is especially interesting. It says fur fur fur EYES NOSE EYES fur fur fur claws and tail. Angel, do the words *you are in my way* have any meaning to you? The words *you are sitting on my book?*"

The cat looked at her drowsily no; purred the louder.

Leslie moved the fluffy weight to her shoulder, and we read in silence for a while.

"Goodnight, little wook," I said, turning out my reading lamp. "I'll meet you on the corner of Cloud Street and Sleepy-Bye Lane. . . ."

"I won't be long, sweetie," she said. "Goodnight."

I squashed my pillow and curled into a sleeping-ball. For some time I had been practicing induced dreams, with minimal success. Tonight I was too tired for practice. I fell off the edge into sleep.

It was a light airy glass house that we saw, high on a greenforest island. Flowers splashed everywhere, a flood

365

of color through the rooms, over the decks and beyond, spilling downslope to a level meadow. A Lake amphibian in shades of sunrise, parked on the grass. Away over deep water other islands scattered, evergreen to mistblue.

There were trees inside the house as well as out, trees and hanging plants under a great square of roof moved away to let in sunlight and air. Chairs and a couch soft-covered in lemon-vanilla cloth. Shelves of books at easy reach, Bartók's glorious Concerto for Orchestra *in the air. The place felt like home to us for the music and the plants, for the airplane outside and the far view, like flying. It was exactly what we wanted for ourselves, some day.*

"Welcome the both of you! You made it!"

The two who met us were familiar. They laughed and hugged us joyfully.

We forget in the daytimes, but asleep we can remember dreams from years gone. The man was the same one who first flew me in the Pterodactyl; he was myself in ten years or twenty, but grown younger. The woman was Leslie-by-the-airplane, more beautiful with knowing.

"Sit down, please," she said. "We don't have much time."

The man set hot cider for us, on a driftwood table.

"So this is our future," said Leslie. "You've done a good job!"

"This is one *of your futures," said the other Leslie, "and it's you who did the good job."*

"You showed the way," said the man. "Gave us chances we wouldn't have had, without you."

"It was nothing, was it, wook?" I smiled at my wife.

"It wasn't nothing," she answered, "it was a lot!"

"The only way we could thank you was to invite you to the house," said Richard-to-be. "Your design, Leslie. Works perfectly."

"Almost perfectly," his wife corrected. "The photovoltaics, they're better than you thought. But I've got some suggestions about the thermal mass. . . ."

The two Leslies were about to fall into a deep technical talk of hybrid solar engineering and superinsulation when I realized . . .

"Excuse me," I said, "We're dreaming! Every one of us, isn't that right? Isn't this a dream?"

"Correct," said the future Richard. "This is the first time we've reached you both. We've been practicing this, on and off, for years—we're getting better!"

I blinked. "You've been practicing for years, and this is the first time you've reached us?"

"You'll understand when you do it. For a long time, you'll only meet people that you haven't seen—future you's, alternate you's, friends who've died. For a long time you'll be learning, before you get into teaching. It will take you twenty years. Twenty years' practice, you can pretty well give direction to your dream-state, when you want. Then you get around to saying thanks to ancestors."

"Ancestors?" Leslie said. "Are we ancient?"

"I'm sorry," he said. "Poor choice of words. Your future is our past. But our future is your past, too. Soon as you get yourself free of this time-belief and on with your dream-practice, you'll understand. As long as we believe in sequential time, we see becoming, instead of being. Beyond time, we're all one."

"Glad it's not complicated," said Leslie.

I had to interrupt. "Excuse me. The new book. You know me and book-titles. Did I ever find a title? Did the book ever get written and printed and I can't for the life of me . . . did I ever find a title?"

The future Richard had not a lot of patience for my doubts. "This dream is not to tell you that. Yes, you found a title; yes, the book got printed."

"That's all I wanted to know," I said. And then, meekly: "What's the title?"

"This dream is to tell you something else," he said. "We got a . . . let's call it a letter . . . from us way out ahead in our future. Your ideas about getting through to young Dick and Leslie, they started something. Now quite a few of us have turned into sort of psychic pen-pals.

"Everything you thought to your younger selves, it got through. Tiny changes, subconscious, but they are alternate people, they may not have to go through the hard times we did. Some hard times, of course, but there's a remote chance that learning how to love won't be one of them."

"The letter we got," said Leslie-to-be, "it said, everything you know, is true!" She was fading; the scene flickered. "There's more, but listen: Never doubt what you know. *That wasn't just a pretty book-title, we are bridges. . . ."*

Then the dream shattered, broke to suitcases stuffed with muffins, a car-chase, a steamboat on wheels.

I didn't wake Leslie, but I wrote pages on the pad by my

pillow, remembering in the dark what had happened before the muffins.

When she woke next morning, I said, "Let me tell you about your dream."

"What dream?" she said.

"The one meeting us in the house you designed."

"Richard!" she said, "I remember! Let me tell *you* about it! It was a glorious place, deer in the meadow, the pond was a mirror for a field of flowers like we had in Oregon. The design, the solar house will work! There was music inside, and books and trees . . . so open and light! It was a beautiful bright-color day and there were Dolly and Angel looking at us, purring back to sleep, fat *old* cats. I saw the new book, our book, on the shelf!"

"Yes? Yes? What was the title? Say!"

She struggled to remember. "Wookie, I'm so sorry! It's gone. . . ."

"Oh, well. Don't feel bad," I said. "Silly curiosity. Quite a dream, don't you think?"

"It was something about forever."

forty-seven

"*I* FINISHED reading *Recollections of Death* one evening shortly after she started *Life After Life,* and the more I thought, the more I needed to talk with her.

"When you have a minute," I said. "Long minute."

She read on to the end of her paragraph and folded the dust-jacket over her page to mark it.

"OK," she said.

"Does it strike you wrong," I said, "does it strike you wrong that dying is most often a messy sort of inconvenient bother, for most people, something that jumps on us maybe just when we've found the one person in the world we love, we want never to be separated from her even for a day, and death says I don't care I'm going to rip you apart?"

"That has struck me from time to time," she said.

"Why does dying have to be that way? Why should we give our consent to such an out-of-control death?"

"Maybe because the only other choice is suicide," she said.

"Aha!" I said. *"Is* suicide the only choice? Isn't there a better way of leaving than this random last-minute dying-by-force custom they have on this planet?"

"Let me guess," she said. "You have a plan that you are about to propose? First you ought to know that as long as you're here, I'm not all that unhappy with dying at the last minute."

"Wait till you hear this. Because this is going to appeal to your sense of order: Why, instead of surprise-dying, don't people reach a time when they decide, 'Done! We've finished everything we came to do, there are no mountains that we haven't pretty well climbed, nothing unlearned we wanted to learn, we've lived a nice life,' and then in perfect health why don't they just sit down, two of them under a tree or a star, and lift themselves out of their bodies and never come back?"

"Like in the books we're reading," she said. "What a nice idea! But we don't . . . we don't do it because we don't know how to do it."

"Leslie!" I said, full of my plan, *"I know how!"*

"Not just yet, please," she said. "We've got to build our house, and there are the cats and the raccoons to think of, and the milk in the refrigerator will get sour and the mail has to be answered; we're just getting started again."

"OK. Not yet. But it struck me, reading near-death experiences, they're the same as the out-of-body experiences in the astral-travel books! Dying is nothing more than an out-of-body, from which we don't return! And out-of-bodies, they can be *learned!*"

"Hold on a minute," she said. "You're suggesting we

371

choose a pretty sunset and leave our bodies and not bother to come back?"

"Someday, yes."

She looked at me sideways. "How much of you is serious?"

"Hundred percent. Really! Doesn't it beat getting run over by a trolley? Doesn't it beat getting separated, losing a day or two, a century or two together?"

"The together part I like," she said. "Because I'm serious, too: if you die, I do not want to live here anymore."

"I know," I said. "So all we have to do is learn out-of-body travel, like spiritual adepts and wolves."

"Wolves?"

"I read it in a wolf-book. Some zoo-people trapped a pair of wolves, mates, in a soft trap, a humane thing that didn't hurt them a bit. Put them in a big cage in the back of a pickup-truck, drove them to the zoo. When they got there, lifted out the cage, both wolves . . . dead. No sickness, no injury, no nothing. The wolves didn't want to be separated, they didn't want to live in a cage. They let go of their will to live and they died together. No medical explanation. Gone."

"Is that true?"

"It's in the wolf-book, nonfiction. I'd sure do it, if I were them, wouldn't you? Wouldn't you say that's a civilized, an intelligent way off the planet? If the whole earth, all space-time is a dream, why not wake gentle and happy somewhere else, instead of screaming that we don't want to leave here?"

"Do you really think we could do it?" she said. It did appeal to her sense of order.

Hardly had the question faded and I was back on the bed with a dozen books from our shelves. *The Study and Practice of Astral Projection, Journeys out of the Body, The Su-*

preme Adventure, The Practical Guide to Astral Projection, Mind Beyond the Body. The weight of them sagged a shallow crater in the mattress.

"These people say it can be learned. It's not easy and it takes a whole lot of practice, but it can be done. The question: Is it worth doing?"

She frowned. "Right now I'd say no. But if you were to die tomorrow, I'd be awfully sorry I hadn't learned."

"Let's compromise. Let's learn the out-of-body part and save the not-coming-back part till a long time later. We've been out-of-body before, both of us, so we know we can do it. Now it's a matter of doing it when we want to, and doing it together. Shouldn't be all that hard."

I was wrong. It *was* all that hard. The problem was to go to sleep without going to sleep, without losing consciousness of ourselves separate from our bodies. Easy to imagine doing that when one is wide awake. Staying conscious with a blanket of sleep heavier than lead dragging one down—that's no simple task.

Night after night, we'd read our astral-travel books, promise to meet in the air over our sleeping bodies, just a glimpse of each other and remember when we woke. No luck. Weeks went by. Months. It became a habit that lasted long after the books were read.

"Remember to remember. . . ." we'd say, turning out the light.

We'd fall asleep programmed to meet overhead; she'd go to Pennsylvania and I'd be perched on a rooftop in Peking. Or I'd show up in a kaleidoscope future and she'd be in the nineteenth century, giving concerts.

Five months into our practice, I woke up, it must have been three in the morning.

I was trying to move my head on the pillow, change position, when I realized that I couldn't do that because the pillow was down on the bed and I was floating on my back, three feet in the air.

Wide awake. Floating. The room was wall-to-wall in dark silver-grey light. Moonlight, I would have said, but there was no moon. There the walls, the stereo cabinet; there the bed, books neatly on her side, a tumbled stack on mine. And there our bodies, asleep!

A jolt of pure astonishment, like blue fire through me in the night, and then an explosion of joy. That was my body, down there; that curious thing on the bed was me, eyes closed, sound asleep! Not quite me, of course . . . me was the one who was looking down.

Everything I thought, that first night, was underlines and exclamation points.

It works! It's so easy! This is . . . freedom!
HURRAY!

The books had been right. Think about moving, and I moved, sliding on the air like a sled on ice. I didn't exactly have a body, but neither was I without one. I had a sense of body—hazy, foggy, a ghost's body. After all our determined practice, how could this be so easy? Extreme consciousness. Compared to this humming knowing razor-life, daily consciousness is sleepwalking!

I turned in the air and looked back. The faintest thread of glowing light led from me to my sleeping form. That's the cord we read about, the silver cord, that links a living ghost to its body. Sever that cord, they say, and off you go.

At that moment a rippling aura blurred from behind me, slowed to hover around Leslie in bed and faded into her body. A second later she moved, turned under the

covers; her hand touched my shoulder. It felt like being
tackled from behind; I was catapulted headlong awake
by the touch.

My eyes flew open in a room darker than midnight . . .
so dark it didn't matter whether eyes were open or closed. I
reached for the bed-lamp switch, heart pounding.

"Wookie!" I said. "Sweetie, are you awake?"

"M. I am now. What's wrong?"

"Nothing wrong!" I shouted quietly. "It worked! We did
it!"

"We did?"

"We were out of our bodies!"

"Oh, Richie, were we? I don't remember . . ."

"You don't? What's the last thing you can think of before
now?"

She brushed golden hair from her eyes, and smiled dream-
ily. "I was flying. Pretty dream. Flying over fields . . ."

"Then it's true! We remember out-of-body nights as flying
dreams!"

"How do you know I was out of body?"

"Because I saw you!"

That woke her up. I told her everything that had happened, everything I had seen.

"But 'seen' is not the word for out-of-body sight, wook. It
isn't seeing as much as it is knowing, knowing in detail
that's clearer than sight." I switched off the light. "The
room's this black, and I could see everything. The stereo,
the shelves, the bed, you and me. . . ." In the dark it was
impressive, to talk about seeing.

She touched her light, sat up in bed, frowned. "I don't
remember!"

375

"You came by me like a rose-and-daisy UFO; stopped in the air and sort of melted into your body. Then you moved and touched me and bang! I was wide awake. If you hadn't touched me that moment, I wouldn't have remembered."

It was another month before it happened again, and then it happened nearly in reverse. She waited till morning to tell me.

"Same as yours, wook! I felt like a cloud in the sky, light as air. And happy! I turned around, looked back at the bed, and there we were asleep and *Amber*, there was dear little Amber curled up on my shoulder, the way she used to sleep! I said, 'AMBER!' and she opened her eyes and looked at me as though she had never left. Then she stood and started to walk toward me and that's the end of it, I woke up in bed."

"Did you feel like you had to stay in the room?"

"No, no! I could go anywhere in the universe, anywhere I wanted to, see anyone. It's like I had a magic body. . . ."

Powerhouse quiet crackled in the room.

"We did it!" she said, excited as I had been. "We're doing it!"

"Another month," I said, "maybe we can do it again!"

It happened the next night.

This time I was sitting in the air when I woke over the bed, and what caught my attention was a radiant form afloat, flawless sparkling silver and gold barely two feet away, exquisite living love.

Oh, my! I thought. The Leslie I've been seeing with my eyes isn't the tiniest part of who she is! She's body within body, life within life; unfolding, unfolding, unfolding . . . will I ever know all of her?

No words required, I knew whatever she wanted me to know.

—You were sleeping, and I was here and I coaxed you out, Richie please come out . . . and you did—

—Hi, sweetie, hi, hi!

I reached to her, and when the light from the two of us touched, there was the feeling we get when we hold hands, yet many times closer, gentle rejoicement.

—Up—I thought to her.—Slowly. Let's try going up.—

Like two warm balloons, we lifted together through the ceiling as if it were cool air.

The roof of the house sank beneath us, rough wooden shingles covered in fallen pine needles, brick chimney, television antenna pointed toward civilization. Down on the decks, flowers asleep in planters.

Then we were above the trees, drifting carefully out over the water, on a night of stray wispy clouds in a sky of stars; thin scattered cirrus, visibility unlimited, wind from the south at two knots. There was no temperature.

If this is life, I thought, it is infinitely beautifuller than anything I have ever . . .

—Yes—I heard Leslie thinking.—Yes.—

—Lock this in that awesome memory of yours, I told her.—You are not going to forget this when we wake!—

—You, either . . .—

Like student pilots on our first solo, we moved slowly together, no quick motions. We had not the smallest fear of height, no more fear than two clouds of falling, two fish of drowning. Whatever bodies these were, they had

*no weight, no mass. We could glide through iron,
through the center of the sun, if we felt like it.*

—Do you see? The cord?—

*When she said it, I remembered and looked. Two
gleaming cobwebs stretched away from us toward the
house.*

*—We're spirit-kites, on strings,—I thought.—Ready to
go back?—*

—Nice and slow.—

—We don't have to go back . . .—

—But we want to, Richie!—

*Nice and slow, we floated back over the water to the
house, through the west wall of the bedroom.*

We stopped by the bookshelf.

—There!—she thought.—See? It's Amber!—

A fluffy light-form floated toward Leslie.

—Hi, Amber! Hi, little Amber!—

*There was a hi-feeling, love-feeling from the light. I
left them slowly, moved across the room. What if we
wanted to talk with someone? If Leslie wanted to see her
brother who had died when she was nineteen, if I wanted
to talk with my mother, with my father just died, what
would happen?*

*In whatever state this is, out of body, questions come
with answers. If we want to talk with them, we can. We
can be with anyone to whom we have some bond, and
who wishes to be with us.*

*I turned and looked back at the two, the woman and
the cat, and noticed for the first time a silver thread
from the cat. It led down through the dark to a basket
on the floor, and a sleeping white fluff. Had I a heart, it
would have skipped a beat.*

—Leslie! Amber . . . Amber is <u>Angel T. Cat!</u>—

As if on cue for a play we didn't know, at that moment our other cat Dolly burst down the hall at maximum wide-open top speed and leaped, a four-legged motorcycle, onto the bed.

The next instant we were cat-stomped, bashed awake, forgetting all.

"DOLLY!" I shouted, but she had caromed from bed to wall and was long gone down the hall again. Just her way of having fun.

"Sorry, wook," I said. "Sorry to wake you."

She switched the light on.

"How did you know it was Dolly?" she asked sleepily.

"It was Dolly. I saw her."

"In the dark? You saw Dolly who is a brown-and-black cat, running top-speed, in the dark?"

We both remembered, the same second.

"We were out, weren't we?" she said. "Oh, wookie, we were together, and we were up in the clouds!"

I grabbed my notebook, fumbled for a pen. "Quick, right now. Tell me everything you remember."

From that night forward, the practice gradually became less difficult, each success clearing the way for the next.

After the first year's practice, we could meet together out-of-body several times a month; the suspicion that we were visitors on the planet grew till we could smile at each other, interested observers, in the middle of the evening news.

Because of our practice, the death-and-tragedy we saw on Channel Five were not death and tragedy; they were the comings and goings, the adventures of spirits of infinite power. The evening news turned for us from grim horror into a broadcast of classes, of tests to be taken, of social investment opportunities, challenges and gauntlets thrown down.

"Good evening, America, I'm Nancy Newsperson. Here's tonight's list of horrors around the world. Spiritual swash-bucklers, you want advancement-through-rescue, listen up: in the Middle East today . . ." She reads, hoping rescuers are tuned in. "Next we have our list of Failures in Government! Anyone out there enjoy repairing bureaucratic disasters? After a brief commercial break, we'll open a crate of Assorted Severe Problems. If you've got solutions, be sure to watch!"

We had hoped from out-of-body practice to learn to be master and not victim of the body and its death. We hadn't guessed that thrown in with the lesson would come a perspective that would change everything else—when we turn from victim into master, what do we do with our power?

One evening after writing, as I poured cat-food and mini-marshmallows into a tray to set out for our nightly visit from Racquel Raccoon, Leslie came to supervise. She had left her computer early, to tune in the state of the world.

"See anything on the news," I said, "that you'd like to invest in?"

"Stopping the nukes, stopping war, as always. Space colonies, maybe; saving the environment, of course, and the whales, endangered animals."

The food tray looked delicious, when I squinted through raccoon-eyes.

"Too many marshmallows," she said, taking some off the heap. "We are feeding Racquel, not Hoggie."

"I thought she might like a few extra tonight. The more marshmallows she has, the less she'll want to eat little birds, or something."

Without a word, Leslie put back the extra marshmallows and went to make a place ready on the couch for us.

I put out the raccoon-food, then curled next to my wife in the living room.

"The best opportunity, I think, is individual advancement," I said. "You and me, learning . . . there's something we can *control!*"

"Not out-of-body flitting off to other levels, did you notice that?" she teased. "Are we not quite ready to say goodbye to our little planet?"

"Not quite ready," I said. "It's enough to know we *can* leave it, now, whenever we want. We may be foreigners on Earth, wookie, but we've got seniority! Years of education in how to use the body, the civilization, ideas, the language. How to change things. Not ready to throw that away yet. I'm glad I didn't kill myself a long time ago, before I found you."

She looked at me, curious. "Did you know you were trying to kill yourself?"

"Not consciously, I don't think. But neither do I think my close calls were accidental. Loneliness was such a problem, back then, I wouldn't have minded dying, it would have been a new adventure."

"What would it have felt like," she said, "to have killed yourself and then found that your soulmate was still on earth, waiting for you?"

The words froze in the air. Had I come closer to that than

I knew? We sat together on our rented couch, twilight fading to dark outside.

"GRF!" I said. "What a thought!"

Suicide, like murder—*uncreative!* Anyone desperate enough for suicide, I thought, should be desperate enough to go to creative extremes to solve problems: elope at midnight, stow away on the boat to New Zealand and start over, do what they always wanted to do but were afraid to try.

I took her hand, in the dark. "What a thought!" I said. "There I am, just having killed myself, separating from my dead body, and then realizing, too late . . . I would have met you, by coincidence, on my way through Los Angeles to New Zealand, except I've just killed myself! 'Oh, no!' I would have said. *'What a goose I've been!'* "

"Poor dead goose," she said. "But you could always start another lifetime."

"Sure, I could. And I'd be forty years younger than you."

"Since when have we started counting ages?" She was laughing at my antibirthday campaign.

"It's not the age, as much as we'd be out of sync. You'd say something about peace-marches or Banthas, and I'd sit there a dull rock and say, 'What?' And another lifetime would be so inconvenient! Can you imagine turning into a baby again? Learning . . . how to walk? Life as a teenager? How we survived adolescence in the first place, it's a wonder. But to be eighteen, to be twenty-four again? That's more sacrifice than I'm prepared to make for at least another thousand years; more likely never, thank you. I'd rather be a harp-seal."

"I'll be a harp-seal with you," she said. "But if this is our last Earth-life for centuries, we should make the very best we can of it. What do other lifetimes matter? Like things we've done this lifetime—Hollywood, living in the trailer, fighting to save the forest—what will they matter in a thousand years, what does it matter tonight, except what we've learned? What we've learned is everything! I think we've got a nice start, this time. Let's not be harp-seals yet." She stirred, shivered. "Would you like a blanket, or a fire?"

I was thinking about what she had said. "Either," I murmured. "Do you want me to fix it?"

"No. Just needs a match. . . ."

The tiny light shed warm glows from the wood-stove into her eyes, her hair.

"For right now," she said, "if you could do anything you wanted, what would it be?"

"I CAN do anything I want."

"What would it be?" she insisted, curling down near me again, watching the fire.

"I'd want to say what we've learned." My own words made me blink. Isn't that strange, I thought. Not finding answers anymore, but giving them away! Why not, when we've found our love, when we know at last how the universe works? Or how we think it works.

She looked from the fire into my eyes. "What we've learned is the only thing we have left. You want to give that away?" She turned back to the fire and smiled, testing me. "Don't forget you're the one who wrote that everything you say could be wrong."

"Could be wrong," I agreed. "But when we listen to somebody's answers, we're not really listening to the somebody, are we? We're listening to ourselves while they talk; it's ourself says this part's true and that part's crazy and that part's true again. That's the fun of listening. The fun of saying is to be as little wrong as we know how to be."

"So you're thinking about giving lectures again," she said.

"Maybe. Would you be on stage with me, we'll say what we've found together? Not be afraid to talk about the bad times or the beautiful? Talk to the ones searching, the way we were, give them hope that happily-ever-after really can be? How I wish we could have heard that, years ago!"

She answered quietly. "I don't think I could do it with you. I can make the arrangements, I'll organize things for you, but I don't want to be on stage."

Something was very wrong. "You don't? There are things that we can say together that neither one of us can say alone. I can't say what you were going through as well as you can; the only way we can do it is together!"

"I don't think so," she said.

"Why not?"

"Richie, when I talked against the war, the crowds were so hostile I was terrified to stand up in front of them. I had to do it, but I promised myself when it was over I would never speak from a stage again. Ever. For any reason. I don't think I can do it."

"You're being silly," I told her. "The war is over! We're not talking about war, now, we're talking about love!"

Her eyes filled with tears. "Oh, Richie!" she said, "Love is what I was talking about then!"

forty-eight

"WHERE DO you get your crazy ideas?" asked the gentleman twenty rows back, the first question in the second hour of the lecture.

There was a mass low chuckle from the couple-thousand people in the Civic Auditorium . . . he was not the only one curious about that.

Leslie sat lightly, looking cool and at ease, on the tall stool next to mine on the stage. For the moment I had walked to the footlights with a cordless microphone, choosing from among the hands raised, remembering to repeat the question so the balcony could hear, and so I could have time to think what to say.

" 'Where do I get my crazy ideas?' " I repeated. In half-seconds, an answer materialized, then the words I needed to say it.

"Same place I get the reasonable ones," I said. "Ideas

come from the sleep-fairy, the walk-fairy, and, when I'm irrevocably wet and unable to write notes, from the shower-fairy. What I've always asked from them is *Please give me ideas that do no violence to my intuition.*

"I know intuitively, for instance, that we are creatures of light and life, and not of blind death. I know that we are not bolted together out of space and time, subject to a million changing heres and nows, goods and bads. The idea that we are physical beings descended from primeval cells in nutrient soups, that idea does violence to my intuition, stomps all over it with football-shoes.

"The idea that we are descended from a jealous God who formed us out of dust to choose between kneel-and-praying or fires-of-damnation, that stomps me worse. No sleep-fairy ever brought me those for ideas. The whole concept of *descent,* for me, it's wrong.

"Yet no one place I could find, no one person anywhere who had my answers except the inner me, and the inner me I was afraid to trust. I had to swim through my life like a baleen whale, taking in great flooding seawater mouthfuls of what other people wrote and thought and said, tasting and keeping bits of knowing the size of plankton, that fit what I wanted to believe. Anything to explain what I knew was true, that's what I was looking for.

"From this writer over here, not one micro-shrimp could I keep, from as much as I could read of her books. From another over there, I understood nothing but this: *'We are not what we seem.'* Hurray! That, intuitively I know, is TRUE! The rest of a book might be seawater, but the whale keeps that sentence.

"Little by little, I think we build a conscious understanding of what we're born already knowing: what the highest inner us wants to believe, it's true. Our conscious mind, though, isn't happy till it can explain in words.

"Before I knew it, in just a few decades, I had a system of thinking that gives me answers when I ask."

I looked quickly to Leslie, and she waved a little wave to say she was still there.

"What was the question?" I said. "Oh. Where do I get my crazy ideas? Answer: sleep-fairy, walk-fairy, shower-fairy. Book-fairy. And in these last few years, from my wife. Now when I have questions I ask her and she tells me the answer. If you haven't already, I'd suggest you want to find your soulmate, soon as you can. Next question?"

So much to say, I thought, and just one day to say it in each town that asks us to come and talk. Eight hours is not nearly enough. How do speakers tell people what they need to tell in one hour? Our first hour, we've barely outlined the framework of how we look at the world.

"The lady there, way back on the right side . . ."

"My question is for Leslie. How do you know when you meet your soulmate?"

My wife looked at me splitsecond terror, lifted her microphone.

"How do you know when you meet your soulmate?" she repeated, calm as though she did this all the time. "I didn't know, when I met mine. It was in an elevator. 'Going up?' I said. 'Yes,' he said. Neither of us knew what those words would mean to the people we are now.

"Four years later we got to know each other and all at once we were best friends. The more I knew him, the more I admired him, the more I thought what a truly wonderful person he is!

"That's a key. Look for a love-affair that *gets better* with

387

time, admiration brightening, trust that grows through storms.

"With this one man I saw that intense intimacy and joy were possible for me. I used to think those were my own special needs, my personal signs of a soulmate. Now I think they may be everyone's, but that we despair of finding them, we try to settle for less. How dare we ask for intimacy and joy when a lukewarm lover and mild happiness are the best we can find?

"Yet in our hearts we know that lukewarm will turn cold; mild happiness will become a kind of nameless sadness, nagging questions: Is this the love of my life, is this all there is, is this why I'm here? In our hearts we know there must be more, and we long for the one we never found.

"So often half a couple is trying to go up, the other half is dragging down. One walks forward, the other makes sure that for every two steps ahead they take three steps back. Better to learn happiness alone, I thought, love my friends and my cat, better wait for a soulmate who never comes than to make that dull compromise.

"A soulmate is someone who has locks that fit our keys, and keys to fit our locks. When we feel safe enough to open the locks, our truest selves step out and we can be completely and honestly who we are; we can be loved for who we are and not for who we're pretending to be. Each unveils the best part of the other. No matter what else goes wrong around us, with that one person we're safe in our own paradise. Our soulmate is someone who shares our deepest longings, our sense of direction. When we're two balloons, and together our direction is up, chances are we've found the right person. Our soulmate is the one who makes life come to life."

To her surprise, the crowd smothered her in applause. I had almost believed what she told me, that she might be less than perfect on the platform. She wasn't.

"Do you think the same way as he does," the next person called from the audience, "do you agree on everything?"

"Do we agree on everything," she said. "Most times. He turns up the radio, and I find that he's the only other person I've known who's enchanted by bagpipes. He's the only other who can sing 'Alone Am I' from *Tubby the Tuba*, word for word with me, from childhood memory.

"Other times," she said, "we couldn't have started farther apart . . . I was a war-resister, Richard was an Air Force pilot; one man at a time for me, Richard's only woman was many women. He was wrong both times, and so of course he changed.

"But at the last it doesn't matter whether we agree or not, or who's right. What matters is what goes on between the two of us . . . are we always changing, are we growing and loving each other more? That's what matters."

"May I add a word," I said.

"Of course."

"Things around us—houses, jobs, cars—they're props, they're settings for our love. The things we own, the places we live, the events of our lives: empty settings. How easy to chase after settings, and forget diamonds! The only thing that matters, at the end of a stay on earth, is how well did we love, *what was the quality of our love?*"

* * *

At the first break, most of the people stood and stretched, some came to the front with books needing autographs.

Others met and talked, without formal introduction, at the place near the stage that we had set aside for them.

While the people were getting back to their seats for the fifth hour of the talk, I touched Leslie's shoulder. "How are you doing, little wook? Are you all right?"

"Just fine," she said. "It's nothing like before! This is wonderful!"

"You are so smart!" I said. "So wise and lovely you are. You could have your pick of any man out there."

She squeezed my arm. "I choose this one, thank you. Time to start again?"

I nodded, switched on my microphone. "Here we go," I said. "Let us continue. Any question ever asked since the dawn of humankind, we promise you, we can answer it to our complete satisfaction!"

So much of what we said sounded crazy, yet none of it was false . . . as if two theoretical physicists stood on stage to say that when we travel near lightspeed, we get younger than nontravellers; that a mile of space next to the sun is different from a mile of space next to the earth because the sun-mile space is curved more than the earth-mile.

Silly ideas, worth the admission price in smiles, but they're true. Is high-energy physics interesting because it's true or because it's crazy?

"Ma'am," I said, nodding to a woman standing mid-audience, wondered where she'd take us next.

"Do you intend to die?"

Easy question; an answer to split between us.

* * *

We sailed that day with the wind of knowing that had changed and taught us, through a sea of questions:

Why do we have problems?

Can death separate us? Since you're going to say it can't, how do we talk to friends who have died?

Is there no such thing as evil?

What's it like, married to an actress?

Have you accepted the Lord Jesus Christ as your own Personal Saviour?

What's a nation for?

Do you ever get sick?

Who's in the UFOs?

Is your love different now from a year ago?

How much money do you have?

Is Hollywood really glamorous?

If I've lived before, why have I forgotten?

Is she as wonderful as you say? What don't you like about each other?

Are you done changing?

Can you see your own future?

What difference does it make, anything you say?

How do you get to be a movie-star?

Have you ever changed your past?

Why does music affect us the way it does?

Do something psychic, please.

What makes you so sure we're immortal?

How do you tell when a marriage is over?

How many other people see this world the way you do?

Where can we go to meet someone to love?

* * *

We sailed through a day lasted a moment long, as though we ourselves were lightspeed travellers.

Swiftly came the hour we shut our hotel-room door behind us, fell on the bed together.

"Not bad," I said. "Not a bad day. Tired?"

"No!" she said. "There's so much *power,* so much love in the air, at one of these things. The joy comes and hugs us all!"

"Let's practice seeing auras, next time," I said. "They say that at a good stage event, there's golden light over the audience, over the stage. Everybody's electrified."

I looked at her blouse. "Permission to touch?"

She considered me sideways. "What does that mean?"

"It's an aviation-cadet custom. Never touch another person without permission."

"You hardly need permission, Mister Bach."

"I just thought, before I tear your clothes off, I ought to be courteous, and ask."

"Beast," she said. "When the man asked if there were dragons left, I should have pointed to you."

I rolled on my back, looked at the featureless ceiling, closed my eyes. "I'm a dragon. I'm an angel, too, don't forget. We each have our mystery, our adventure, don't we, going our million ways together across time, all at once? What are we *doing,* in those other times? I don't know. But I'll bet you a strange thing, sweetie," I said, "I'll bet that what we're doing now . . ."

". . . is tied with ribbons of light," she said, "to what we're doing then!"

I shocked awake as she finished my sentence.

She lay on her side on the bed, seablue eyes locked with mine, knowing me, knowing so much more.

I spoke as gently as I could to the life that sparkled and danced behind those eyes.

"Hello, mystery," I whispered.

"Hello, adventure."

"Where shall we go from here?" I said, full of the power of us. "How shall we change the world?"

"I saw our house, today," she said. "When the lady asked do we know our future. Remember our dream? That house. I saw the forest on the island, and the meadow. I saw where we're going to build the house we went to in the dream."

One corner of her mouth curved in a tiny smile. "Do you think they'd mind, all those hundreds of other usses everywhere at once beyond time and space? Considering what we've been through," she said, "do you think they'd mind if we built our house first, and *then* changed the world?"

forty-nine

THE LITTLE earth-mover roared over the hill, saw me by the meadow, rolled down to meet me, its steel bucket half-full of topsoil for the garden.

"Hi, sweetie!" Leslie called, over the roar of the engine. Workdays, she wore heavy white coveralls, her hair swirled up under a yellow tractor-cap; hands disappeared in heavy leather gloves on the steering-handles of the machine.

She was master of the earth-mover, these days, glad to work at last on the house she had built for so long in her mind.

She shut the engine down. "How's my darling word-smith?"

"Doing fine," I said. "Don't know what people are going to make of this book. They're going to say it's too long and too sexy for the likes of me to write. But I love it. And I found the title today!"

She pushed her cap up, touched her forehead with the back of a glove. "At last! What's the title?"

"It's already there, it's been there all along. If you find it, too, that's what we'll call the book, OK?"

"Time for me to read it now, the whole manuscript straight through?"

"Yep. Just one chapter to go, and it's done."

"One more chapter," she said. "Congratulations!"

I looked down the slope past the meadow, out over the water to the islands floating on the horizon. "This is a pretty place, isn't it?"

"Paradise! And you ought to see the house," she said. "The first of the photovoltaics went in, today. Hop aboard, I'll ride you up and show you!"

I stepped onto the bucket with the topsoil. She pressed the starter.

The engine roared to life, and for a moment, I could have sworn the sudden rumbling blast was the sound of my old biplane, started in the meadow.

If I half-closed my eyes, I could see . . .

. . . *a mirage, a ghost from years gone by, moving in the meadow. Richard the barnstormer, started the engine of the Fleet for the last time and settled down in his cockpit, touching the throttle, about to take off in search of his soulmate.*

The biplane crept forward.

What would I do if I saw her now, he thought, if I saw her walking through the hay, telling me wait?

On silly impulse, he turned and looked.

There was a sunlight blur in the field. Through the hay to the airplane, long golden hair flashing behind her,

ran a woman, ran the most beautiful . . . Leslie
Parrish! *How did she. . . ?*

He stopped the engine at once, dazzled to see her.

"Leslie! Is that you?"

*"Richard!" she called, "Going up?" She stopped
breathless at the edge of the cockpit. "Richard . . .
would you have time to fly with me?"*

*"Would you . . ." he said, all at once out of breath
himself, ". . . would you want to?"*

I turned to my wife, as startled as the pilot by what I'd
seen.

Dirt-streaked, glorious, she smiled at me, tear-bright radiance. "Richie, they're going to try for it!" she said. *"Wish
them love!"*